Sort of a place like HOME

Remembering the Moore River Native Settlement

Sort of a place like HOME

SUSAN MAUSHART

FREMANTLE ARTS CENTRE PRESS

First published 1993 by
FREMANTLE ARTS CENTRE PRESS
193 South Terrace (PO Box 320), South Fremantle
Western Australia 6162.

Consultant Editor Bryce Moore.
Designed by John Douglass.
Production Coordinator Sue Chiera.

Typeset in 10/12 pt Times
by Fremantle Arts Centre Press
and printed on 100gsm Masterprint A
by Lamb Print, Perth, Western Australia

National Library of Australia
Cataloguing-in-publication data

Maushart, Susan, 1958 -   .
Sort of a place like home: remembering the Moore River Native
Settlement.

ISBN 1 86368 060 8.

1. Moore River Native Settlement (W.A.) - History. [2.].
Aborigines, Australian - Western Australia - Moore River
Region - Reserves - History I. Title.

994.120049915

Contents

Acknowledgements

In 1989, Dr John McGuire, an associate professor of history at Curtin University, introduced me to Annette Roberts, who introduced me to Edie Moore and through Edie to the subject of Moore River. Annette gave me the transcript of an extraordinary oral history interview she had recently conducted with Edie, including a short segment about an institution called the Moore River Native Settlement. A newcomer to Western Australian history, I was astonished by what I read — and ashamed of my ignorance. The next day, I headed straight for the library to find out more.

That was nearly four years ago.

The ensuing quest has been the adventure of a lifetime — intellectually, spiritually and professionally. I am proud to have been allowed to act as catalyst and, later, as assembler and scribe for the inspired team of storytellers and story-listeners who joined me in the search.

By far the most important of these have been the former children of Moore River themselves. Represented by seventeen courageous informants — Hazel Anderson, Jim and Myrtle Brennan, Robert Bropho, Eric Conway, Ken Colbung, Doreen Dalgety, Elizabeth Dalgety, Ralph Dalgety, Jack Davis, Olive Hart, Vincent Lambadgee, Ned Mippy, Phyllis Mippy, Edie Moore, Alice Nannup, Angus Wallam and Bella Yappo — their interviews yielded some two thousand pages of raw remembrance, reflection and revelation. It was from this goldmine of Aboriginal Australia that the present volume was largely dug. I am in no position to 'thank' these people. Quite simply, this book belongs to them.

When invited to direct the oral history component of the project, Annette Roberts — a self-described 'farmer's wife from

Dandaragan' — couldn't decide whether to be exhilarated or scared witless. She bravely joined the team anyway, and in the end conducted nineteen of the twenty interviews herself. In her own modest and unerringly polite way, Annette proved our best inspiration and most acute critic. But her special genius — and it is evident on every page of this book — is to listen. For an historian, I can think of no higher accolade.

Dr Joan Wardrop, a scholar of enormous breadth and skill, gamely agreed to tackle the Moore River archives. The perspicacity and attention to detail of Native Affairs bureaucrats found their match in Joan, who would eventually present me with a phonebook sized binder bristling with her quarry. The librarians at the Battye will remember her as the one who spent much of first semester 1990 weeping into her laptop. For this compassion, as much as for her encyclopedic research feat, Joan's contribution is gratefully acknowledged.

Dr Will Christensen, Head of Curtin University's School of Social Sciences and a distinguished anthropologist of Aboriginal Australia, acted for all of us as facilitator, mentor and conscience. His participation as consulting anthropologist opened door after door that would otherwise have remained closed to our fumbling. His unqualified support as Head of School meant we had the wherewithal to explore each of them unencumbered, and in our own good time.

It was our great good fortune that the first of these doors was the one leading to Cedric Wyatt's office. As Commissioner of the Aboriginal Affairs Planning Authority of Western Australia, Cedric provided a generous research and travel grant, without which the Moore River Project would probably have remained an intriguing but rather sketchy proposal mouldering somewhere in the graveyard of my hard disk. Cedric took a big gamble on us, and I have no higher aspiration for this book than that it justify his staunch faith in us.

Maggie Garton, Cedric's right-hand, made me laugh harder than anyone, even when I was pregnant. Ken Colbung, who is related to everyone, conducted a series of invaluable community consultations and introduced us to a vast network of Moore River alumni. Curtin

University's Centre for Aboriginal Studies, under the direction of Pat Dudgeon, also provided helpful support during the project's planning stage. Marjorie Bandy, Eileen Isbister Neal and, especially, Sister Eileen Heath spoke freely and fearlessly about Moore River from a non-Aboriginal perspective. Phil Prosser's courage and generosity in sharing his mother's remarkable Native Affairs file made possible this book's most eloquent chapter, 'One Half Caste Girl'. I am also grateful for the technical assistance provided for this chapter by the ever-efficient John Priestly, Information Officer at the Department of Social Services. Project Secretary Sharon Bonner expertly transcribed most of the interviews, and Samanttha Wilson's exhaustive research assistance gave substance to the idea behind Chapter Five, 'The Moore River Scrapbook'. That idea, incidentally, was a last-minute inspiration of my editor Bryce Moore, whose ability to understand what I was getting at even better than I did was sometimes unsettling.

Susan Maushart

Fremantle Arts Centre Press receives financial assistance from the Western Australian Department for the Arts.

Publication of this title was assisted by the Australia Council, the Federal Government's arts funding and advisory body.

Sort of a place like

HOME

Introduction

One: The Place

3 January 1930

Mr A O Neville
Chief Protector of Aborigines

Dear Sir:

I am fowarding the composition about the Settlement that you asked me to do when you were here. I hope you will like it as I did my very best to have every word complete.

Yours respectfully,

Gilligan

"The Settlement"

The Settlement lies on the bank of a river which is called the Moore River, the hills surrounding it making it look quite a pleasant little home.

The houses are opposite each other, and the trees on each side which are of good height form an avenue.

There is also the patch of young pines of one year's growth, which are all growing rapidly. They were grown by Mr. Neal the Superintendent of Moore River.

Every morning the girls and boys get up at half past six which gives them time to dress for breakfast, the breakfast takes place at

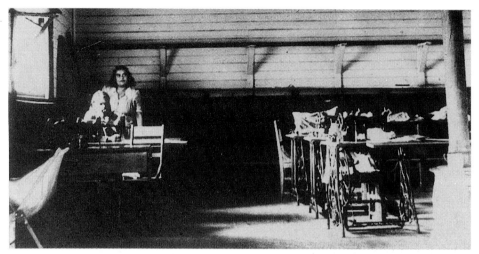

seven. When breakfast is over the children have what they call cubby houses in parts of the compound where it's bushy.

There they play until it's time to have their hair combed. The Matron sees to that. At 8:30 the sewing bell rings and the girls go down to the workroom immediately they hear it ring, and set to work with the things that are given to them to do.

Nurse Crosse who is the sewing mistress sees that every thing is done right in the work room.

Then at nine the school bell rings and the children come skipping along chattering and laughing from all directions, then they form two straight lines and march into their places quietly.

The roll is called, when that's over they set to work doing arithmetic etc.

When school is over at play hours the girls and boys scamper over to the playground which is a treat to them. Then the school bell rings again at eleven and the children immediately leave off playing and come to school.

The dinner is ready at twelve.

The bell is rung three times, to make sure everybody hears.

The first bell rings when the dinner is being given out, when the second bell rings everybody comes to the dining room.

When the third bell rings everyone goes in and stands quite still until the Nurse who's on duty comes in. Grace is said, and they sit down and have dinner.

The same is done at teatime except for the "Lord's Prayer" which is said after tea.

During the Summer seasons the girls and boys often go swimming or fishing.

Large numbers of fish are caught in parts of Moore River.

When fishing, the smaller children often have long reeds beside them.

When they catch a fish they stick the smooth part of the reed through the fish's head and let it slip down to the bottom.

At the bottom is a cluster of seeds, that prevents the fish from falling through.

The favourite spot for girls is Honey Pot, where they generally swim in the Summer.

At Saddle Hill the beautiful Geraldton wax plant grows. It looks beautiful when in bloom. It is exceedingly showy, the trees don't grow very tall only of medium height.

Everybody loves picking them.

At the beginning of Winter the school children and the bigger girls look forward to mushroom picking which they gather in barks.

The camps lie in a sort of valley in a row. Most of the couples have a kangaroo dog which they take out in the weekend to catch kangaroo and rabbit, which are multiplying rapidly around Moore River.

Saturday is the bath day for all the girls and boys. There are three large baths in the bath room. After their bath they bring their clothes they have been wearing to the Nurse, and the Nurse puts down a stroke against their name. The boys have their bath first and the girls have theirs.

Everybody here appreciates the goodness of the Government and Chief Protector in providing food and clothing, and are thankful for the kindness of the Matron and the Superintendent and Staff for the good work they have done for them, particularly the teacher who has taught them to read and write which is the most important thing to know.

As Mr. Schenk of Mt. Margaret Mission said a little while back, some of our colour who are still uncivilised are being cruelly treated by some of the bad white people.

The people here are very thankful for all they have got and they are all trying hard to help one another.

Introduction

Two: The People

JIM BRENNAN

Born: 9 October 1917
Mother: Aboriginal, name unknown
Father: Tony Blankard, Maltese

... They tried to appeal to the police there that they adopted me. They were Catholic, good Catholic and they christened me as a Catholic, and we was goin' to church every weekend, and they were really upset over it. I didn't know what to do. I keep running and the police keep bringin' me back, and they end up tied me up ... yeah tied me over and then they, then the caretaker, a lady, white woman was lookin' after me at the time, she told 'em, told the police, 'Leave us alone', and they told her to go and mind her own business. They put me in a cell in Laverton that time and I shouted and cried and tried to get out [laughs] of the place, but didn't work ... Yeah, there were about, might be about eight or nine of us kids all tied up. Then we all got sent, they draft us out in different colours, and if you're whiter than the other kids, you half-caste, quarter-caste or quadroon or whatever it is, they draft us out like that and I was drafted out to be sent to Moore River Native Settlement there, and when I got there every Aboriginal looked like meself, same colour ....

MYRTLE EVANS (CORDELLA) BRENNAN

Born: 1 August 1927, Lake Darlot, Western Australia
Mother: Daisy Cordella, Aboriginal
Father: John Evans, Irishman

... They used to hide me in the bush, my mother and father, because they were afraid of losing me. See in those days they used to take away part-Aboriginal kids and send them to Moore River. When I was born I was carried around in a suitcase. That's only way they could hide me. They had a little hole in the suitcase so that I wouldn't get smothered, and they carried me round till they couldn't carry me any more in the suitcase.

When we were caught we was at a place called Poke's Find — Dad was prospecting there — and the police came out there and Mum and I were just coming back from hunting, and saw the motor there and we're just going to run and he told us, this policeman, 'Stop or I'll shoot!' I was still pulling my mother, I wanted to keep going, whether we got shot or not, but she pulled me back and we went back and then we was taken to Wiluna ... We got on the train from Wiluna and we went to Geraldton and straight through to Perth there. My mother was still with me, and there was a policeman with us. Anyway, when we went to Perth we stopped in Bennett House. That was the place there where the Aboriginal people used to stop before they go up to Moore River. So I don't know how long we stopped there — just couldn't recollect now — but at the end, it might have been a week or a fortnight, and we went to Moore River then.

Oh, I didn't like the place. No, it was sort of too many people and it wasn't a place you could live in — I thought. You get these bugs and things, fleas eating you. And then we was drafted away from our parents, like the women's dormitory was next to ours, and the children's dormitory was next, all in that same area. But you was locked away from your mother ...

24

ELIZABETH RAY DALGETY

Born: c1922, Balladonia Station
Mother: Dora Ray, Aboriginal
Father: Bob Ray, European

I was on the station when I was born until I was 'bout five, as I said 'bout five or six, they took me away. I don't know why. I suppose because there's no schooling there and I was too white for my mother and father. Yeah, I remember the day that the police from Norseman came there to pick me up and took me to Norseman. He took me to Norseman and then left me and I had to stay at the police station with them, him and his wife. Oh I felt awful. I cried all night. Tell you the truth, I cried and cried. I wanted to go back to my mother and I couldn't go back. All he said was you got to go to this place where you have to go to school, that's all, he didn't tell me where I was going. My mother, well, she stood there as they, as I got in the car and went and she just cried and cried. I can see her crying, you know. I can see her standing there crying and I just couldn't do nothing, just standing there. Nothing she could do, nothing at all. She just stand and watch me go away.

I never seen her again. When I got married and went back to Norseman to see my mother, they told me that you're a week late because your mother only died a week ago ... Never even had a photo of her.

I went by train to Perth and they put me to the Bennett House, you know East Perth. I was there for two weeks then the Moore River truck came down and picked me up and took me to Mogumber and when I got off I seen all these kids running and I thought to myself, 'Oh this is must be the place where I got to stay', and I see all the kids running and all swarmed around the truck to see who was the strange girl. You can hear them saying, 'Oh that's the new girl, who's her name?' One of the blokes said, 'Oh that's Lizzy Ray', and then they want to know where I come from and who was my parents, big mob of kids.

So this old nurse took me to the dormitory where we had to sleep, took me there and showed me dorms where we are to sleep and all

25

the beds and mattresses and she said, 'Oh you can make friends with
your little girls and boys', she said, 'because you have to stay here
now'. When she said that, I could remember I was crying, I didn't
want to stop there, and a couple of days after I asked one of the kids,
I said, 'When I'm gonna go home?', and girls that works in the dormitory they said, 'I'm sorry, my dear, but you won't be able to go
home yet, because Neville and Bray took you away from your parents. You have to go to school here in the Mogumber Mission now.'
Oh I didn't like it, I tell you, at first I didn't like it. I cried for weeks
I did, and you know they used to come and talk to me, kids used to
come and 'Oh don't cry you'll get used to being here, you'll meet
your friends'. But I would say, 'I want my mum, I'm going back to
my mum and dad in Balladonia', I used to say to them ...

BELLA ASHWIN YAPPO

Born: 11 February 1917, Leonora, Western Australia
Mother: Winnie Ashwin, part-Aboriginal
Father: George Dunn, Scotsman

Q: What age were you when you went to Mogumber?
A: Fifteen, I think.
Q: And how was it that the family came to go down to Moore River. Why was that?
A: Well there was no school, education was the reason. Most of the people were sent there for school.
Q: How did you feel about that?
A: Well I didn't learn anything, I was too old to learn anything.

ANGUS WALLAM

Born: 1 October 192?, Moore River Native Settlement
Mother: Beatrice Kearing, part-Aboriginal
Father: Lewis Wallam, part-Aboriginal

Q: Were both your mother and father at the settlement?
A: Yeah, both of them, yeah.
Q: And whereabouts had they been living before they went to the settlement?
A: They were all working on farms, all around Goomalling and all them places.
Q: Do you know why they went to the settlement, why they would stop working?
A: Well I think the what's-its-name, the department people, Neville and them, I think put them in there.

ALICE BASSETT NANNUP

Born: 17 October 1911, Abydos Station,
                   Western Australia
Mother: Dot, Aboriginal
Father: Tom Bassett, European

... and one day Mrs Campbell out of the blue came and said, 'Well Alice, you and Herbert and Doris are going to Mogumber'. I said, 'Where is that?' She said, 'I don't know', she said, 'but Mr Neville wants youse to go to Mogumber and go to school there because there's no school here'. I thought to myself, well, this is it, you see, and 'When do we go?' and she said, 'Oh in a couple of days' time'. So they took us into Broomehill, picked Doris up and took us to Broomehill and put us on the train and that was the last of it ...

28

DOREEN MAY THOMPSON DALGETY

Born: 1923, Dongara, Western Australia
Mother: Dora Leyland, part-Aboriginal
Father: Arthur Thompson, Irishman

... We didn't like it very much, but we just sort of had to go, I suppose, it was Government rules.

... It was very cold that morning. That's what I could remember. And so my father and mother made up a plan that if he stayed with us — they had us in the gaol house in Mingenew — while he stayed with us (we all had to sleep there in the cell), she'd make a break for it. I don't know what her plans were but she didn't get very far. It was night-time and the police constable caught her, and brought her back and she was brought back to the prison cell and we had to go from there the next morning and it was very cold, and we was put on the train and went to Mogumber.

[The family left after five months.] But when we were taken away the second time to go to Moore River we just were taken on our own. That was in '36, because my father had an accident. A motorbike hit him and broke his leg, and he was in the old public hospital. And see my mother got a bit depressed and things like that that she'd take off and leave us children on our own. We were living in Dog Swamp then. And we just had tents and tin humpies but we were more or less sort of secluded, you know. We weren't in contact with the other people. I was thirteen when my brother went with this other boy, and they got caught in a house stealing apples and food, and the man told them — he caught them — and he told them to sit down and eat the apples, and then he got the police. So the police took my brother away first. My other older sister, she was already in Moore River. She'd been taken some couple of years before. And then they took us to court and all this charges come up about my brother and so forth that we were being neglected children. So we went to Moore River the next couple of days after the court hearing.

VINCENT LAMBADGEE

Born: 12 March 1924, Moore River Native Settlement
Mother: Annie Calgaret, Aboriginal
Father: Jack Lambadgee, part-Aboriginal

Q: Do you know when your parents went there or how they came
   to go there?
A: No I really don't know how they got there. My mother was
   telling me, but she didn't say how they got there. I know that
   my father came from the nor'west, and that's about all.
Q: So were your parents living at the camp?
A: Yes, I think they would have been down there. I wouldn't really know before because we don't, we never ask questions.

RALPH DALGETY

Born: c1923, Dalgety Downs Station, Western Australia
Mother: Ivy Wolga, Aboriginal
Father: Mort Fitzpatrick, Irishman

... Our old man *owned* the station. And while he was away they came in and just grabbed us, sent us into Carnarvon, on the boat down to Fremantle and up to Moore River. And I don't even remember leavin' the station or gettin' on a boat or nothin'. Oh I must have been only about two or three years old I suppose.

Mum was with us too. Oh yes, she went down to Moore River

31

with us and she died down there then. I don't even remember her ... I believe she was upset all the time, died more or less of a broken heart I think. She wanted to go back home again. I don't even know what the old boy, old man looked like ... I had two sisters, five of us, three boys, two girls. That's from *my* mother, but the old boy, he had some more kids from another woman. Yeah. And there was four of them. But we all went together. They took the lot of us, put us all on a boat, both families ...

NED MIPPY

Born:	1 January 1919, Mandurah, Western Australia
Mother:	Clara Harris, Leyland part-Aboriginal
Father:	Arthur Mippy, part-Aboriginal

... Oh I reckon I was around three, three or four, when my parents put me into Carrolup [Native Settlement]. I think it was that Mum and Dad couldn't look after me, couldn't care for me, and whether they were drinking or not I couldn't say that, but for the good of me own health, that's why they took me ... [Some time later Ned was transferred to Moore River, where his parents had taken up residence.] I just thought they were some other people when I arrived at Mogumber. They had to posh me up and kid me round before I believed them. I remember getting off the train there and I was really looking for a motor car, and there was a sulky there with a horse in it, and they came over, and a couple of the boys was there to con me into the thing ... Otherwise if I'd 've seen a white man there I might have took off in the bush ...

ERIC CONWAY

Born:	1932, Mulga Downs Station
Mother:	Blanche (Naijong), Aboriginal
Father:	Spiros Cosmos, Greek

... I did some chasing up with Community Services — a bit of chasing up of some records of history as to when exactly we were picked up from up there ... The record states that both of us, Harold and I, were picked up from our parents in 1937. I remember when the policeman arrived there, two policemen, sorry, and the Native Inspector arrived in this mustering camp, it was about eighty-odd k's south of Port Hedland, called White Springs, and they used to just come on to the camps like that when they were going out searching for kids. 'Ooh, where's your kids?' 'Ooh that one, that one, that one, that one.' Well, they looked straight at Harold and I, 'You two get your swag and get on that truck,' 'cause we were the two half-castes, left our full-blood ones behind. We didn't know the reason for that, we just thought we were going for a ride. 'Come on, Harold!' Chuck our little blanket on and away we go.

Yeah anyway they got us into Port Hedland, they picked up two of our cousins and a sister. They were living on nearby stations, that's right, Rosie our sister and Reggie and Margery our cousins and we're all half-castes, kept in Port Hedland to be checked ready for the journey to Perth. I can remember then we were loaded in a basket, taken out in a dinghy 'cause the big ship, the old *Koolinda*, couldn't get into the harbour in those days, they had to anchor it just out of Port Hedland, took us out in dinghies and loaded us into this basket and hoisted us onto the state ship like that, three kids at a time ...

HAZEL COLBUNG ANDERSON

Born: 4 October 1918, Mount Barker, Western Australia
Mother: Emma Harris, part-Aboriginal
Father: Joe Colbung, Aboriginal

... Couldn't say what year my father died, but I know after that we moved to Moore River in 1924, see. I was six. Nearly six when we moved there. Funny part of it, they wanted to take us away when our father was living, but he said no. They say they want to grab all the family what got school children see, that's what they was looking at, the school kids. Yeah, but Mum told me that my dad said that they not takin' us to the settlement, to the Moore River Settlement, when he can work and keep us ...

This policeman, he was a nice sergeant, he told us we had to pack up and, 'cause we were going, got to catch that train. We were going up to the Moore River Settlement. We got ready. We had a dog, we asked, our kangaroo dog it was only young dog, so

Mum asked the sergeant could we take the dog with us and he said yes. So we all went to the station and got on. My mother, she didn't say much. I think she was worried too, but see I thought, where we was goin' to that I knew no one, because the people

used to tell us down home that 'If you go away, don't go to that place 'cause there's people that eat people up there', Nyoongahs like us. Must have been telling us to frighten us, I suppose. That's the reason why, that's the reason why my brother wouldn't come. When we said we was goin' he said, 'I'm not goin' up there to be ate! Ate by Nyoongahs.' ...

OLIVE MORRISON HART

Born: 1919, Katanning, Western Australia
Mother: Martha Orchard, part-Aboriginal
Father: Samuel Morrison, part-Aboriginal

... After Mum died we were all sent away up there, Moore River Native Settlement. Dad came up there, stopped a week with us and he had to come back to shear, see, come back and did his shearin'. He took us up there and left us. We took the Albany Progress to Perth, and then we caught the eastbound train goin' out that way, up north way, to Mogumber. Got a big truck to pick us up like a load of cattle [laughter] or, you know, sheep or anything else, it had big sides on it so the kids don't fall out ...

PHYLLIS NARRIER MIPPY

Born: c1927, Moore River Native Settlement
Mother: Rose Brown, part-Aboriginal
Father: Frank Narrier, part-Aboriginal

... My parents met in the settlement, see. My mother went to the settlement when she was a little girl, and my old dad was put in there. That's where they met and they got married ...

EDITH MADELINE WORRALL MOORE

Born: 29 March 1918, Moora, Western Australia
Mother: Clara Worrall, part-Aboriginal
Father: Leopold Websdale, part-Aboriginal

... Well, my grandfather had gone out on one of these trips, like he'd go way, like way past Walebing onto these farms to try and find work, and it was one of those times that he was out there when the sergeant from Moora came out and Tilly Michael, she had two daughters, and he took them, you see, because someone must have said these girls were there, and because they talked about herding kids up to send them to the Moore River Settlement. Well, then, because she went in and asked why did they take her two daughters and left me? So therefore the following week he comes out and collects me. And I was sent down there, you see, to go to school. And then I only had eighteen months and they sent me out to work. Well, I'd hardly had time to learn a thing.

The first three months I just cried and cried. Especially because I didn't see my grandfather to say goodbye to him, and in that time I got a message to say he died, and that made it a darn sight worse. So then my grandmother — you see, they still had my sister and they didn't want to lose her and they kept moving. They put her in, I think they put her in to New Norcia because they felt New Norcia was different. You could go there, and you could take your children away. Where the settlement, the government took you and shoved you in there, and forgot about you ...

38

KEN COLBUNG

Born:	2 September 1931, Moore River Native Settlement
Mother:	Eva Colbung, part-Aboriginal
Father:	unknown

... Yeah, I was born on the Moore River Native Settlement. My mother had me because she was raped in Fremantle when she worked for the Grosvenor Hospital, down at Beaconsfield. She was then sentenced back to the boob, put in the boob, because that was the pattern of life in those days with the Aboriginal people ... My mother was in Moore River when the family first came up in 1924. The whole family was taken there. First of all, Madge was taken up there, then the rest of the family, and Auntie Josie was left at Katanning and then she was sent up there. And then everybody was there. They told them they had to go there but they had to give

39

themselves freely or they would just send them up by warrant, because they executed warrants against the Aboriginal people in those days to get them off the land that the white people wanted, and Grandfather Joe applied for land and because he did that I think they had a set against him and wanted to get him away from that area ...

JACK DAVIS

Born: March 1917, Subiaco, Western Australia
Mother: Alice, part-Aboriginal
Father: Billy (Bung Singh) Davis, part-Aboriginal

... Mr Neville, who was Protector of Aborigines at the time, rang my dad, got in touch with my father and said how would he like to send his two, two of the older boys — that's my brother Harold and myself — to Moore River Settlement where we would learn about farming. I think they needed those sort of boys who were educated — had a bit of common sense — because not too many Aboriginal people in those days had education and of course we were educated. We'd been through the school system. He thought we might make good employees for some employer ...

ROBERT CHARLES BROPHO (BROPHY)

Born: 9 February 1930, Toodyay, Western Australia
Mother: Isabelle (Bella) Leyland, part-Aboriginal
Father: Thomas Brophy, Aboriginal

... For being in the company of adult Aboriginal men older than myself, receiving stolen clothes, we all went to the Bunbury court in Bunbury. That was south of Perth. They went to the adult court, and when I went into the children's court I was confused because I was confused with the words which I didn't know then but I know now what the difference is. 'Institution' and 'execution' is two different words. 'Execution' is you gonna be, you gonna be done away with, or you're gonna be killed! 'Institution' is put away into some place because you're under age. And I stood in the court and I was sentenced to an institution which was Moore River Native Settlement.

I come back into the prison yard where the older boys were and they said to me, 'What happened to you?' And I was quiet, 'cause I said, 'They're goin' to execute me!' [Laughs]. I was real quiet, and I said, 'I think they're gonna execute me', and then they all busted out laughing because they knew and I didn't know! And they sung out to one of the police constables to come and get him to explain it to me. So he come and told me ...

chapter 1

A Day in the Life of Moore River

Observers of the Moore River Native Settlement have tended to describe the place in dramatic terms — 'a woeful spectacle', 'a concentration camp', 'a day and night brothel'. Yet to the inmates themselves, settlement life was a good deal more prosaic. Particularly for the children, many of whom had no basis for comparison anyway, the institutional routine was simply a set of unfortunate but inalienable facts of life. Conditions at Moore River were a bit like the weather — everybody griped about them, but no one seriously believed anything could be done to alter them. Life in the compound was dreary, and at times downright degrading. But it had the virtue of consistency, and its boundaries, though narrow, were clear for all to see.

No one is better qualified to tell the story of everyday life at the Moore River Native Settlement than the children who lived there. This chapter is narrated by two of them, a boy and a girl. Although strictly speaking they are fictional characters, their words are not drama but documentary. The alternating monologues of the boy (Roman type) and girl (italic type) have been constructed, like vast jigsaw puzzles, from the pieces of eighteen interviews with the former children of Moore River. All the incidents described in these monologues actually happened. The language in which they are described is also faithful to original sources. Time sequences have been altered or compressed, some of the names have been changed and certain details have been sharpened or shaded to enhance the accuracy of the whole.

The quoted material that appears throughout this chapter is drawn largely from archival sources and should be read as a commentary on the children's stories. In some cases, this material amplifies or explains a point made in the main text. In others it counterpoises an 'official' version of reality to that which the children have experienced and expressed.

Because they shoulder the textual responsibility of 'standing in' for so many individual children, an attempt has been made to render the characters of the boy and girl as representative as possible. At the same time, each child has a distinctive personality and point of view. The boy, who is the first to speak, is about nine years old. With his mother and other relatives resident in the camp, his experience of settlement life is more or less positive — an accurate reflection of how most male informants recalled their childhood experiences. The girl is a few years older and a more recent arrival. She has no family at the settlement, and her perspective on compound life is both gloomier and more resigned than the boy's. Again, this reflects accurately the majority experience of female informants — particularly those who had been separated from their families. By contrast with the boys, who were allowed quite extraordinary freedom of movement, the girls generally had more responsibilities, greater restrictions and fewer gratifications.

The realities of settlement life altered substantially from decade to decade and at times from year to year. A decision was made to set 'A Day in the Life of Moore River' in, roughly, 1939 — the final year of A J Neal's career as Superintendent. Chronologically and in other ways, this year is a midway point in the life of the institution. At about this time, the settlement reached its apex in administrative efficiency and in the quality of staff, while standards of nutrition and hygiene remained at pre-Child Endowment lows. Finally, while it cannot be argued that the year 1939 was 'representative' of the Moore River experience over more than three decades, it is the period about which we are best informed, owing largely to the ages and memories of those interviewed.

*

long	6.30am	shake a leg
short	7.25am	stand by
long	7.30am	breakfast
long	8.30am	roll call
short	10.30am	morning tea [staff]
long	11.50am	hospital, trackers camp
short	12.00noon	stand by
long	12.05pm	dinner
long	1.30pm	roll call
short	4.55pm	stand by
long	5.00pm	tea
short	6.15pm	stand by
long	6.30pm	dormitories

Daily Alarm Bells, Moore River, c1946

Yeah, well, when Mum passed away, I mean, we were more or less lost. We had no relations down there.

None at all?

No.

How did that feel?

Terrible, terrible. See they bunged us in the dormitory when Mum passed away, see. We were only tiny.

How did you get on with the other children?

All right, good. I loved 'em, loved 'em, all me little mates, yeah. That's the first thing I think about when I go back to Moore River and have a look around there.

1990, Ralph Dalgety to Annette Roberts

'Wakey, wakey boys — come on, rise and shine. Up and do your work before school!'

That's Kingy (he's a tracker and he can *yell*). Goin' up and down the rows, beltin' a board with a stick. Us kids, we hidin' down in our beds, see, 'cause it's too dark to get up. Too cold too! Soon (not

45

Kingy, c1938. 'Wakey, wakey boys — come on, rise and shine.'

soon enough but) Kingy, he go off across to the girls. Good ol' boss, yeah. We can hear him bangin' on the walls over there. They just the other side, see? We can hear 'em squealin' if we listen hard.

Six o'clock always come too soon. In my bed, we got three (or four — who's that lump down the bottom?). A lot warmer that way, see, with all our blankets together. We got iron beds, those fold-up ones — you know, kick the leg underneath 'em? There's one for almost everybody. But when it gets cold, we just pile up them ol' mattresses on the floor. Can't fall out that way! (Some of them mattresses stink, but. See, if the little kids wet theirselves at night, it just kinda soaks in there. Trackers come and throw 'em under the cold tap of a morning — the kids, I mean. The mattresses, they just sit there.)

Too dark to see much but rows and rows of bumpy beds, and bumpy lumps a' boys. Always dark in here — jarrah walls we got, more blacker than Kingy, and windows stuck over with mesh. Too dark to get up ... And it's freezin' out there. Can't you hear that rain? Hear it? Over there by the door (it's locked up, see) wind's blowin' bits a' straw all round ... Maybe I'll just pull this blanket up over me ears and ...

Oh no! Here he come now through the door! Run! Strap swingin' — come on! There's boys screamin', yellin', jumpin' out a' their swags. I'm laughin' at the little kids. They scared a' Kingy. Don't know any better yet. Soon he's gone out the back to his own place, gone to boil the billy. We got any time later, we crowd round that fire and get warm, yeah. Maybe he chase us with strap, but never catched us yet. He's a good old boss, is Kingy. Good ol' fella.

*

Blast that man! We just fall asleep and it's time to get up again. Rather be scratchin' from bugs in me old bed than shiverin' outside it. Bugs must love that stuff that come off a coconut (that's what they put in the mattress).

Gracie had a bed full o' maggots once and Matron got mad and Gracie start cryin'. But Matron, she was only mad at the maggots. She lovely to us, she is.

Here she comes now — second wake-up call, but we pretend like we don't hear. Wakey, wakey! Rise and shine! Girls startin' to

Standard issue Tuffnut clothing, c1938. 'No night-dress, no day dress, just dress.'

groan and move. No sense jumpin' up yet, 'cause there's nothin' to do but freeze between now and breakfast. Here she come again — really yellin' now — OK, OK. I gotta rise but I ain't gonna shine.

Don't take but a second to make up the bed. No sheets to fuss with. (Except once I seen 'em, when Mr Neville come to visit. We scrub everything then, and from somewhere they get sheets. We not allowed to touch 'em. They gone before we ever get in bed.) Some girls got pillows. Most have two blankets like me, one to lay on and one to cover. Keep the bed bugs warm, yeah!

I see all me little mates gettin' up slow, scratchin' heads — if it's not the bugs it's the nits, they everywhere now. I get up too. Shake myself like a puppy dog, all over. Smooth my dress what I slept in but it's so stiff, like a paper sack. No clean clothes till Wednesday.

No night dress, no day dress. (Nowhere to put 'em even if we did.)
Just dress — all the same, all made out a' some stuff called Tuffnut
what's hard to rip. The colour is like dirt (Nurse says 'khaki'),
which we girls hate. We get 'em off the shelves in the mending room
of a Wednesday and a Saturday. Underwear too (whoever heard of
Tuffnut bloomers?) but that's only Saturdays.

Now I'm almost with the big girls I try an' wash out me vest and
pants between times. That's them hanging off the bedstead. Oooooh!
Still cold and wet! Never mind. 'Be clean in thought, word and deed'
is what Teacher learnt us in Girl Guides. Wish I had a piece of soap
like Olive. It's Sunshine and she bought it herself in the store. That
cardboard box under her bed — that's where she hides it at night.
Carries it around with her the whole day, too. Sometimes me and me
mates steal bits of soap what come down the drain over the laundry.
We walk along the drain and pick those little pieces of soap up. Take
ourselves off to the river then and wash our things. We look nice then!

Nana Leyland (she's the attendant) comin' round now make sure
we've had a wash. Supposed to go have a cold shower. Even if I could
stand to freeze, I can't stand the stink in that washroom of a morning.
See, some of the girls use the basins for toilets and — yuck! Can't
blame 'em, but. It's hard findin' that little bucket in the middle of the
night. Just one round bucket for all us girls — maybe a hundred —
well, it fills up too soon! (The big girls get newspaper every night, but
not us little girls.) They put that phenol stuff in the bottom but it sure
does stink anyway. We sooner wash in the sun in the river later.

> ... the children were using the floor in most cases because
> ample sanitary conveniences were not available to the
> children. The lavatory was covered each day with dry
> sand and the following day the sand with the refuse was
> taken away and fresh sand thrown over the floor. This
> practice, as you have no doubt noticed, is very bad and
> does not reflect any credit on the person who inaugurated
> the idea ...
>
> Deputy Commissioner of Native Affairs to
> Superintendent, September 1946

One of the nurses used to say to me, 'I always have to
have a cigarette before I go in there in the morning'.

Sister Eileen Heath

*Nana off tryin' to comb the little girls' hair. (She don't worry
about my hair, 'cause I gone baldy. I stop crying about it now, if
anybody make fun I pretend I don't see. Matron had to shave me for
the head lice, but it's cruel not lettin' me wear a cap to cover it,
cruel's what I call it.) Everybody use the same comb, everybody use
the same towel. It's not hygiene, Matron says, but where we got to
put our combs or towels? (Olive has hair slides, she keeps 'em in
her box.) Things just go missing an' dirty, so we share and don't
worry too much.*

*There's the bell for shake a leg! We gonna be late again — and
late to breakfast mean no breakfast. Bed's made — that's the easy
part! Now us bigger girls (I'm eleven, see) got to sweep up all
around with a big broom. Do you believe the mess us girls can make
in one night! There's crumbs (at night we eat the bread and fat we
steal at tea — hide under our pillow till lock-up and then have a
good feed) and squashed up berries (those go under the bed, see)
and bits of coconut straw and hair and dead bugs — aw! Then wipe
it over with a bucket and a rag and some more of that phenol stuff,
then ... STAND BY BELL!!! We gone!*

*

Kingy must a' had his cuppa already — he's back herdin' us like a
mob a' sheep into the washroom. Them big ol' tubs is full of cold
water — like ice, it is, never heard of hot water in there. You have a
wash or you have a strap. Not sure which one feels worse but.

Chores now, before breakfast. Wish I had me cuppa tea out here.
I'd pour it on the sand and stand on it to warm my feet, yeah! Them
two there, they go over the butcher shop and cut the meat up for the
day. Lucky! 'cause they might get a knuckle bone to roast for later.
Me four mates over there get to bring in the cows for milking (that's

50

good too when there's a fresh cow pat to stand on, ahhh!). The little boys, they got chores too. They the street cleaners. Every morning they gotta rake the main street — it's a big wide sand track — all the way from the dormitories across to the staff quarters and the school and back over the Big House.

Me and this mob here, this week we get the worst job of all. We gotta help cart away all the buckets from the whole place. Matron calls 'em 'sanitary pans' but they sure don't smell sanitary to me! One of the campies drives the old cart while we boys trot out with empty buckets and take away the the full ones. Dump 'em behind the hospital somewheres in little rows. Sometime we do out the buckets every day, and that's bad enough. But sometime the men get slack and it's only maybe twice a week ... There's that many flies you can't see. Sure can smell, but.

That stink's still in my nose by the time we hear 'Stand By'. That's the bell tell us get ready for breakfast and we run like hell to the dining room. All the kids does — see 'em come flyin' out from everywhere. You line up on the verandah, see (the trackers, they make sure the lines is nice and neat), and wait for the second bell to go marchin' in. Man, are we hungry! Course, we always hungry. But specially for breakfast, 'cause we had tea at five o'clock and now it's half past seven, and that's a long time between bread and fat.

As we go in I see some kids come tearin' down from the river. They ain't gonna make it, not this morning. Nothing till dinnertime for them kids, unless they got theirself some fish down there. Wish they'd give us some fish up here (there's plenty cobbler in that ol' river) but it's always the same: bread and scrape and porridge with funny milk.

'Cept for them coppers clanking where they put the fat — and our plates are tin and clanky too — and the tea kinda sploshing into our mugs, it's real quiet. We ain't allowed to talk, see. You just try it, and you'll have Kingy and Bluey over there show you what happens. (Mostly they just yell at you — but they could whip you if they wanted, they could.)

Anyway, we too hungry to talk, and sometimes if you eat fast they'll give you another piece of bread and fat. (If it's jam day you get this jam made out of melon rind or black treacle.) We like to

sneak it out (you just shove it down your shirt when Bluey's chattin'
up the kitchen girls) and toast it over a fire before school. Tastes
better, somehow, outside and with the fire. You can talk then, too,
without anybody smacking you.

*

*After breakfast, the boys and the littlest girls get to run around and
play. We gotta stay here, though, and clean up: scrub them big pots,
about six or seven of them, that's my job. When I finish that I get
down my hands and knees and scrub that floor. You gotta do it right,
too, or they just lock you up in here. One day I just had that floor
clean and the nurse come (she ain't no nurse really, but that's what
they make us call them) and she just got the water, hot boiling
water, and chucked it all over the floor again. That's how she
punished me. Now do it right, she says. Still, us girls work in the
kitchen — peelin' vegies, settin' the table and that — we can have
some fun when nobody there to watch over us. And most of the time,
the white staff rather have smoke-o anyway than look out for us.*

> Anybody could apply for a job, and anybody could get it.
> Whether they had any training or experience or not, it
> didn't make any difference ... [The staff] were just
> marking time, really ... I don't think they expected any
> improvement. They certainly didn't get any. There was
> no forward looking that 'Oh, well, things are going to be
> better next week' because they weren't. It was just the
> same old routine, day after day.
>
> Sister Eileen Heath

*Never seems to be enough of anything here — except time, and there's
so much a' that everybody's just tryin' to kill it somehow. Not enough
food, not enough clothes — not even enough rags to wash up with.
Sometimes we got to use the same ones for scrubbing the floor and for
washing up our dishes both. I always rinse 'em out as good as I can but.
   Some of the other girls, they helpin' out in the laundry before
school, hangin' the clothes on the fence to dry, or maybe some of*

Renee Hart, Lizzie Eyre, Rosie Wood, Myrtle Cordella. Front: Edie Harris, c1940. 'Some of us girls got jumpers.'

them in the bakehouse carrying bread around to the white staff (they get butter). Best job we all think is helping Miss Marshall over the kindergarten. We love them little kids — gettin' them ready for their little playschool and helping to clean the kitchen (they got their own one) and all the little cots where they sleep.

We feel sorry for them little kids, 'cause they got no mums or dads down the camps, or even aunties and that, like some of us do. And they got to stay in their little pen, like, and not mix with the big ones or go for a walk down the river or anything like that. Still they got sheets and toys and books and milk and Miss Marshall (she's got a piano), which we ain't.

An attempt has been made to segregate about 30 native children with the purpose of giving the same educational opportunities as the whites. They are housed in separate buildings, and it was intended that these children should not contact the natives of the settlement, especially the camps of the adults. The project seems doomed to failure, as limited facilities have compelled the transfer of kindergarten children to the main school.

Education Department Report, 1941

Sometime we finish early — sometime we don't do nothin' at all but stand around. Today it's so cold, we go and stand around the side of the bakehouse. The sun shines down there, see, and the baker (he's a blackfella too) sometimes he lets us clean out the tins. Some of us girls got jumpers — Gracie Comeagain knit a whole bunch for the little girls but I made my own and so did Lizzie. They give us the wool. (That's not her real name, Comeagain, they give her that name when she came here. Sister Eileen said they prob'ly couldn't say it right, that's why. Lots of us named for stations: Milli Milli, Dalgety. Orange and Lemon Ah Kim, their dad is a Chinaman greengrocer. I had a Nyoongah name but I can't remember it anymore.) I guess if we thought about it we'd be really cold. Lucky we don't think about it. And we run around a lot.

*

After breakfast we finally get to eat something. Berries, mostly. That's why we come down here, see. Those over there are my favourite: we call 'em snotty gobbles! All us kids know where to find berries and which ones are poison and when they're ripe and that. We got a fire going over by the river — we always got a fire goin' somewhere. The Boss, he say it's in our blood. (We carry plenty a wood to the Big House, but. Make you wonder about his blood!) See, a minute ago all we got was just plain bread and fat — now it's toast and dripping, yeah!

54

Me mate Arthur, he's showin' me this shanghai what he made, so I can make me own. Plenty of parrots up there in the trees — not for long, eh! After school, we'll be back here to get 'em. A course, some kids never bother even going to school — there's no one to make us — but us, we like it.

In our class we got Teacher Perrett, there's about maybe fifty kids. She's a nice lady — young, like, and smiley. She wasn't a teacher before she came here. Teacher Brenchley, she got the bigger boys and girls all the way up to the top — that's standard four, see. We all in the one room — same one what's our church on Sundays with the desks turned around the wrong way for pews. Us boys are on this side, girls on the other. Bubs sit near the door and it goes up like that to the top class. There's a boy and girl reading fifth standard books up there for a while, but they sent them down to Perth.

Teachers Marshall, Perrett and Hall, 1938. 'Just when you get used to 'em,
they leave, see?'

We never do much of work — just do a little bit and then play
time come, and go out to play and come in again. Too many of us
for much work. And then the teachers keep coming and going. I

remember Teachers Brown, Mitchell, Rae, Neal, Steen, Millen. Just when you get used to 'em they leavin', see. We says to the last one, 'Oh teacher, why do you have to go away — why do you have to go away?' And she says, 'Because we don't have enough money'.

School was spasmodic. There was a time when there was only one teacher ... It was not under the Education Department [until 1941], so there was no compulsion about hours or work curriculum at all, and the teachers did the best they could with the children of all ages. Some were almost beyond going into an infant class because they were far too old.

Sister Eileen Heath

*

For this new morning and its night
We thank you, Heavenly Father.
For rest and shelter of the night,
We thank you, Heavenly Father.
For health and strength and food and friends
For all your love and goodness sends,
We thank you, Heavenly Father.

After we all says our prayer (Sister Eileen learnt us this and Our Father) then we start doin' some copying or something. We still in bubs but we too old. Hate it when the little kids could read better than us — just want to die if Teacher asks me stand up and recite. Just won't look! When I first come here, and we had them slates, I didn't know how to make one mark on it. When I give it back, my slate was just the same way how the teacher gave it to me. Lucky she didn't notice. My sister said to me, she said, 'Look, you wanna put something down there', I said, 'What I gonna put on? I don't put nothing on.' That's how dumb I was, see, first time I go to school. My sister showed me how to make ABCs and now I can write as good as anybody almost.

Then, see, I liked going to school because I met me mates there,

all the kids and that. I stopped cryin' then because I had somebody
to go and play with, and make friends with, and it was all right then.

I find that most children adapt very quickly to a different lifestyle, and most of those that I have kept in touch with have quite happy memories of the settlement, and they're not that anti at all. You might have one or two that say we did and what we didn't have ... I think a lot of them are quite grateful for having had that education, to be able to read and write.

Marjorie Bandy (Perrett), Teacher, 1937-42

... we should confine [their education] to reading, writing and a little elementary arithmetic ... Anything further than this, except in very exceptional cases, is only creating false impressions in their minds, and causing future unhappiness through striving after that which they can never attain.

1921, Ernest Mitchell, Superintendent, MRNS (1918-21)

Chief Protector A O Neville. '"Mr Devil" is what the campies say. We just call him Mr Cup and Saucer Face.'

This morning we doin' singin', which is real good. We gotta practise for when Mr Neville come to inspect us. He like to hear us sing his favourite songs — that 'Way Down Upon the Swanee River' and 'Rule Britannia'. Those are good, but my favourite is 'Misery Farm'. See, it's all about these animals that didn't do this and didn't do that — you know, hens won't lay, we can't make hay, we work all day and get no pay. I think whoever wrote that song must of stopped here at the settlement! Oh, and 'God Save the King', too. Mr Neville, he like that one a lot. (We act we real glad to see him, but we ain't. Don't know why us kids don't like him, but we just don't. Mr Devil, I hear the campies say. We call him Mr Cup and Saucer

Face 'cause he look just like one of them cups that got a face kind of comin' off it.)

I wonder whether you could let me have a photograph of yourself which I could have enlarged, for the purpose of hanging it in the kindergarten at Moore River. If you can, I am sure the staff and children alike will be very pleased.

1942, Acting Commissioner of Native Affairs Bray to A O Neville, retired Chief Protector of Aborigines

Sometimes Teacher or maybe a monitor like Myrtle (she's a big girl helps out at school all day) take us out bush for a walk to look at the birds and flowers and that. We like that best of all, and then come back and write a story about what we seen. I always do real good at that. Sometime Teacher put a poem up and we make up pictures about it or maybe some flowers in a cup to copy.

Oh, I don't think we learned history. I don't think we learned — I don't think we learned geography. We learned, hardly learned anything ... More or less little bit of spelling or arithmetic ... I could barely spell 'cat' when I left Mogumber.

Vincent Lambadgee

Sometimes we march around outside for awhile to keep us all busy. Hate doin' sums but. Never can see how that answer comes. Can't really see what Teacher's doin' all the way up there most times. Can't hear neither — it's just a buzz, like. My sister explain me some of that stuff — she went to a real school once before we come here — but she's gone now, gone off to work somewhere down in Perth. (Mr Neville give her a bible with his autograph in it when she left. He always does that.)

She just loved school, my sister did. Read like anything. But when you fourteen, that's it, you're outa school, it's off to work. Sometimes it feels that way, they keep takin' something away from you. Each time something good happens, it get taken away. Gracie

— she's a monitor too, see — tell us long time ago in school they had toys and plasticine and dolls and that. Then one day they just disappear. That's what Gracie say. Where our dolls go? the kids ask Teacher. Take 'em away, she says, 'cause the Boss said so.

I started with ideals and hopes of success in the training of the half-caste children, but with so much interruption and lack of understanding I feel my work is at a standstill ...

Teacher Marshall to the Chief Protector, July 1940

Most times we love school but sometimes I just get hard-headed. I won't do what I'm told. Oh dear! Then Teacher — Burgess, this is — she whack me across the leg with the cane. But she lovely just the same. Well, even if she hit us in the morning, later when we leavin' she'll call us up and say, 'Hello, my dear, and how do you feel? You gonna be good tomorrow?' 'Oh yes, we'll be all right tomorrow.' 'Well, we're friends now', she always says to me, 'we friends' Oh, she's lovely, her.

*

Mostly we like school pretty good, but it don't last too long anyway — between monitor takin' us off to play, and then there's dinnertime and by the time we get back and in our places it's just about time to leave, see. We boys supposed to get farm trained, too. That's what me dad say when we come here. You gonna learn how to farm, he says. You listen, he says, and be good and learn something. But the only farm I ever seen is Bluey's garden down the river — and not even that too much, 'cause he chase us away with a strap for stealing the vegies.

The policy of the Department is to train every child so that he or she will be capable of earning his or her own living as soon as old enough ...

1921, Secretary, Department of Native Affairs

61

> So the training you expected to get there ...
> ... was non-existent.
>
> Jack Davis to Annette Roberts

They take a lot a' trouble with our noses, but. Never can figure that out. We all get some soft paper stuff every day now and then they count to three and we got to blow one side — 'Everybody blow!!' — then count to three (and take a breath or you blow your eyes right outa your head) and the other side — 'Everybody blow again!!' That's nose drill, and we never miss that. Works real good when you got that paper, but you just try it with a shirtsleeve.

> I was glad to find that the Department has no idea of forcing these children into competition with white children in the schools. It is certain that their endowment in 75% of cases makes it impossible for them to go beyond the work of standard 3 ... The remaining work will be very slowly mastered, if there is skilful teaching, but it should not be begun so early. Many of these children have not the mental power of a six-year-old white child until they are eight or nine ... The early years at school and fully half time in the later years should be devoted to practical lessons:
>
> a. the building of a shack
> b. the making of a bed
> c. the making of a fire
> d. cooking
> e. simple pottery
> f. making coarse soap for camp use
> g. nose drill
> h. disposal of waste
> i. simple laundry exercises
> j. use of knife and fork and spoon
> k. how to clear and set a table, wash dishes
> l. how to sweep a room, beat a carpet
> m. how to prepare soil for seeds.
>
> Psychologist Miss E T Stoneman, Report of June 1926

Pearlie Cross, on the day she left for Sister Kate's, c1937. 'That's where they put the fair ones.'

Twelve o'clock now — stand-by dinner!! You hear that bell, you *run*! Up to the dining room, up onto that verandah: two lines, quiet and neat. Well, neat, anyway. Hmmmmmm! Can't you smell it! It's terrible stuff, that ol' soup, but still you never get enough of it. Never know what you gonna find there — sometimes some meat and fat but funny bits, like from the insides, and tough. Peas make it seem thicker sometime or beans. Today I got a little lump of flour stuck to the bottom. Beauty! Dumplings!

We supposed to have more bread but just look at it. Even me mates won't eat that stuff: some days (like today) it's so sour-like and wet inside it make you sick. Never mind. We go down the camps after school and get somebody give us some flour for a damper, yeah! Tell those little kids it's OK. We get them a damper or something later, down the camps. Me mum's down there, see — she'll give us a feed if she can.

Domestic training class, c1939. 'Like, we did some laundry last week, and today we gotta clean out the staff kitchen.'

When I was at the settlement on the 11th inst. the following women came to see me, headed by Mrs. Mary Morden: Mrs. Mary Morden, Mrs. Hart, Mrs. Morrison (May), Mrs. Mogridge, Mrs. Oscar Little, Mrs. Jack Doherty, Mrs. Annie Stack, Mrs. Jackamarra. Mrs. Mary Morden, who was the spokeswoman, said they wanted to ask why they had to give up their children to have a cottage. I told Mrs. Morden that the position was that they had to give up the children if they wanted a cottage.

A O Neville, 1938

When we first come here she got so mad the Boss make us live up here in the compound — but that's the only way she get a place to live, see. I get to see her after school most days. My brother, he from mum's second family, he got sent away from here last year. Sent up Sister Kate's in Perth. That's where they put the fair ones. And I think them little kids — only just tiny — I don't think they like goin' away from the settlement. They was reared up here, but they take 'em away in a big truck just 'cause they look whiter. It ain't their fault. It's so sad, you know, seeing little kids goin' away. We stand on the dining room verandah watchin' 'em go.

> Ken [Colbung] was taken out there, he was taken away, and he was sent to Sister Kate's ... Well, I think it was pretty hard because we were all friends together ... After when I woke up to this it set me thinking. 'Wonder why Ken ended better educated than me?' Only thing I can come up with is his colour was fairer than mine. So he was more educated, which he is pretty educated now. Why? Because he had the right teacher.
>
> Vincent Lambadgee

*

Today us girls gotta go to domestic training, see, 'cause in a couple years we goin' out to service like me sister and we gotta know how to conduct ourselves proper and do some cookin' and that. That's what Miss Marshall say — she take us girls for a class couple times a week. Well, it's not a class so much as ... well, like we did some laundry last week, and today we gotta clean out the staff kitchen. We like it better if we got to cook something like a rock cake. Miss Marshall, she say maybe we do that one day if she can find some sultanas, but with fifty of us girls — that's a lot a' sultanas. I tasted 'em before (Sister Eileen give us a few once) and they is heaven.

I ask Darcy (she's me sister) what you do in that job where you work? Well, she say, I just do what youse do already — scrub floors, wash dishes, do some washin'. Only she get paid for it, see. (They send her pay to Mr Neville and he let her buy some dresses with it some times.) She be fifteen soon.

Big girls what work here at the settlement makin' government clothes every day, they get good training, but. Learn how to use the sewing machine, and cut out and make buttonholes and mend and that. I heard some womens talkin' say it's not fair 'cause the sewing room girls, see, they don't get a pay. But I know that's a lie — they get chocolates every Saturday, I seen 'em myself.

Some of the girls went out to work and got quite good jobs, were well looked after, I think, but they eventually came back, most of them, came back pregnant and either went back down to Matron Campbell's at East Perth or came back and had their babies, and their babies were put in the nursery, and they were given jobs ...

Sister Eileen Heath

As you will realize, there are very few girls here who are properly trained, and those few have up to the present gained their experience away from here. This was probably quite unavoidable, as the Domestic Classes here last year were only held on two afternoons a week. You must admit that in that amount of time it would be impossible to train a native girl, as you must be constantly with them, and constantly training them to get a really successful result ...

Acting Matron Gregory
to the Commissioner of Native Affairs, 1943

Such utter bosh — there was no training at MRNS and no likelihood of such a thing.

Mr and Mrs Henry (former staff couple) to Minister Coverly, 1944

*

Three o'clock and school is OUT! Now the day, it's ours! Two whole hours till tea bell — no chores, no sums, no prayers. Now we FREE! We get to roam everywhere (long as we can still hear that bell) — mostly down the river, go fishing and swimming when it's warm (even when it ain't), hunting rabbits, parrots, anything what moves. Winter now, so first thing we do's build us a good fire. That way we keep warm, see, and it's all ready to cook what we catch. Just bung 'em in the ashes once it gets real hot. Fish beautiful that way, yeah!

What else we got? Ned over there, his dad work in the bakehouse and he pinch us some burnt up bread — only half burnt up, but. It's good bread — from what they bake for the Boss up the Big House, see. We got shanghais what we made this morning, so we could catch a parrot too — roast 'im in the ashes. Mmmmmm! Then we have a good feed. And nobody out here to tell us how to do or say or we gotta line up or anything like that.

One kid he drowned out here — just a little kid, he was. Trackers just found a little pile of clothes by the river next morning. That was sad, that was. Some kid say it the woodarji man got 'im and killed 'im. That woodarji — we seen him once or twice and we run and hide. He kill you just as soon as look at you, he would. All us kids know that. He stay around mostly at that place they call the morgue — you know, that big iron shed place — that's where the dead ones go. We make a big circle around there when we go down the river — big circle! Don't get near to those dead ones.

Sometimes the Boss, he's out makin' a coffin from boards — he might chop up a table or somethin'. For babies, I seen him use them little cartons — you know, them wooden ones? (when we had the whooping cough last year, I remember seein' it a lot). Sometime

67

they just lay the big ones on a board, just a bare board, and sew a rug around it and that's it.

*

Us girls — we go down the river when it's warm — we love to swim there. (We got our pool what's private to us — don't let nobody see us.) But us girls, we don't hunt or nothing like that, so when it's cold we just kinda hang around the compound tryin' to get warm. We like sittin' here on the verandah but sometime the staff they throw a bucket a' water to make us move. We ain't got nowheres to go to, see. Teacher, she says us kids should have a place for reading some books she's got (comics too — we love those comics) with a stove and some rugs. Maybe next winter, she say. Sometime, see, we just ain't got nowheres to go.

> There is plenty of shelter about the settlement ... but natives will run about in all weathers, and sometimes they become wet in running about in the rain. This is unavoidable with native children in view of their abandon to games and playfulness, and I think it would require quite a large staff to refrain them from such tendencies ...
>
> Acting Matron Gregory
> to Commissioner of Native Affairs, 1943

> Last Sunday I noticed that the toddlers at the kindergarten are placed in boxes for want of proper playgrounds. Not only does this method of control restrict the child severely, but the practice creates a very bad impression on visitors ...
>
> Acting Commissioner of Native Affairs, 1947

We know how to make our own fire, but — and if it ain't too wet, we sit around that maybe. Or we go down the camps and watch 'em play two-up, or get us a feed and play with some a' the kids live down there (lots of kids do — mostly like tiny tots what live with

68

their mums cause they too tiny for school. And the kindy, see, they
ain't allowed in there. That's for the kids without no mums). Some of
the campies, they real nice to us girls. Like, they let us come on
weekends sometimes and out campin' in the bush. But Matron, she
don't like us down there so much, and we gotta stay 'round the
compound lookin' for some sun to sit in. Olive's got a mum down
the camp. Got her own cottage, she does, cause her old dad he goes
out to work. That Olive, she got a mum and a dad down there, see?

What I didn't like about it, I didn't have any love from
my own parents. You know, being taken away like that,
lot of kids would have had love from their parents if they
had of stayed, and would have felt more better inside if
they were with their own parents. We didn't, because we
didn't have somebody to love us, sort of business. If
you'd been loved, I think it would have been a different
story, but we had nobody to love us. We had to just find
our own way out, most of us, in the world without love.

Lizzy Dalgety

We like Thursdays, 'cause Sister Eileen, she take the whole mob
of us Brownies and Girl Guides out bush walkin' or we do some
sewing in a little room what they give her. (The sewing room girls,
they made us our uniforms too. We love 'em! Sister keeps 'em in her
room so they stay nice.) Sometime Matron, she come out from the
hospital or down the camps and she hold our hand and walk with us.
She always dressed in white with a kind a thing on her head what
they wear in church. She's beautiful, she is. I never seen her hit
anybody, never.

But the Boss — you don't try to hold his hand — he'd put the
boot in your backside quick! He got a big moustache and a little
white dog follows him everywhere. We scared to death of that little
dog — he's mean, he is. He ain't bit nobody yet but we give 'im
room anyhow. Yeah, I run up a pine tree I see that dog. Some kids
says the Boss, he got shellshocked when he in the war. We always
say, 'Oh, look out now'. See, he might think he's in a war and start
beltin' you.

69

Matron Neal, c1937. 'I never seen her hit anybody, never.'

I know he must've been strict because he was strict with us, but he wouldn't have been cruel, I'm quite sure. Maybe they thought he was cruel because they'd never had anyone command them to do anything. They'd been allowed to roam around, and when I look at it in that light I think, well, maybe they did think he was cruel.

Eileen Neal Isbister,
daughter of Superintendent Arthur Neal

> They [the Neals] were only there to sort of run the thing, like. They had no part of providing these things, like the food or anything like that. They just had to do the best they could with what they had provided by the Government. That was just their job ... I mean, I wouldn't like to ever hurt their feelings.
>
> Edie Moore

Here at the settlement, us kids learn to watch out for ourself. See, the staff, some of them real mean and give you a smack or swear at you and that. And some of the girls is tough, too. When you come, see, they ask you, 'Where you come from? where you come from?' And if you from the north, and they from the sou'west, well, that's it. Some a' them girls, they sure can fight. When there's a mix-on, I get scared with everybody screamin' and yellin'. Plus there's full-bloods and half-castes and some kids look so white you can't hardly tell 'em from the staff kids. Nurse says they oughta go to Sister Kate's 'cause it's not right to hold back the fair ones. If anyone call me 'black' I still get mad, but. Sister Eileen says I shouldn't ought to, 'cause black's what makes the music nice or something. But I still do.

> I said, 'What's the trouble?' and this little black one said to me, 'Sister, she called me black. I'm not black, am I?' And she was black as black. And I said, 'Well, look, go and put your heads under the tap, both of you, and then come in and talk to me.' ... So I sat them down, and I said, 'What are you really fighting over?' and Ruthy said again, 'Oh, she called me black.' And I said, 'Well, Ruthy, you are black ... You're black and you're half black and I'm white.' And I said, 'None of us can help our colour. Fighting over it won't change us a bit. We've just got to accept the colour we are. All those flowers out there in my garden, they're all different colours. But if they were all just the one colour it wouldn't be half as nice. You look at the little organ of mine in there. It's got black keys and white keys on it. I don't play on the white keys all the time, and I don't play on the black keys. I

use them both, and that's what makes the nice music. It
doesn't matter what colour you are outside. You can't
change it, and we just make the best of what we are.

Sister Eileen Heath

*

Five o'clock already? Geez, we gotta get up the compound quick
smart now. It start to get dark and rainy now and we runnin' — see,
the bell, it rung already and if you don't get there on time that's too
bad. Your tea go to someone else. It ain't far, but when it's gettin'
dark and you hungry and you gotta go by that morgue place ... Well
no sense takin' your time. Girls always get there before us — always
hangin' out on that verandah, they are.

'For this good food, dear Father God, accept our thanks and
praise.' Yeah, that's what we gotta *say* but tea ain't much, and that's
the truth — just some more bread and fat and another cuppa tea (no
milk, no sugar, we never see sugar, only the white staff see sugar,
not us). We can get another piece of bread (they give us two, see) if
we ask but only to eat in here. Can't take it away to have later in the
dormitory or nothin' (that's why I steal it down me shirts sometime.
See, you just kinda stick it down there flat when Kingy ain't lookin'.
Five o'clock to breakfast, it's a long long time. Lucky we got berries
under the bed, but!). See that nurse? She stand guard by the door and
check out you got any bump in your shirt ('What's that there? You
give it here now!') so make sure it don't show.

*

Straight after tea, we gotta go back the dormitory, see. As you go in
they call your name out. If you missing, well, they just send the
tracker for you. Lot a' times girls go missing — sometimes five or
six or seven or more. Run away, see. It's good fun. I done it once
with some a' me mates and we got up past Regan's Ford before the
tracker got us. He brung us back and made us front the Boss. And
then he give us a hiding with the cat o' nine tails, and we was cryin'

72

and sayin' we never do it again. (But we might!) We was headin' to
see me Aunty out at Dandaragan, see, and get us some tucker.
The big girls, they run away all the time. Go to see their
boyfriends up at New Norcia or somewheres. Always drag 'em back
but. Throw 'em in the boob then for a couple of days or a week or
so. But them big girls, they don't care, see. Give 'em half a chance,
and they just bust out all over again. We watch 'em go sometimes.

Escapes by girls from the dormitories at night are preva-
lent. It is effected by using the trap door through which
the night pans are placed. Wooden traps have been tried
but these are ineffective. I instructed the Superintendent
to requisition for iron grills of suitable size and these,
when locked, should prevent escapes ...

Report to Commissioner of Native Affairs,
March 1944

Sister Eileen, she come in and tell God to watch us and keep out
the bad perils of the night and that. Then they lock the doors. We
supposed to go have a wash — them cold showers again. But I'm
ashamed sometimes 'cause the bathroom, it's all open like — there's
no walls or nothing in there. Same for the big girls (more like
womens, they are, like working girls) next door. See over there, we
broke that hole in the wall between us. Sometime we peep over at
the big girls washin', showerin'. They chuck water in our faces and
all. We do it for fun, but.

We got some light to see by — not electric light, nothing like that.
Just kerosene lanterns. Only got a couple little windows, see, so that
kerosene, it gets right up your nose. But that's better than bein' in
the dark, ain't it? Us girls, we hates the dark. (We get us a little
light from the staff quarters just over there, 'cause they got the elec-
tricity till ten o'clock.)

It's too early to be tired, so we play some games and run around
and yell for a while — some girls fight and some of the little ones
what just arrived, they cry. We always try and give 'em a cuddle.
Sometime we clear out a big circle and everybody play this game
where you run around and throw a cloth behind someone's back.

And then you got to try and get round and catch 'em before they wake up to it was them, see. It's a good game! We like singin' too at night — like we take a song and make up funny words to it about the settlement and the Boss and that.

We got all the noise from the dormitory when the children were locked in, as they were at sundown. They were all locked in, and they had nothing to do, no way to amuse themselves, so they'd sing at the top of their voices, or else they'd fight, and the noise on some nights was simply dreadful.

Sister Eileen Heath

Sometime if you really tired, like if you sick and coughin' (and lot a' girls is 'cause it's so cold), you just can't fall asleep if even you want to. See, the other girls just run around singin' and yellin' till they drop and if you tell 'em to stop, sometime they come over and pull your hair or smack you and then you gotta fight 'em, and then you never get to sleep. See, ain't nobody here to make 'em stop. (Only sometime it get so bad somebody over the staff quarters call Matron, and she come and pull apart the ones what's fightin'. Then we can get some sleep. We tired the next day, but.)

Frequently the children in the dormitories make a great noise until long after all growing children should be asleep. Consequently the next day teachers are wearing themselves out trying to teach dozing and fractious children. Neither is it good for the children to lose necessary sleep.

Jean Birt, Head Teacher,
to Commissioner of Native Affairs, April 1943

Personally, I see no great harm in this type of rowdiness, and as a youngster I often indulged in pillow fights, etc ...

Commissioner of Native Affairs to Minister, 1943

74

*

Kingy lock us boys in hours ago. It must be about midnight or something by now, 'cause them lanterns is flickerin' and ready to go out any minute. Most of us boys is asleep in little piles all around the floor. Some of us had a wash (we get a hot bath tomorrow, anyway) but what we wear to bed is same as what we run around in all day with: trousers and a shirt. But like I said, tomorrow, it's Saturday and we get a hot bath then. We make the fire under the copper ourselves and carry water back and forth, see. We're allowed to cut the wood up during the day and then we stack it inside. Maybe five or six of us kids use that same lot of water, and then we go and heat up some more.

Saturday's the best day at Moore River, all right, 'cause they let you just wander around anywhere or just do what you want to do. Like, I might go hunting tomorrow, if somebody invites me (see you gotta wait for that, we never push our way into the camp people what got families). Like if Ralph's dad is gone hunting, he say, 'Oh, can my mate come, can two mates come?' Then it's up to the father, and he say, 'Yes all right you can bring them two.' Mostly we go away for the day and get back late. If it's for more (like if you gonna spend overnight at the camp) then you gotta get permissions. But you ain't allowed to do that much, 'cause it's much safer when they keep you locked up, locked away.

We take some dogs, see, and get a kangaroo and roast it right over the coals. Can't beat that! Damper, too, and vegies if we have any — like spuds, and you push them down inside the roo, like, and onions too if we have any. We have a good feed then. Sometime we just stay down the river and Matron she give us a lunch and we take that down the river and just fish or hunt rabbits and that. See, the staff they go to town (we hear lots of 'em come back drunk on the Saturday night), so we can do what we like on the weekend.

We go huntin' or campin' or anything, we gotta be back the compound for Sunday service. But that's all right, 'cause we like that — specially standin' up there singin' hymns. I'm mad on singin'. We got a choir (I'm in it — boys get to wear a white robe) and we rock the house down, this choir.

We attended church on Sunday nights and thought it
rather ironic to see those young fellows standing in rags
singing their praises to God ... That poor crippled ragged
Reggie Yorkshire with that glorious voice just like an
organ giving thanks to God for what?

Mr and Mrs Henry (former staff couple), May 1944

The church is Church of England, see, that's what Sister Eileen is.
(Some kids is Catholics, but, and they got their own priest come up
from New Norcia. And then all us kids, we turn into Catholics too. That
priest, he bring along apples, see, and give 'em out to the Catholics.)

Course, a lot of the kids duck Sunday School — go down the
river instead. But the little ones, they love it. They do their little bit
of painting or hear a story and that. Back when I was a little kid, I
used to go and listen to Sister Eileen tell bible stories. It was just the
way she used to do it, see, you just used to sit there and listen to it.
Well, you just wanted to be part of it. If you was a little kid, I mean.

They had a respect for the church — the choir and everybody that came to church. They were far more reverent
and quiet in church than a white congregation would be,
and they listened.

Sister Eileen Heath

*

*I'm tryin' to sleep now (soooo tired!) but sometime I itch so bad I
just think I gonna scream. See, like I was tellin' you, we got all these
creepy crawlies. Bugs and fleas in the bed's bad enough but there's
head lice too (on the girls what got hair) and the rest of us now has
the body crabs: like little white bugs, like. You don't notice 'em so
much during the day but at night seems that's all you can think
about.*

*It's noisy too. There's always girls got a nasty cough in here —
they go on like that all night. See, that's why they give us the fish oil,*

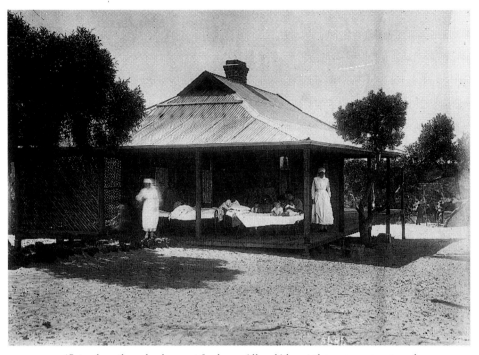

'Saturdays they check us out for bugs. All us kids got the same — sores and runny noses and bugs.'

I think. Every Saturday (that's tomorrow) they dose us up with this fish oil. We gotta line up for it on the dining room verandah. Awwww! Some of the girls, they vomit it right out again. But I'm cunning. I take it all in my mouth, and then I just run around the corner and spit it out! We hate that stuff. You get a lolly to take the taste away, but. We like the lolly, but sometime it still just tastes like a fish oil lolly.

Saturdays they check us out for bugs, too, and other stuff. Like they scrub off these sores here — hurts like anything! — and paint 'em with yellow stuff (sometime we gotta eat it on our bread too and I seen 'em burn it inside our dormitory here). All us kids got the same — sores and runny noses and bugs. Oh yeah, and you prob'ly saw how some of the kids, they look like they crippled or something,

77

the way they walk. Well, that's nothing. That's just the old stone bruise, see. Lucky I'm real tough — got feet like a goat, that's what me mum used to say. But me eyes get sore sometime and I rub and rub and rub and never feel no better.

Doc Myles, he come around sometime and look in our eyes and stuff. We afraid a 'him, but I just always watch the ash on the end of his cigarette, see — take bets with meself just how soon it's gonna drop. Some kids got these pot bellies — stick straight out to here. I feel sorry for 'em. Matron she say it's some kinda worm thing but it must be more like a snake to get that big.

I never had that, but last year I had mumps terrible. All us kids did. They put us in this big isolation ward, see, boys and girls each side. They just locked us in that old place, and we used to lay around like poisoned dogs, just laying there. Some kids had beds and some of us just chucked mattresses on the floor. Had to stop there two or three weeks till that mumps go right down. But what I hated was they used to lock the door — it was like a big gate thing. Lock us in. Meals was brought there and just put on the cement floor. There was kids goin' in there day and night for months and months last year, what with mumps and then whooping cough. Even closed the school, they did.

Ooooh, that was a bad time, that was. We have lotsa' bad times here, I guess. Good times too. Never think about it much, but. You only feel bad if you do — so it's no good feelin' anything, is it? It's like me mum. Don't even know where she is. I ain't never asked nobody neither. We don't ask questions, see.

Would you change anything about your childhood, if you could, when you were growing up?

About me childhood? No, I had a lovely childhood down there. I was happy, that was the main thing, yeah.

Do you think your life would have been very different if you hadn't ever gone there?

I don't know, tell you the honest truth. I suppose I

would've been ... if a man got to know his mum, you know? I don't know what it would have been like. Not knowin' your parents, you don't know a hell of a lot ... I miss me mum. I really miss her, I'd like to seen her. I haven't even seen a photograph of her, you know, or the man. Don't know what they looked like ...

Ralph Dalgety to Annette Roberts

chapter 2

Bread and Fat

Perhaps more clearly than anything else, the children of Moore River remember what they ate, and what they didn't. This is hardly surprising. For human beings, food is always more than mere nutrition. Food helps give life colour and form; it flavours (as we often say) our moods, our relationships, our experiences. But for the young, food assumes far greater importance. It is through the sensitive medium of the stomach that every infant gains its first experiences of security and sociability. To the young child, food is nothing less than love made edible.

At the Moore River Native Settlement, the institutional diet was grossly inadequate in both quantity and quality, and most of the children were hungry most of the time. In the words of one woman who spent her childhood there, 'it was terrible and you never got enough of it'. Over the three decades of Moore River's operation, the precise make-up of the menu varied with the shifting fortunes of the Aborigines Department. But the staples always remained the same: bread and fat and sugarless black tea — supplemented sparingly by porridge, soup and mutton by-products. For many years, Aboriginal children at the settlement received no fruit, no fresh vegetables, no eggs, no milk that wasn't tinned or watered down and no sweets except bulk jam and black treacle. Knives and forks were considered unnecessary; children were taught instead to use spoons and fingers.

There were allegations that the Moore River diet caused widespread illness and even death. Although impossible to substantiate, these charges seem plausible. Luckily, however, the children of

'It was terrible, and you never got enough of it.'

Moore River were never completely at the mercy of their overseers. Meals at the compound were doled out of enormous coppers as long lines of children shuffled silently to their benches. But less than a mile distant, in the wild land along the river, fresh fruit, game and fish were available in abundance. The bush offered the closeness of mates, and full tummies at last. Best of all, it helped nurture the conviction — despite all the official messages to the contrary — that Aboriginality was not a taint, but a privilege.

The contrast between bush and compound is a recurring motif in the Moore River story. In fact, it is no exaggeration to speak of competing institutional 'cultures' — the official (European) culture of the compound versus the outlaw (Aboriginal) culture of the bush. But Moore River also gave rise to a distinctive culture of childhood, which proved astonishingly successful at providing its small members with the security and gratifications which neither of the adult systems — for quite different reasons — could offer.

This clash of cultures is an important tool for understanding the ambivalence of so many Moore River memories. To some, the settlement has become enshrined in memory as a 'sacred site ... our home'. To others, it never seemed more than a prison. But most of the people who spent their childhood there see the light and the shadow mixed, and their recollections resonate with the tension between nostalgia and bitterness.

*

On the subject of diet and nutrition — as on just about every subject at Moore River — there was a yawning gap between theory and reality. On paper, the settlement was designed as a splendid place: a self-supporting community where Aboriginal people would learn new and marketable skills, where part-Aboriginal ('half-caste') children would receive the education the wider community had unjustly denied them.

Whatever else we may condemn them for, those responsible for the planning of Western Australia's settlement system never envisaged the grim reality of the Moore River Native Settlement. On the contrary, they saw the site thirteen kilometres west of the Mogumber siding as a potential Eden. But the land that was to have flowed with milk and honey stubbornly refused to cooperate. In fact, it was no time at all before the dream of milk and honey gave way to the realities of bread and fat.

Although the settlement was officially established in 1917, it was not until 1919 that the boys' and girls' dormitories were completed and the compound dining room began operation. Until that time, children lived with their families in the camps, and were issued weekly rations in accordance with the prescribed government scale. For children between the ages of two and twelve, this provided two kilograms of flour, 340 grams of sugar and fifty grams of tea. It was assumed that these rations would form a supplement to a much fuller family diet. But it quickly became settlement policy that all children 'excepting babes in arms' would reside in the compound. As Chief Protector of Aborigines A O Neville explained it:

> every child should at least be fed in the compound when
> sufficient space is available. The camp children cannot

be fed in the same way as the compound children, as they get what their elders choose to give them, the cooking very often being exceedingly bad ...

Simply put, Aboriginal mothers and fathers were regarded as too irresponsible to feed their children. This was a matter for government control.

In theory, the original Moore River diet scale, while dull, would probably have been sufficiently nourishing and, by the standards of the day, even generous. It included a breakfast featuring porridge with milk and sugar or treacle; bread with dripping, treacle or jam; and a cup of tea or coffee. For dinner, there was to be hot roast meat once a week, and hot boiled meat once a week, with cold meat, stew or meat pies on the remaining days. Tea was planned as a rather spartan meal of bread and a choice of spread (fat, honey, jam, treacle or butter), washed down with a cup of tea or cocoa. For boys, extra bread was to be available for the asking. The scale also provided for two vegetables a day, plus puddings or stewed fruit, with school children receiving a morning tea of milk or lime juice and water. Sundays were set aside as red-letter days, marked by special treats like plum pudding, salads and fresh fruit. It was taken for granted that the 'fresh milk, butter, eggs, potatoes, vegetables, fruit and meat are to be the produce of the settlements'.

In 1920, when the Commissioner of Native Affairs requested an evaluation of the Moore River diet scale from the State Children's Department, he was assured that the 'scale is a very liberal one', comparing favourably with similar institutions. But what was Moore River similar to? In later years, we know that it was prisons, not schools, that were held up as yardsticks of appropriate nutrition for Aboriginal children. In 1943, F I Bray, Commissioner of Native Affairs, suggested that the children's diet be modelled on the one in use at Bartons Mill Prison. In evidence before the 1934 Royal Commission, however, A O Neville, his predecessor, had bristled at the suggestion that prison rations be used as a guideline. He considered them extravagant. 'I have stated that more food is required by the natives at settlements and elsewhere', he conceded, 'but if we fed them [as suggested at the hearing] on such a diet as is supplied at

It was taken for granted that the 'fresh milk, butter, eggs, potatoes, vegetables, fruit and meat are to be the produce of the Settlement'. But year after year, the dream of self-sufficient farming yielded to the realities of bad managment, bad land and just plain bad luck.

Broome Gaol, I feel that we should have a community of idle natives. What we need is a well-balanced diet not in excess of requirements.' Neville got his wish. At Moore River, as former inmate Ralph Dalgety has wryly observed, 'nobody was overweight'.

The problem was that the 'diet scale' existed only in the mind of its creators. The reality — what inmates actually consumed — often bore strikingly little relationship to it. As early as six months into the operation of the compound kitchen, Superintendent Mitchell admitted to Head Office:

The scale is not being adhered to in its entirety as laid down. Nevertheless the scale is used as a guide & the food of the children is alternated [sic]. Such articles of diet as coffee and cocoa are not being supplied. My contention is that any undue attention in the way of providing diet for the compound children that is different from that which they have been used to ... is not going to be conducive to the well being, happiness, & discipline of the settlement.

The dietary scale of November 1920 shows Mitchell's handwritten amendments. Puddings now appear only twice weekly, but 'boys and girls can always obtain more bread if required, especially in cold weather'. Salad is crossed out. A year later, the Secretary confessed to the Deputy Chief Protector that at neither Moore River nor its sister settlement, Carrolup, were the prescribed dietary scales being adhered to. The inmates, he hastened to add, 'are all looking particularly well, and are well nourished and in view of this, I do not think it advisable at the present stage to lay down a definite diet scale. To do so would probably mean increased expenditure.' The files for this period feature repeated calculations of the official (but discarded) ration scale; actual expenditure is often up to forty per cent less. In January 1923, for example, the value of rations actually issued was £153.19.8, while the cost of the approved diet would have been £252.16.1.

The rhetoric used to defend such economies ranged from hardheaded avowals of economic necessity to high-minded flights of historical fancy. As Superintendent Ernest Mitchell wrote in a 1921 minute:

It is a very simple thing to recommend a liberal scale when dealing with other people's money ... We have to remember that we are not dealing with white children whose forbears have been used for hundreds of years back [to] food such as we have. Speaking from years of experience and knowing these people in their wild state, I am of the opinion ... it is wasteful and foolish to provide these children with food they would never eat had the Department not taken them into its keeping, and will never have as regular diet after they leave the settlement.

86

Although Mitchell argued that the principal staple of the native diet should be solid meat (not stew), he felt strongly that Aboriginal children should be discouraged from developing a taste for such delicacies as eggs. 'It is superfluous to give them egg puddings', he decreed, 'excepting when eggs are plentiful and then only as a luxury'.

But Mitchell's argument went even further. The 'natives', he implied, did not deserve anything better, for 'they have absolutely no feeling whatever about waste, it is necessary to watch every mouthful they eat, the whole thing needs the very closest supervision by the staff without relaxing ...' In similar vein, he suggested it was not only too expensive but 'wrong to supply them with tea at midday — I have cut out the use of cocoa and coffee for the compound children, it is sentimental waste'. Mitchell's logic leads him at last to the conclusion that 'It is necessary at times to cut them down to help them appreciate their good fortune'.

On the basis of rationalisations like these, the respectable dietary scale with which Moore River began was utterly abandoned within a few years. For the next two decades, the children of the settlement subsisted largely on bread, fat and tea. Amazingly, however, most managed to retain enough energy and resourcefulness to supply their own needs. What the system couldn't or wouldn't provide, they found — or bought or begged or pinched — for themselves.

Bread

The carpenter packed up and walked off one morning because settlement bread was served in the staff quarters one night, in an emergency.

Department of Native Affairs Inspection Report,
December 1947

Bad bread seems to have been something of a settlement tradition. As early as 1924, Superintendent Brodie noted that inmates were purchasing 'considerable quantities' of bread from the settlement store, 'although they have been getting too much bread' as part of their regular rations. The contradiction is not as puzzling as it sounds. Ned Mippy, whose mother and father worked in the bakehouse throughout the thirties, remembers the rationed wholemeal loaves well. His parents, he recalls, would be told to 'stick some of that stuff in what you give to horses — bran or some blooming thing'. It's no wonder everyone craved the softer white bread, which was only available for purchase.

But any bread beyond the two-slice-a-meal ration was better than none at all. (In 1935, Ned's parents were using an average 170 kilograms of flour a day to make 250 one-kilogram loaves.) As bakers, the Mippy family found itself in a privileged position. 'Well, we got first preference', he explains. But they also devised ingenious ways and means of sharing their modest wealth.

> The kids, they'd come and they'd want a feed, see, and they used to grease the tins for us. I'd say, 'You want a feed?' 'Yes.' Well, I said, 'don't grease the tin' because you've got to clean the tins after and it would all stick to the bottom. They'd be sitting there eatin' round the corner, yeah.

Ned also remembers that his parents would use the oven to make an unofficial damper or two. Kids used to literally beg to be allowed to help. Unfortunately, Ned remembers, the omnipresent trackers — the settlement's Aboriginal police force — would be standing guard to ensure that only a few were selected.

Before the arrival of the Mippys, Angus Wallam's father was employed in the bakehouse. Angus, who was born at Moore River and had a large, extended family resident there, also remembers his father's generosity. 'I'd get a bit of bread from him — a lot of the other blackfellas, too, see. He'd sneak 'em bread or a bit of flour ... If he got caught, he'd get six months.' Phyllis Narrier, who met and married Ned Mippy at Moore River, recalls that the bakehouse bread was a big improvement on the stuff that preceded it.

Problems with bread baking plagued the settlement for years. In July 1940, a visitor, Frederick Wilson, reported seeing several batches of bread actually buried. The following year, Acting Superintendent Tanner stoutly observed, 'In my opinion the inmates of this settlement are not over fed, but appear to be reasonably fed, in view of world conditions'. But even Tanner was forced to admit that the bread seemed a bit off, 'both quality and quantity'. He was sure that the problem had much less to do with the inferior ingredients than with the shiftless natives themselves. 'With natives as bakers', he explained, there was too much 'guess work'.

In 1942, the bread being supplied for native consumption was so bad it actually became the subject of a Public Health inspection. 'We are having some difficulty in getting the natives to eat wholemeal bread', reported Medical Inspector Dr Musso to the Commissioner of Public Health. His investigations revealed some very good reasons why — including the fact that it was causing rampant diarrhoea ('I do not think ALL suffer, but apparently some do', he confirmed). Musso also reported that the bread was not only soggy, coarse-grained and sour, it was badly leavened. In fact, mere words failed him, and he arranged for a loaf of the bread to be sent to Head Office for inspection.

The 1946 annual report suggests using the bakehouse as a training centre for Aboriginal boys. 'I fail to see why splendid results should not be obtained', wrote the Superintendent. Yet the idea — rather like the wholemeal flour — was inexplicably left to moulder. A no-nonsense report by Accounts Clerk B Crooks helps explain what was going wrong:

> The bakehouse is appalling from every point of view. Before you even approach the door you are welcomed by a stench from ground contaminated by recently removed refuse, which had evidently been allowed to gather ... Windows are broken with bags hanging over them, the oven itself looks very like a quarry inside ... The actual bread tins resemble a pile of scrap tin ... It is an impossibility to bake decent bread with the facilities provided ... It is not a very good advertisement for the bakehouse when we find that supplies of bread for the staff are purchased from an outside source, and this is not to be wondered at ... From a hygienic point of view it is appalling ...

'The bakehouse is appalling from every point of view ... Windows are broken with bags hanging over them, the oven itself looks very like a quarry inside ... The actual bread tins resemble a pile of scrap tin ...'
(Inspection Report.)

Even the Deputy Commissioner of Native Affairs was forced to agree that the situation was desperate. 'I had a meal at the Staff Quarters and the bread which was placed before me beggars description', he confided.

But reports like this were simply filed away, and the only thing that seemed to shift was the burden of responsibility. By 1947, the institution had completely exonerated itself. The bakehouse, the report for that year claims, 'is a constant source of loss through the poor baking efforts of the native bakers, attributed both to their lack of skill and facilities'. The loss 'through crumbling' is estimated at about fifty per cent daily — translating into about seventy-five pounds a year. The cause, it is reiterated, is 'not attributed specifically to the state of the oven, but more so to the lack of skill of the native bakers'.

The following year, bread-baking facilities were again reviewed, this time as part of a settlement-wide inspection carried out personally by the new Commissioner of Native Affairs, Stanley Middleton. Middleton condemned the bakehouse as 'most unsuitable for preparation of food'. The concrete floor was badly broken, as were the windows. There were no fly doors and even the walls were 'cracked and broken'. The oven itself was near collapse and the only things in good working order seemed to be the flies. A few months later, Middleton noted tersely, 'Waste here colossal. Bread being produced and issued not fit for pigs to eat.' The bakery was finally abolished in January 1949. As Superintendent Ethell explained, 'a good 75% of the local product is wasted and sent to the farm for pig feed. Daily cost of bread production on the settlement is in excess of £2.10.0, whereas all normal requirements can be supplied from Moora and delivered here for not more than £2.5.0 per day.'

Fat

> They had all these big bakin' dishes, and they'd melt the fat in that and they'd have all the bread there, and they'd just dip one in and hit the other one on like that [claps hands together] ... That was breakfast.

Ralph Dalgety

> Gee, I think of the cholesterol in those days!

Eric Conway

The ubiquitous fat — known as 'dripping' to the bureaucrats and simply as 'scrape' to the inmates — is the single food item most readily identified with the Moore River Native Settlement. Fat sandwiched between slices of sour wholemeal bread was the centrepiece of what must surely rank as one of the most dismal diets in twentieth century institutional history. But from the point of view of Head Office, fat was a positive luxury. It was not, after all, included in the official listing of 'rations to indigent natives'. As the Secretary of the Department of Native Affairs reminded Superintendent John Campbell in September 1922, 'Dripping is not one of the usual items supplied to natives, although it is recognised it is advisable to supply it at times in limited quantities, and you must guard against the too general or generous issue'. But this directive was swiftly forgotten, or ignored. Government provisioning lists for this period show that the monthly consumption of fat averaged between two hundred and three hundred kilograms.

A O Neville was particularly sensitive on the subject of scrape. In evidence before the Moseley Royal Commission in 1934, he protested that 'the so-called fat is the best Wyndham Meatworks dripping'. Over the course of a fondly remembered childhood in Moore River, Ralph Dalgety would have consumed several hundred pounds of the stuff he calls 'the national feed'. 'Oh yeah', he agrees, 'it was beautiful fat, no two ways about it, nice and clean, oh yeah. [Did it taste good?] Well, I s'pose so [laughter]. Used to it.'

Like most of the children of Moore River, Vincent Lambadgee had no particular objection to fat. But it was no substitute for butter. 'Never, never, ever had butter spread on our bread', Vincent remembers, 'always fat. And yet I would put out twenty or thirty cows that gave milk, and ... they separated and made butter only for the whites, where they could have fed us all with butter and bread, but they didn't.' Mr and Mrs Henry, a former staff couple who took their complaints about settlement administration to the press in 1944, alleged that Superintendent Mark Knight and his wife routinely appropriated as much as two kilograms of butter weekly of native rations, with the excuse that 'they had to entertain a lot of people'.

Phyllis Mippy and her mates were sometimes so desperate for a decent feed of bread and butter they would steal it from the staff dining room. If they were lucky, they might also pinch a bit of honey as a break from the hated black treacle 'that used to sicken me'. She remembers that the staff 'used to have this funny sort of butter, big bulk butter. Well, I used to go in the [staff] dining room and ... I used to put it under my jumper.'

From the point of view of Moore River's Aboriginal children, the staff 'lived like lords', in the wistful words of Eric Conway. 'They had the best of everything', he remembers. Yet most of the kids had never known anything different, and the inequities between 'them' and 'us' were accepted as simply another unpleasant fact of life. As Eric puts it, 'We thought that was it, that they are the staff, and that's the sort of food they've got to have. "Wish we were staff", we used to say, and "Look what they get, they have bread and jam and cream on top!", we used to say.' Not only cream, apparently, but puddings, pies, fruit, fish and dozens of other items never seen on a compound dining table. According to a June 1932 report, while the Aboriginal children ate fat, the white staff were consuming a pound of butter a week each, in addition to daily rations that included a pound of meat, a pound of bread and over a pint of milk.

Tea

> They used to put tea out for us, and it had no sugar in it but molasses or something was in it. When you put your face to it, you know, you could smell that. Oooh — putrid! ... They reckon they steamed the tea all the time, you know, just popped a few more leaves in and boiled it up [again]. Anyway, we never drank the tea. Couldn't drink it.
>
> Alice Nannup

Like children, tea at the Moore River settlement was graded into castes. There was 'tea' — which is what the staff drank, or what could be purchased in the settlement store — and then there was 'native tea'. When one observer indignantly described the latter as 'coloured water', the Commissioner of Native Affairs was not amused. He insisted that if the tea was undrinkable it must be the fault of the natives themselves, who 'would be inclined to do this ignorantly'. According to other witnesses, however, even the water used to brew the tea was tainted. In 1934, former inmate John Egan informed the Moseley Commission that 'the tea was made with the water from the pools where the girls swam'.

At some point sugar seems to have disappeared altogether from the tea cups at Moore River, a fact immortalised in the title of Jack

Davis's powerful drama of settlement life, *No Sugar*. The words are taken from one of the compound kids' favourite songs — a parody they had devised from a familiar hymn. The official version went:

There is a happy land
Far, far away,
Where saints in glory stand
Bright, bright as day:
Oh, how they sweetly sing,
'Worthy is our Saviour King!'
Loud, let His praises ring,
Praise, praise for aye!

and the unofficial version:

There is a happy land
Far far away
Where we get bread and scrape
Three times a day.
Bread and butter we never see
No sugar in our tea
While we are gradually
Starving away.

The children found it hilarious.

In tracking the case of the missing sugar, government provisioning lists offer little help, for sugar continued to be ordered, paid for and presumably eaten by the hundredweight. The question is, who was eating it? Ralph Dalgety has clear memories of unloading consignments of sugar along with other stores. 'Yeah, there was bags of sugar there', he confirmed, 'but when you have your cup of tea you don't ever see it. [So who had the sugar?] Gawd knows. Cooks, I s'ppose. Fatten themselves up. I don't know honestly.'

Oral history evidence suggests that the sugar ration was eventually replaced by saccharine and/or treacle before sweetener was eliminated from the tea altogether. But in the twenties, sugar was still an important — possibly a much too important — element of the institutional diet. In the early years, white sugar was ordered in amounts up to half a ton at a time. Both staple and luxury, sugar was seen as a cheap price to pay to keep the natives happy. 'With reference to your recent requisition,' wrote Head Office to Superintendent Campbell in July 1922, 'I am sending white sugar, as the difference in the cost of white and brown would only be about £1, and, under the circumstances, I do not think it advisable to send brown sugar, as the natives do not like it, and it is hardly worth while upsetting them for the sake of saving £1 ...'

With or without sugar, native tea at Moore River was nearly always black tea, for adults and children alike. Indeed, there is evidence that during certain lean years, the camp children received no milk at all. Despite settlement policy that all children reside in the compound, overcrowding — coupled with lax administration — ensured that there was usually a sizeable 'underground' population of children at the camps. In March 1943, for example, the dormitories were full, and there were fifty children residing in the camps. In evidence before the Moseley Commission, former farm assistant John Thomas Hedges testified that 'Milk should be issued to the children'. He added:

> I have seen babies drinking tea without milk from their bottles as no milk was available.
> Q: Was that your experience during the whole of the time you were there [1929-1933]?
> A: Yes, on many occasions.

The rations for camp children during this period consisted of half a loaf of bread daily, not more than one hundred grams of fat twice a week and forty grams of sugar weekly.

Edie Moore recalls that, in 1930, milk was seldom seen at all, even in the compound dining room. Ned Mippy agrees. 'You all sat along the side. There were stools, not chairs. You'd sit along, pass this and pass that. Time the milk got to you, there might not be any left. The strongest survived, that was the attitude there.' Eric Conway remembers that in the 1940s the children received skimmed milk with their breakfast porridge. The cream and full cream milk were reserved for the adult white staff.

'I have seen babies drinking tea without milk from their bottles as no milk was available.' (Testimony before the Moseley Royal Commission.)

Hazel Anderson was six years old when she came to Moore River with her mother, and remained until her marriage in 1937. Interviewed in Perth at the age of seventy-two, her memories of mealtimes remain vivid. She relates that the tea was served not in ordinary cups but in small jugs: 'We used to have to battle with that. All us little ones too.' Before the jugs, she remembers, they had tin pannikins without handles. The tea stayed so hot in these that, by the time it was cool enough to drink, it would be time to leave. Edie Moore, who came to Moore River as a teenager in 1930, remembers drinking tea from tin cans. 'I remember Mr Neal making some mugs for us out of condensed milk tins', she explains. 'Where he got them from I'll never know ... but he had a heck of a lot of tins, and he put handles on them. Soldered handles on them. And they were our mugs for a while until they went black.'

Meat and Vegetables

The food the natives get is not fit for an animal to eat, and I can say that to anyone.

Mary Warmadean,
inmate of Moore River, early 1930s

No vegetables are grown at the settlement, and a totally inadequate supply is imported ... There is an insufficiency of meat, and, if such articles as fruit and eggs were occasionally supplied, fewer children would go to the hospital. This view is supported by the doctor and the nursing sister.

*The Report of the Royal Commission
on the Condition and
Treatment of Aborigines,* 1934

Supplementing the 'national feed' of bread, fat and tea, were porridge, a kind of soupy stew (or stewy soup, depending on your point of view) and extras like bulk jam, tinned vegetables, sago and — during certain periods — even solid meat. For camp families, however, rations were even more spartan. Issued through the cook-house window, breakfast of two slices of bread and fat per person (no porridge, and no jam) was available promptly at 7.00am. Each family would bring its own tins for tea. Solid meat was rarely offered to the camp population, although 'the stew as composed makes a plentiful, thick, soupy stew with a definite quantity of solid meat in it for workers'. Women and children received no solid meat at all, nor any milk.

There were various rationalisations offered for the lack of meat. For one thing, the camp cookhouse had no oven; it was equipped only with coppers. For another, the natives were not to be trusted to prepare their own meat. As the Deputy Chief Protector pointed out, 'To give the food raw for the natives to cook offers too much possi-bility of using the food as a means of gambling'. In fact, it was tobacco that became used as a means of gambling. As Jack Davis recalls, 'Of course there would always be a game of two-up, and people would play their tobacco [ration] to try and win some more, 'cause if you won some more you could use that to exchange for potato or an onion or tea and sugar or flour, if you were a bit short'.

As the settlement's scarcest resource, food was both commodity and currency. Few Aboriginal workers were ever paid a cash wage of any kind. The sewing room 'girls', for example — women often working eight hours a day, six days a week manufacturing govern-ment-issue garments — were paid in chocolates: approximately one a day, distributed on a Saturday. A wage for the forewoman of this factory was finally introduced in 1943: ten shillings a fortnight. During the twenties, treats such as tinned jam, sardines and con-densed milk were dispensed as rewards for services rendered. But it was not long before Head Office attempted to nip such incentives in the bud. 'The issues appear altogether too heavy', the Deputy Protector fumed in a September 1925 minute.

> Why so many sardines? In cases of sickness I should
> have thought that beef-tea, soups, or other foods much
> better [sic] than sardines. Why were so many tins of jam
> used? There was a plentiful supply of bulk jam on hand.
> The milk used appears excessive also. Allowing for the

'Too much meat ... only feeds and cultivates the grosser animal passions.'
(Superintendent John Brodie.)

shortage of sugar and the use of condensed milk in tea it
appears heavy. I should like Mr. Brodie's further
comments.

A handwritten note indicates how the problem was resolved: 'discussed with Brodie at settlement — free issues for good work to be
stopped'.

Meat supplies to the compound children improved dramatically
after the war, but until that time the institutional diet featured only
shreds of it. Alice Nannup recalls that the main meal of the day in
the mid-1920s consisted of 'watery soup with sheep's heads'. In the
summer, dead blowflies would often be floating on top. The superintendent during this time, John Brodie, was apparently acting upon
his stated opinion that the natives not be allowed 'too much meat
and tea which only feeds and cultivates the grosser animal passions'.

A small flock of sheep was always kept on the settlement, but precious little meat ever found its way into the kitchen coppers.

Soon, Brodie was running the butcher's shop himself to ensure that 'no food is wasted or given out indiscriminately'.

A decade later, in Ned Mippy's time, the recipe for the children's main meal had not varied much. In typically vivid language, Ned explains that the soup was so thin 'you could see through it'. It retained only the memory of meat or vegetables — 'You could see where a couple of peas had been, or meat ...' Hazel Anderson explains succinctly, 'That soup we used to have, it used to make me sick. We used to call it slops.' Mary Warmadean, who lived at Moore River in the early thirties, gave a memorable description of the preparation of the children's main meal of the day:

> They fill up the copper with water and then they chop up the meat and put it in a dirty old kerosene tin. Then they put the kerosene tin into the copperful of water and boil the tin with the meat in it. Then they half fill the copper with split peas and boil the copper full of peas and the tin as well. That is how we had our food cooked there.

A small flock of sheep was always kept on the settlement, but precious little of the meat ever found its way into the big kitchen coppers. Edie Moore still remembers the squalidness of the 'killing pen'. Eating the meat 'there in the dining room, it was all right', she explains, 'but when you went to see where it was prepared, it turned you off'. The Commissioner of Native Affairs apparently agreed with Edie. Following an inspection of the pen, he wrote angrily to the Superintendent in 1943, 'I believe sheep skins and entrails were lying about all over the place, and the position was very noisome indeed'.

Edie Moore recalls, 'I don't know how many sheep they killed — I suppose they'd have to kill a few. But we got the flaps and whatever, the neck ... and stuff like that.' According to Hazel Anderson, the only mutton the kids ever saw was tripe or trotters. 'We used to eat those trotters when we was goin' to school, sheep trotters', she explains. 'We used to go and get them and get some matches from somewhere and go down along the river and make a fire and cook and eat.' Hazel suspects that, during the 1920s, children died from lack of meat at Moore River. Vincent Lambadgee, who lived at Moore River from 1924 to 1939, recalls that a baked dinner was served exactly once each year, at Christmas.

Occasionally during this period an attempt was made to supplement the mutton 'memory' with local kangaroo, Hazel Anderson remembers. The files confirm this. In August 1924, Head Office advised that 'a more determined effort appears to be necessary on the part of the natives to procure kangaroo flesh ... Please deal with the matter expeditiously.' Like just about every other element of the Moore River diet, however, the kangaroo was boiled in coppers, Hazel remembers — 'and that's the worst thing you could ever eat is boiled kangaroo'.

Doreen Dalgety was a teenager when she moved to Moore River with her father in 1936. During her five years there, she was one of the few inmates lucky enough to eat meat regularly. It was issued as her father's 'wages' for working as the compound butcher and carpenter.

He never got paid for any of those things but ... he could take as much meat as he wanted to and use for his own eating. And he had me brother there with him for a while and he used to come around too, like we all did. Plus we had all the school mates of me sisters, they'd all come around too and we'd feed the kids left, right and centre.

Doreen's father also used to trade meat for damper rolled in fat and cooked in the bakehouse oven. There are other examples of meat being used as a reward or 'perk' for services rendered. As a child, Ned Mippy used to envy the sewing room workers their portion of meat, and Edie Moore remembers that the girls who helped out in the kitchen 'always used to make themselves a nice little oven dish'.

After World War II, meat rations improved dramatically. Eric Conway remembers lunch as 'cold meat of boiled shanks and mutton legs' while stew almost invariably appeared at the evening meal. It was the dreary sameness of the meat issue that Eric remembers. The presence of an official visitor, however, could produce instant and sweeping reforms to the bill of fare. When the acting Commissioner inspected the dining room in November 1946, he was gratified to observe a nutritious meal of saveloys and mashed vegetables, baked apples and custard, bread and butter. It is no wonder he reported that 'All the children appeared to enjoy the meal, and they ate heartily'.

The Dining Room

Mealtimes at Moore River were heralded by the ringing of bells: one 'to get ready' and one 'to go'. On the first bell, children all over the settlement would race to the dining hall verandah to line up, boys on one side, girls on the other. As Angus Wallam explained, if you were late, well, you just missed out. The lines of hungry children were kept in order by the trackers, who were given a surprising measure of discretion in their bid to keep the peace.

The atmosphere of the 'dining room' — a very proper name for a very shabby place — was as unfriendly as the meals themselves. A

1944 report observed, 'The windows were indescribably filthy and choked with all manner of scraps of food-stuffs. The kitchen floor was dirty despite the fact that some of the girls were idle. One girl was found sleeping in a blanket in the dining room and the girls had their clothes hanging around the walls.' The children were strictly forbidden to talk to one another during meals. 'They had trackers there to come and watch', Phyllis Mippy remembers, 'and this tracker, he was always goin' for my little gang, and yet two of them little girls was his nieces ... He used to always hit us ... Whosever lips he see moving, he'd just come and whack us with a strap right across our back.'

By the mid-forties, the diet had improved and the trackers were somewhat more discreet, but the no-talking rule persisted. It made mealtime into yet another duty, and eating a task to be performed strictly for survival's sake. 'If you were chatting', Eric Conway recalls, 'you were told to be quiet, and if you did it again you were asked to leave the room, whether you had your meal or not'. Nevertheless, the dining room remained 'controlled by the strap' and pervaded by fear: the fear of not getting enough, and the fear of getting more than you asked for. Eric remembers some of the disciplinary measures of the dining room as 'downright cruel' — particularly the practice of force-feeding vegetables.

> The tracker would hold you while the grown up would force that spinach down your throat, 'cause kids just didn't like spinach — especially the way it was cooked those days, just boiled in a copper. None of us liked it, but oh we used to eat it and swallow it and just sit there and say nothing, 'cause everything was controlled by the strap ...

Interviewed at age sixty, Eric's memories of Moore River are almost palpably acute. He has spent a lifetime reflecting on his experiences there. A man of infinite courtesy, Eric's pain has been tempered by the hard edge of intellect, and cushioned by natural humour. So many of the rules, roles and routines he grew up with still seem inexplicably cruel, or downright pointless. Yet there

103

remain aspects of his harsh Moore River upbringing for which Eric is grateful. One of these, ironically, was the good manners not merely encouraged but, to use Eric's apt metaphor, 'forced down people's throats'.

Before 1945, the children had neither knives nor forks. 'Until then, everything was by a spoon ... and then you had to use your hands and fingers. But they taught you to be clean while you were doing that.' Kids who chewed with their mouths open once rarely tried it a second time. 'They stopped all that caper', Eric explains, adding 'Today, I agree with that'.

The absence of proper eating utensils had nothing to do with wartime shortages. Things had always been that way for the inmates of Moore River. Samuel Isaacs was forced to take his two sons to the settlement after his wife died in 1919. Isaacs continued to visit the boys, his heart broken to find 'they had sores and scabs on them and were filthy'. A well-educated man with a good living as a horse driver, Isaacs recalled taking them

> to a Perth restaurant for a meal and they did not under-
> stand the use of the knife and fork. They said they had
> not seen knives and forks at Mogumber. I asked what
> they used and they said, 'Fingers, with a bit of bread.'

In 1934, Superintendent Neal was compelled to confirm this under a Royal Commission grilling:

> Q: I noticed some of the children eating with their hands?
> A: Yes.
> Q: One witness said recently that when he got his boys
> from the settlement they did not know what a knife
> and fork were for. I did not see any spoons today?
> A: We generally have a supply of spoons, but owing to
> the matron's absence some have been lost. I have
> ordered new ones.

But Royal Commissions were no better guarantees of action then than they are now. It would be another eleven years before the children of Moore River enjoyed the privilege of knives and forks — and then it was only owing to the generous donation of the outgoing army regiment that had been stationed there. They couldn't have lasted long. An inspection report in July 1945 noted that 'no one present had a plate, knife or fork; in fact, most were without even a cup or spoon'. A year later, a different inspector reported with obvious disgust:

> I made it my business to be present during at least one breakfast dinner and tea, and it was not a pretty sight to see. Children at breakfast time pushing food into their mouths from broken and buckled plates ... The attendant in charge of the kitchen said that lack of culinary utensils and other facilities made it impossible to serve any variety of food, particularly second courses of sweets, as the plates required ... were not available.

On the other hand, as Ralph Dalgety philosophically explained, 'You didn't need a knife and fork anyway for soup'.

Treats

The diet at Moore River was not all bread and fat. Occasionally, the institution itself would provide special treats — vividly remembered oases in the great, dull desert of ordinary mealtimes. When settlement families became eligible for Child Endowment payments in 1941, the variety and quantities of these increased enormously. And of course there was also the settlement store, which stocked luxuries like tinned fish and 'real' jam (not the bulk stuff made from melon rinds) for those with money to spend.

From a nutritional standpoint, the lack of fruit was probably the most serious deficiency in the settlement diet. The white staff enjoyed an abundant supply of local melons, apples, grapes and figs. But the children of the 1920s and 1930s (whose only reliable source of vitamin C was the shreds of cabbage that appeared in the daily soup), had only the bush berries they scrambled to find between meals.

The absence of fruit from the dietary scale was noted as early as 1920, when the State Children's Department suggested to Neville that private donors might be encouraged to supply some, and in fact, donations of fruit were occasionally received. But oral history testimony suggests that very little ever found its way to the native population. Mary Warmadean testified before the Moseley Commission that fruit was regularly donated by the Benedictine community in nearby New Norcia; nevertheless, 'whenever the natives wanted fruit, they had to buy it'.

But even this practice was discouraged as being 'too risky' by Head Office. In 1944 — when fruit was proving particularly difficult to procure — Superintendent Leeming asked permission to allow a Slav hawker, 'a local man, with an unpronounceable name', to sell 'rather nice fruit, grapes mostly' to the natives. He explained, 'It's the only chance many of the natives have of getting any fruit at all'. Head Office found two grounds for opposing the request. First, it was pointed out the Slav could bring in 'intoxicating liquor' and second, he might smuggle messages to and from the natives. Later, the Commissioner reluctantly gave his approval, with the rather obscure warning that 'unless you watch the Slav hawker I am sure he will cause you trouble in due course'.

According to 1935 official records, apples were distributed to the children about twice a week, but Aboriginal informants who were there during this period have no memory of this. Elizabeth Dalgety recalls that shortly before her marriage in the late 1940s fruit became more widely available. 'Well, in the end we had apples ... They used to have two big green bags of apples sent up to Mogumber. We did have apples then to eat.' Before that, she insists, there was 'no fresh fruit. That's why we ate the berries, that's the only fruit we had'. In 1945, the practice of issuing each child with an apple at morning recess was begun. Eric Conway remembers eating tinned fruit, which — like most other settlement foodstuffs — arrived in bulk in four-gallon tins. A case of apples would be delivered each week, he adds. 'That mainly lasted two days, but at least you were getting an apple certain times.'

Ice cream made its first appearance at Moore River during the war, according to Eric, who remembers 'the army had a lot to do

'We'd have our epsom salts every Saturday, and you'd get a lolly to take the taste out of your mouth.'

with that'. The files show that ice cream was occasionally supplied by a private donor. In December 1944, for example, a Mrs Fiora of Guildford sent up twenty litres of ice cream by rail, and 'Mr. Knight opened the churn on the verandah and invited all the children to partake of it'. Eric's recollections confirm this. 'Ice cream used to come up from Perth, just one container, and you all had to line up and have that. We thought it was heavenly.' In the settlement's final years of operation, the children received ice cream weekly.

Inmates with money to spend could always eke out a more varied diet from the settlement store. (Credit was given to staff; for the natives it was strictly cash only.) The most popular lines included bread, tobacco, sugar and jam — despite the fact that these were all rationed items. Samuel Isaacs recalled in 1934:

> A nephew of mine, quite a small boy, an inmate of the settlement, was in very poor condition. I asked him what was wrong, and he asked if I would lend him a shilling. He went to the store and bought a loaf of bread and a tin of treacle, and said, 'I am going to have a good feed now'.

Other items available included exotica like tinned fish and fruit, butter and soap. Doreen Dalgety remembers the store as a fairly basic place. 'You couldn't buy a lot of things', she explains, 'you couldn't buy any luxuries or that ... Mostly they'd have biscuits or chocolates.' Although usually only the white staff had enough money to buy them, 'all fruits and vegies [were] sent up from the metropolitan markets and all the cuts of meat and sausages and saveloys'. Olive Hart was lucky enough to avoid the dreaded Moore River porridge by buying Vitabrits at the store, using money left in trust for her by her father. Although Olive worked in the kitchen, she received no pay of her own.

Phyllis Mippy, both of whose parents lived in the camps, remembers her mother occasionally giving her threepence or sixpence to buy sweets: 'just them plain, plain sort of lollies'. Otherwise, the only lollies the kids ever saw were those used literally to make the medicine go down. As Ralph Dalgety recalls:

> I'll tell you about sweets! They used to get them in a, like a four-gallon bucket. We used to call 'em kerosene tins. We'd have our Epsom salts every Saturday, and you'd get a lolly to take the taste out of your mouth. Old Matron Neal used to give us that.

Eric Conway grew up to associate lollies with the Church of England. He still has fond memories of an Anglican priest who visited the settlement monthly to conduct services — and to woo the children with sweets. 'We used to look forward to that gentleman, and oh, he was a gentleman. He'd bring bags of lollies. He spoilt us. And I think the mission must've realised that too, because they started to buy lollies occasionally, not every day.'

After 1941, the settlement food budget increased slowly but steadily, thanks to the influx of Commonwealth Child Endowment funds. Moore River received ministerial approval for participation in the scheme, even though 'any institution wholly or mainly dependent on government funding' was originally deemed ineligible. It was later decided, however,

> that aborigines should not be forced to leave settlements for the purpose of receiving endowments ... It is only reasonable that if a native family, resident outside a settlement, is in receipt of endowment, those native families who are inmates of a settlement will at once make all endeavours to leave the institution for the purpose of collecting the endowment.

Only those children with parents in residence were eligible, however. In 1941, out of a total of 196 children, there were sixty-seven who qualified. An amendment to the Child Endowment Act dealing with payments to the settlements specified that the money would have to be spent for the benefit of the children. From this time, whenever families arrived who had been receiving Child Endowment, they were required to turn their books in upon arrival. The goal, as the Commissioner of Native Affairs put it in 1942, was to 'gradually step up the welfare of the native children from native to white standards'.

The first Child Endowment cheque received at Moore River was for the enormous sum £563.0.10, or about £8.3.0 per eligible child. Not surprisingly, food was the first item on the priority shopping list — particularly extra milk and fruit. Other planned purchases included knives, forks and spoons, glass cups and saucers, plus — strangely, considering other shortages — tablecloths for the big girls' tables. The evidence supplied by oral history informants, however, suggests that none of these additional items was ever purchased. Yet there is no doubt that considerable sums of money were spent, as specified, 'for the benefit of the children'. Hazel Anderson recalls that it was only after her marriage, 'when that Endowment come out first, that's the only time we see butter and eggs, cheese and vegies and fruit. That was for the kids. Well, we thought that was great too because we never seen them things.'

Soon after the scheme began operating, Superintendent Paget boasted to Head Office:

> There has been an extra supply of food as follows: Eggs, Butter, Cheese, fruit, and salads. Tomatoes etc, these added to [the children's] ordinary ration has made a wonderful change in the feeding, as time goes on further additions such as ingredients for puddings will be included ... you may rest assured that everything will be done to put the best food on the tables when obtainable. ... I am in communication with several farmers re the purchase of milking cows and, hope in a day or two to secure a few which will keep up our milk supply.

Two years earlier, although the dairy herd numbered more than forty, the milk supply was just as bad. By 1948, the new Commissioner of Native Affairs, Stanley Middleton, wrote bitterly, 'In the past, failure to secure results from the milking herd has been due mainly to neglect on the part of the member of the white staff delegated for this duty and the utter disregard by the Superintendent of the responsibility for supervision'.

But the promise held out by Child Endowment funds was never realised. Meals improved, certainly. Yet this comparatively huge influx of funds ought to have made a dramatic difference to life at Moore River, and it didn't. In 1948 alone, for example, £2,600 in Child Endowment funds were spent on provisions. There is no evidence of any conspiracy to divert the funds, and no one appears to have used the money for personal gain. Like just about every other resource that found its way to Moore River — from personnel to livestock to tinned jam — the Child Endowment funds just seemed to evaporate. It was probably a case of not-particularly-benign neglect, of an administration not so much evil as just plain incompetent.

The Deputy Commissioner practically admitted as much in 1945, when he wrote:

ever since Endowment has been granted I have striven to provide better meals for the native children ... but not with much success. Plenty of food stuffs are supplied ... in bulk but I have not made much progress in providing meals which are both appetising and in addition with considerable variation day by day.

That there had been any improvement at all, he conceded, was probably owing not to any influx of government money, but to the culinary skill of inmate Gladys Thompson, who had been put in charge of the kitchen. Head Office took the unusual step of rewarding Gladys with an actual weekly salary of five shillings, placed in trust.

The amount of wasted food will never be known, but isolated reports over the years suggest the losses were tremendous. A Head Office inspection in 1946 noted 'piles' of decaying lettuces and beetroots in a corner of the kitchen. 'When asked what was the position, [I] was told that the natives were not eating it and did not like it in the present season ...' It was quite apparent in so far as the settlement was concerned, they were quite happy to sit by and let the food continue to be ordered — and to rot unused. The same inspector observed a dining room meal in which eighty children attempted to eat a meal using thirty-five plates, twenty-three bowls and twenty-one dessert spoons. An inspection two years later showed much the same state of affairs — 'despite the fact that during the year, and every year, hundreds of the above items are issued'.

One permanent improvement after Child Endowment was the appearance of cheese as part of the regular diet. Unfortunately, however, the children hated the cheap 'loaf cheese', and more of it seemed to end up in the bin than in their bellies. In 1943, the Acting Matron was practically pleading with Head Office to permit a change to Kraft cheese. 'Kraft cheese is even flavoured', she wrote, 'and therefore more palatable to children, and although we might only get half the quantity for the same amount of money it would be plenty for their requirements'. The Commissioner replied that 'common cheese' would have to do. 'I would suggest', he concluded icily, 'that the issue be reduced to those who are not too fond of it.'

Other uses for Endowment funds were downright scandalous. In October 1946, for example, Superintendent Harvey was requesting increased quantities of spaghetti, custard powder and jellies. But the reason for this sudden generosity soon became evident. Harvey had determined that giving the natives sweets and other carbohydrates at midday 'consequently allowed for the lightness of the evening meal and so balanced expenses'. Nevertheless, in that same year, a sample menu shows how much the children's diet had been improved over the 'old national feed' of bread and fat. Breakfast offerings now included eggs, frankfurts, spaghetti and fried polony. Dinner featured much more solid meat — sausages, saveloys, boiled mutton, roast and braised meat, in addition to vegetables on alternate days. According to this report, tea was positively scrumptious, with everything from salads and fruit to scrambled eggs and pies with custard on offer. But the words of Eric Conway, who turned fifteen that year, lend a different perspective to the official record: 'We never used to get enough to eat', he remembers. 'Never used to get enough ...'

'The Produce of the Settlement'

The original settlement dietary scale — the fictitious one praised for its 'generosity' — specified that 'the fresh milk, butter, eggs, potatoes, vegetables, fruit and meat are to be the produce of the settlements'. In fact, for more than twenty years, not only were most of these foods not produced at the settlement, they were not included in the diet at all. When Moore River closed down in 1951, the dream of self-sufficiency remained unrealised. In fact, it was as far off as ever. Ironically, the Moore River Native Settlement became instead a model of almost comic inefficiency: a place where the bakehouse operated day and night to produce inedible bread, where mutton was left in the summer heat to rot by the hundredweight, and where precious manpower was wasted tracking nanny goats and stray ounces of tobacco. Edie Moore remembers a song the kids learned in school that seemed to sum the whole thing up:

In the early 1940s, produce from the Settlement Farm included tomatoes, peas, beans and lettuce. They were reserved for staff consumption.

We've got a farm, a barn of a farm
Right in the middle of a swamp
There ain't any charm in our little farm
Right in the middle of a swamp.
Nothing's grown since the day we came
'Misery Farm' is our farm's name.
We're miserable, so miserable, down on Misery Farm
So are the animals, so are the vegetables,
Down on Misery Farm
The hens won't lay, we can't make hay
We work all day and we get no pay
We're miserable, so miserable, down on Misery Farm.

Neville had always envisaged farming as the hub of his settlement scheme. But by the late twenties, it had become clear that the sandplains of Mogumber were stubborn enough to resist even the best-laid political plans. Neville lobbied hard for funds to cultivate more land — a mere thousand pounds for equipment was all that was required — but the request was knocked back by the Premier, a slight Neville long remembered.

Nevertheless, when A J Neal came on board as Superintendent in 1928, he was confident that within a few years the settlement would be returning two thousand pounds a year 'over and above our own requirements' from the sale of sheep and wool. Neville — the son of an Anglican minister — tended to cast his arguments for self-sufficiency in a moral framework. 'Raising up the natives to the white standard' was his chief concern, saving money an important, but secondary, consideration. Neal, who fancied himself a man of action, had no patience for theology. 'We have to keep the natives for all time whether they work or not', he reasoned bluntly, 'so that the sooner a start is made to make the place produce something the better it will be for the State'.

It is really not remarkable that Western Australian bureaucrats hit upon the idea of a work camp as an answer to the 'native question'. It was, after all, a time-honoured solution to the problem of governing indigenous people. What is remarkable is how spectacularly the idea failed. Year after year, the dream of self-sufficient farming yielded to the realities of bad management, bad land and just plain bad luck. But the greatest of these factors, without a doubt, was bad management.

Consider, for example, the case of the goats that went walkabout. As the first of many money-making pastoral ventures, the quest to keep and raise goats for meat sounded like a reasonable proposition. 'Goat meat', wrote Superintendent Brodie, a bit uncertainly, 'is quite as good as mutton but some people won't eat it, that is the difficulty'. 'Some people', it turned out, included virtually the entire Aboriginal population — whom nobody had bothered to consult before the first herd of ninety goats was delivered. As settlement administrators would later learn, 'The Natives object to eating them or killing Nannies. They reckon it is like killing and eating a human being.'

Goat cultivation was first attempted, with dismal results, in 1918. Seven years later, despite Head Office reminders that the original herd had given 'no end of trouble', Brodie insisted on forging ahead. Admittedly, times were tough. There was no mutton for sale locally, and the settlement farm was not even producing enough feed to keep its own small flock alive. Mutton was reserved for staff only, while the natives made do with the despised boiled kangaroo. In his request for another herd of goats, Brodie wrote, characteristically, 'It is the cost I'm thinking of'.

What he failed to consider was the fact that nobody liked goat meat, that the goats would eat anything that wasn't nailed down, and that they would inevitably make a break for the bush, where they would gorge themselves on poison plants and die by the dozen. In fact, the stubbornness of the beasts was matched only by Brodie's own. Grimly refusing to admit defeat, when the goats took to the bush, Brodie dispatched three of his best trackers to ferret them out. Billy Kimberley — a big man fondly remembered by many Moore River children — knew a good thing when he saw it. After an absence of five days he had found only four of the runaways. Brodie was unamused — 'Kimberley I find hung about [with the neighbours] a good deal & incurred unnecessary expense', he wrote sourly — and his Commissioner even less so. Throwing good money after bad was becoming a hallmark of settlement administration.

The episode of the runaway goats was particularly absurd, yet essentially the same story is repeated time and again throughout the next three decades. Sometimes the schemes seemed fairly sensible; at other times they were downright outlandish. Almost always, they would die a slow death by administrative ignorance, sloth or mismanagement. Among the more bizarre ventures was a suggestion by the Deputy Commissioner that Moore River's manpower be harnessed for the cultivation of parrot seed. As the *West Australian* noted, 'Mr. Bray felt that as most of the seeds were produced by dark labour [i.e. in South Africa and Queensland], experiments should be made at some of the native settlements in this State'. Superintendent Neal found the idea laughable. 'As you know', he wrote, 'there is a very small amount of decent land ... and what little

115

bit we have, we require for a better purpose than growing sunflowers — that is, feed for stock'.

New superintendents often came to Moore River brimming with fresh ideas for economising through 'self-sufficiency'. Mitchell came up with one such plan, which actually sounded feasible: to stock the local pools of the Moore River with perch and other freshwater fish, to supplement the settlement diet. As he wrote to his Commissioner in 1920, the natives were catching plenty of these small fish within the boundaries of the settlement. Mitchell set about the project scientifically. He even went so far as to test the heat and depth of a sample pool, and contacted the Chief Inspector of Fisheries as well as the Secretary of the Parliament 'Acclimatisation Committee'. Probably through no fault of Mitchell's, the scheme was apparently never even attempted. The file — like so many in the Moore River archives — simply dwindles away.

In 1932, it was Neal who got a bee in his bonnet. He wanted to start an apiary, he told Neville, because 'there are a lot of bees around here ... New Norcia [Roman Catholic mission] procured about three tons of honey this year, and I think we could do the same and more.' But Neville's Deputy only replied testily, 'We had bees at Moore River once before, and it was quite hopeless on account of the attacks on the bees by numerous ants, which Mr. Neal knows very well exist there'.

Rather more successful was Paget's idea to establish a settlement piggery. In 1941, he persuaded Head Office to supply a handful of pigs 'with a view to fattening same for Pork or bacon' and reselling back into the market later. By September 1941, the piggery had earned thirty-three pounds and was proving 'a profitable sideline' — although the idea that some of the pork might be used to supplement the children's meat ration does not seem to have occurred to anyone. Instead, Paget regarded the piggery as a kind of personal hobby. It certainly kept him busy, and he took obvious pleasure in recording every detail of the purchase and sale of each of his 'weaners'.

At the same time, however, less than a quarter of the total farm area (320 hectares) was under cultivation or in use. Although tomatoes, peas, beans and lettuce were grown, they were reserved for staff consumption only. There was also a continual problem with water supply, and for this reason the proposal to create a small garden at the Superintendent's house was dismissed by Head Office as 'impractical'. As Neal's Deputy (soon to succeed him as Superintendent), Paget nevertheless remained optimistic about the settlement's chances of farming success. Subtly, however, the rhetoric had changed. No longer was self-sufficiency for the Aborigines the goal, as it had been for Neville. Now the bureaucrats began to speak expansively about making the farm 'a payable proposition' for the Department of Native Affairs.

By the time a white farm supervisor was appointed in 1940, Bray — who had just succeeded Neville as Chief Protector — had twisted his former boss's utopian vision beyond recognition. He brazenly announced his plans to transform Moore River from an ineffectual 'clearing house' to a scientifically administered work camp. To this end, he favoured restricting the main settlement to 'females, school children, kindergarten and hospital, and certain married couples essential for the carrying on of the actual settlement itself. All others it is proposed should be removed to the farm where they could all be employed usefully.'

Paget agreed with enthusiasm, and looked forward to 'Being able to get rid of all these half-grown men ... away from the girls, there is plenty of clearing and fencing to be done'. Head Office was delighted, and the Commissioner began to consider other ways in which the work camp might prove useful. 'I heard a day or so ago that the Matron had had to submit to some bad language from one of the elder girls. I do not like this, and think we should endeavour to get rid of such foul-mouthed persons by transferring them to the farm, even if they are women', he wrote.

A year later the farm was at last thriving, and was finally supplying the settlement with potatoes, wheat, oats, field peas, subclover and onions. But somehow, Bray's chilling vision of a detention centre/work camp had failed to materialise. In fact — in an ironic twist — it turned out the farm was being run not by black slave labour, but by paid whites. Following an inspection with the Minister, the Commissioner reported with ill-concealed disgust their discovery that

117

white men were engaged in digging the potatoes, and elsewhere on the farm, and natives were noticeable by their absence ... All of us were very dissatisfied to learn that white men were working for natives instead of the natives themselves being employed in producing vegetables for their own consumption. It was rather a shock to know that this had been going on.

Even more shocking was the cost. The scheme that was to have been 'a payable proposition' was proving yet another in a long line of liabilities. (Earlier, Paget had protested that the work camp scheme would have to wait until more native labour became available. 'Every man is usefully employed in essential jobs', he explained, 'also the boys ... In fact I could use more native labour if I had it. There are thousands of cement bricks to be made for the Detention House ...')

From this point on, the fortunes of the farm declined steadily until the appointment of a new manager, Ellis, in 1944. Aboriginal people who were at Moore River at the time remember Ellis's efficiency and kindness. Officially, he was acknowledged to 'have a flair for handling the native boys ... this not always being a very simple matter'. A year later, there were eighteen Aboriginal people living at the farm, employed as poultry and yard boys, horse boys, general hands, camp cooks and laundry girls. It was beginning to seem that Ellis could work miracles.

In 1946, the farm is described as being in 'excellent condition'. There were 300 fowl 'starting to lay very well', some 1500 cabbages, 'unlimited radishes', and beans, peas, cauliflower and swedes 'making splendid progress'. It all seemed too good to be true. And it was. Ellis left in 1946 and his replacement, a local man named Donegan, quickly re-established the accustomed disorder. Donegan had a singular genius for chooks, however. In no time, he increased average egg production from twenty-one dozen to 132 dozen a week! Eric Conway remembers this time vividly. There were 'all the eggs in the world ... stacks of eggs ... eggs were popping out of everybody'. That same year, Head Office noted with disapproval, 'Except in respect to egg production I am not aware that the children are benefiting in any way from the general farm production at Moore River'. Nevertheless, the farm was costing upwards of a thousand pounds a year to run — a lot of money for eggs, even stacks of them.

When Stanley Middleton was appointed Commissioner in 1949, the pretence of 'self-sufficient' farming was finally over. With characteristic honesty, he wrote:

> Careful inquiries have revealed the fact that the Moore River settlement Farm is an economically unsound proposition and ... has ceased to have any institutional value [i.e. as training ground]. Being a job for which only a 'pocket money' wage was paid, employment on the farm was never popular with the trainees.

'I am sure', he concluded, 'they would be much happier, and probably more usefully and economically employed, if permitted to engage in proper apprenticeships on properties in their own districts of origin.'

Bush Tucker

> I still reckon the food we used to get from the bush kept us survived there.
>
> Ned Mippy

Not at all surprisingly, the administrative records of the Moore River Native Settlement tell an administrative story. It is one version — and a vital one — of 'what really happened' there. But, like any institution, Moore River had both an official life and an unofficial one. Front stage were the bureaucrats, their staff and that dim, undifferentiated mass called 'the natives' they tried so hard to control. But backstage — away from official eyes and ears, away from institutional walls and whistles — was where the Aboriginal inmates of Moore River really lived. Among their families and mates, they were able to express themselves naturally — speaking their own language, sharing their own jokes, finding their own food.

For the children especially, the bush was both the symbol and the site for this other, more authentic life. The bush offered much more than a critical food supply of berries, fish and game. For many of the children of Moore River, it provided the only positive experience of growing up free and Aboriginal. It was thanks to the hunting and gathering expeditions into the bush around the Moore River — snatched in between official duties during the week, or in the delicious weekend interval between Saturday bathtime and Sunday School — that so many of these children managed not only to survive, but to thrive.

On a more prosaic level, the children needed bush tucker to supplement a grossly inadequate diet. They were at great pains to seek it out simply because they were very, very hungry. As Ned Mippy remembers it, 'we lived on berries ... On Sundays you went out, you conned your way into a family what'd take you ... You can eat till you bust, they'd make sure that you had a feed.' Ned remembers a time when the land around Moore River yielded more than thirty different types of berries, including sandplain or golberries, crown berries, butter berries, emu berries, swan berries, scenty berries and ball berries. 'Now you can't get them', he explains, 'because the white people came in with that spray stuff, theys killed all those little things what we used to eat'.

Much, much later, Ned Mippy — as a widely revered elder — taught Aboriginal culture and spirituality to children in the Moora schools, and his knowledge of bush tucker was prodigious. Ned was lucky enough to have both his parents resident in the camps. Thanks to them, he never lost contact with his culture. But the generosity and concern of the camp families ensured that many of Moore River's 'orphans' also learned what the institution was designed to destroy. Although most were deprived of a full sense of their Aboriginality — few learned any language, for example — almost all experienced something of their own culture. Not surprisingly, the emphasis was on survival skills. Many cannot recall exactly how they learned to identify bush tucker or trap game or start a fire. The knowledge was just, somehow, there.

Phyllis Mippy remembers that she and her little gang of mates used to head up to One Mile Hill for berries before school. 'We used to go over the hill there, and in a big hollow there was a berry patch ... Oh, we used to think it was great.' Officially, it seems the practice was tolerated but not encouraged. Phyllis is still not certain why. 'I don't know', she muses. 'They sort of didn't like us bein' happy or something, I suppose.' While the boys would stuff berries down their shirtfronts, the girls tied a string around their waists to make a big pocket. 'We used to come with a lot of berries in our bosom', Phyllis laughs. They would race back to the dormitory and hide their loot under the beds. 'Then, after school, when the dormitory door open, we all rush for our berries.'

Angus Wallam had a huge family at Moore River, including his grandparents, who taught him much about surviving in the bush. He remembers searching the bush for carnopes, a large fruit about ten to thirteen centimetres across. 'You dig 'em out from underneath the rocks', and they tasted like boiled potato.

Ralph Dalgety was one of the boys Ned Mippy went berrying with. The two remained close friends until Ned's death in 1992, sharing fond memories of the settlement which, for all its faults, they still regarded as 'home'. Ralph recalls, 'We used to do all right there in the bush with the bush tucker. Plenty of rabbits, there was millions of rabbits there.' The boys would use both traps and dogs to catch the rabbits, which would then be cooked on the coals.

Although the official bill of fare never once featured chicken in all the years of Moore River's operation, the children had no lack of game birds. After school, Ralph remembers, they'd 'just roam around the countryside, chasin' birds and rabbits and whatnot. We nearly cleaned up every bird in the place up there.' Parrots were caught with stones and shanghais. Eric Conway remembers occasionally killing swans for food — a memory he has somewhat mixed feelings about. 'I think that's sad today', he says, 'but the beautiful thing of it was we never wasted them, we ate them'.

Many also remember fishing in the Moore River for cobbler and other fish. At one point, the Department of Native Affairs actually supplied Aboriginal adults at Moore River with hooks and fishing line. Their response is unrecorded. But we do know that they taught the children the art of spear fishing. Angus Wallam remembers, 'Oh, we would make this knife from a bottle, sharpen the point of it, and we'd go up to where the narrowest part of the river, you know where the mouth of the river comes in shallow? And wait there till the school comes past.'

For the boys especially, the depressing sameness of institutional life was made bearable by weekend hunting expeditions that, by contrast, were charged with challenge and adventure. Jack Davis recalls:

> I think the happiest times we used to have was when half a dozen of us boys, that's fourteen- and fifteen-year-olds, and maybe a couple of the small kids would come with us ... and we would go hunting. We would leave the settlement say at eight o'clock in the morning and come home at dusk that night, and of course we'd get a roo or a rabbit or whatever and take salt with us, a billy can of water, and we would go hunting, we would just go out and hunt and eat and bring some meat back to the camp for the older people.

Hazel Anderson remembers the almost intoxicating freedom of weekend camping expeditions with her family. For once, they were able to make their own decisions — to do things their own way. She explains:

> We'd make our dampers and cook our meat ... if we wanted to have soup, we'd have soup. We'd have potatoes and onions and things like that, and if we didn't have any potatoes and onions, we'd just cook our meat, kangaroo meat, on the coals. We used to like it that way, too, cooked on the coals. [Did you always have enough to eat when you were in the bush?] Yeah, we all had enough to eat.

*

Contradictions

Don't you run my home down. We never starved. We come out of there fat, and look at me, we're still fat.

Bella Yappo, quoting her friend
Lawrence Withemayer

Although there are those who would wish to tell a simpler tale, the story of Moore River is full of contradictions. The 'authorities' — the people who spent their childhood there — are in agreement about much. But just as completely different lives can be lived within the same house, childhood at Moore River was experienced variously as 'all we knew of heaven' and 'all we need of hell'. It is not the job of the historian to decide which of these realities was the truer one. Both were experienced; both therefore existed. At times, they were equally true at one and the same instant.

This is why it is possible to be fairly certain what the children ate, and what they didn't, but it is not possible to understand precisely what this meant for them. It is tempting to condemn the system outright, to reject flatly its priorities and procedures. But even here mere observers must tread cautiously. As Ralph Dalgety explains: 'She was rough, oh she was a rough place, oh yeah, as far as meals were concerned. But we didn't worry because it was our home, you know, more or less, and we had our friends there. That's all we wanted.'

chapter 3

Recalcitrant Natives

Lord, Remove our guilty blindness,
  Hallowed be Thy Name.
Show Thy Heart of loving kindness
  Hallowed be Thy Name.
By our heart's deep-felt contrition,
By our mind's enlightened vision,
By our will's complete submission
  Hallowed be Thy Name.

T Rees, 1916
The Mirfield Mission Hymn Book

It was like a prison, but we thought that was the norm.
You grew up like that. You know — to see a window
without steel mesh on it, you thought something was
wrong with it.

Eric Conway

He that spareth his rod hateth his son, but he that loveth
him, chasteneth him betimes.

Proverb 13, Verse 24
As quoted by Superintendent
Phil Leeming, 1944

This chapter and the next, which examine punishment and reward at Moore River, reveal the institution at the worst of times and the best of times. The decision to focus on extremes has been a conscious one. From its inception, settlement life was defined by extremity and paradox. Founded on a philosophy both supremely racist and superbly utopian, and guided by a staff that included sadists as well as saints, Moore River offered its Aboriginal inmates a haven in the image of a prison cell. Claustrophobically crowded, it remained as isolated as a colony on Mars. The adult population were treated as children. And the children were treated as animals — occasionally as pets to be indulged, more often as wild beasts to be hobbled and tamed.

Moore River has cast so much darkness over so many lives that it is tempting to paint its portrait in shadows. But to do so would be to ignore a light quite stubbornly apparent to those with the only vision worth trusting: the people who lived there. Life at Moore River, their reminiscences assure us, was far from unremitting doom and gloom. A few have even confessed — quite astonishingly — that they miss most of all the 'freedom' they knew there. There are many others who were permanently scarred by the sheer brutality of institutional life.

But for everyone who spent time there, life at Moore River was intensely experienced. There is no doubt that when it was good, it was very, very good — and when it was bad, it was horrid. At the same time, for both staff and inmates alike, the most commonly experienced emotion was neither anger nor fear; it was boredom. Settlement life — apart from occasional giddy highs and terrifying lows — was rather like the landscape on which it unfolded: arid, monotonous and almost preposterously predictable. Against this backdrop of institutional tedium, positive and negative extremes tended to be thrown into dramatically high relief.

*

It would be a mistake to imagine everyday discipline at Moore River as a reign of racist terror, the children cowering in fear before swag-

Staff March 1940. J Stewart, J Marshall, J Ash, I Turner, M Brenchley, Mrs Wilson, G Campbell, F Wilson, Mrs Stewart, A O Neville, R Paget, E Paget, Sister Eileen, M Perrett, M Rowe. Most of the staff at Moore River were not hostile. They were simply indifferent.

gering white overseers. In fact, most staff were not particularly hostile at all — at least not to the children. They were simply indifferent. There were notable exceptions, of course. At least one Superintendent had violently sadistic tendencies, and there was no lack of staff who took occasional satisfaction in humiliating their captives. But, although the children were often harshly punished, active persecution was rare. The real story of their mistreatment is one of passive neglect: of an administration that simply couldn't be bothered to provide more than survival strictly demanded.

In fact, most of the evil committed at Moore River was committed in the name of nothing more exalted — or more dastardly — than bureaucratic expedience. The practice of locking children and single women in their dormitories for twelve out of every twenty-

four hours is a perfect case in point. With no access to books, games or any other amusements, the boys and girls learned to supply their own diversions. That these included fist fights, vandalism and absconding ought to have surprised no one. The practice of locking up children 'like fowl', as one indignant newspaper report of the day put it, was motivated by the desire to save labour and to save money — both exceedingly scarce resources. It was regarded as a perfectly rational solution to a complex administrative problem.

Discipline is a potent form of schooling — and from that point of view the children of Moore River received a first-class education. They may not have done much history or science but every child quickly learnt his or her place and how to stay there. All disciplinary efforts were ultimately directed at maintaining the rigid social boundaries segregating white from black, half-caste from full-blood.

The physical boundary separating the Moore River Native Settlement from the world outside was a cattle fence any child could climb. The psychological boundaries of the place were so formida-

ble that nothing more was needed. Sister Eileen Heath recalls a staff
member telling her, 'There should be a sign over the entrance:
Abandon Hope, All Ye Who Enter Here'.

The Aboriginal inmates were required to abandon much more
than this. The relinquishing of adult rights — and the suspension of
adult reponsibilities — was the basic condition of entry to Moore
River. This was the 'discipline' to which every adult inmate was
subjected daily. Control over their children, over the food they ate
and the homes they lived in, over their amusements and recreations,
their finances and work lives, over the language they spoke and the
people they spoke to: all these matters of individual and cultural
choice were now dictated by institutional policy. It was the price the
state exacted for 'protection'. No wonder Aboriginal people wanted
to know, in the words of inmate Peter Jackson, 'Is there not some
law that will protect me from the Chief Protector?'

Settlement life was dominated by the urge to defend boundaries.
This is precisely the reason that the so-called half-caste was per-

ceived as so fearsome a threat. Neither black nor white, half-castes violated the most fundamental social boundary of all. The institutional arsenal was a formidable one, ranging from alarm bells and roll calls, locks and enclosures, to a private police force armed with sticks and straps. It is no coincidence that so many of Moore River's administrators boasted a military background and aspired to a military ideal of precision and order. But somehow their vision always eluded capture. Despite the enormous expense and energy of defending them, the boundaries kept right on crumbling.

But this is all an historian's privileged view of the matter. It is interesting to observe patterns which can only be spotted from the air. But life on the ground is usually a very different matter. It was particularly so for the children of Moore River.

How did they experience the discipline of settlement life? Although the written evidence is silent on this question, the evidence from oral history testimony is thunderous. But it is also full of tension and contradiction. Quite obviously, different people experienced settlement discipline in very different ways. To avoid insisting on a single 'correct' version of this very complex reality, it may help to imagine the disciplinary structures of settlement life as comprising a strong but invisible web. Like all webs, this one gave support to some lives even as it ensnared others.

For many of Moore River's children — denied access to the traditional discipline structures of their own culture — these early lessons in boundary-setting would prove a virtual lifeline. 'You know, there was a lot of discipline, strict discipline', Eric Conway explains, 'and I appreciate that today ... it did a lot of good for us'. It's a sentiment echoed by many others. Institutional discipline may not always have been just, but it was at least coherent.

There were others, however, who experienced the discipline of settlement life as a straitjacket from which they continually, and vainly, struggled for release. Not surprisingly, most of these were female. Like their sisters in the world outside the settlement borders, the 'big girls' were subject to far tighter control than their male counterparts. At the same time, the outlets available for discharging their physical and creative energies were far fewer. The only form of self-expression many of them were able to manage was flight. And flee they did, often and repeatedly, both singly and in mobs. Displaying a fierce and often reckless courage, these young women showed their contempt for institutional boundaries separating blacks from whites, children from parents, boys from girls. And their punishment was tailor-made to fit the crime: imprisonment in the 'boob', an isolation chamber whose tight iron boundaries left barely enough space to breathe.

The Trackers

Vivid in the imagination of every child who ever spent time at Moore River were the omnipresent 'black trackers', the handful of Aboriginal men who comprised the settlement's in-house police force. In some they inspired fear, in others downright contempt. Yet there were many fatherless children who loved them. On the whole, however, the trackers were regarded uneasily with what might most accurately be described as mixed feelings. It is not hard to understand why.

Straddling both sides of the institutional fence dividing white from black, the trackers were highly ambiguous figures. Moore River's adult Aboriginal population tended to regard the trackers as 'Uncle Toms' who had sold out their own people in return for white protection. Resentment was fanned further by tribal differences — the trackers tended to be northerners while the majority of the settlement population was from the south-west. This, certainly, is the portrait painted by Jack Davis in *No Sugar*, in which a fictionalised version of the real-life tracker Billy Kimberley emerges as a self-serving, dim-witted buffoon. In Davis's retelling, even the children despise Billy, whose heavily caricatured, pidgin-style English provides welcome comic relief.

In fact, to Moore River's compound kids, the trackers were hardly a laughing matter. As role models, they loomed particularly large in the lives of the boys. After all, the trackers were black, they were male and they were highly visible authority figures. Few of the compound boys would have had fathers living in the camps — if one parent was present it was much more likely to be a mother. Those lucky enough to have resident fathers usually managed to see

In some, the trackers inspired fear, in others downright contempt. Yet there were many fatherless children who grew to love them.

132

them only on weekends. Ned Mippy, whose dad worked as the settlement baker, was one of the rare exceptions, and he was keenly aware of this privileged position. The trackers, by contrast, lived quite literally side by side with the boys — in lean-to quarters attached to their dormitory. Theirs were the first faces to greet the boys every morning, and the last each night. Armed with blackboy sticks, they haunted the dining room, the schoolroom, even the bush.

But the presence of the trackers was not only pervasive in space, it was also uniquely constant over time. Particularly after the departure of the Neals in 1939, when staff turnover reached almost epidemic proportions, they constituted virtually the sole point of stability in a constantly erupting human landscape. It is little wonder that Eric Conway, for example, who arrived at Moore River in 1938, unselfconsciously refers to tracker Bill Lewis as 'Uncle Bill'. Eric, who was taken from his home at Marble Bar at age six, had no adult kin at the settlement. For him, the three trackers — two of them full-bloods — offered a model of male Aboriginality that was both dignified and nurturing.

Eric recalls that Bill Lewis was originally sent to Moore River on warrant, 'but he became a tracker, and a good one at that. Nothing could get away from him. He knew how to track, that fellow, and he took his job seriously. But at the same time, he had a kind heart. Well, they all did really.' For boys like Eric, it was important to grow up alongside Aboriginal men whose traditional skills were so highly valued, but who were also able to show a caring side. As Eric explains, 'I've seen the times when they gave you a hiding and felt sorry for it after, you know, but they just felt that they were only doing their job'.

To the younger children, the trackers seemed all-powerful. But their apparent autonomy was an illusion — just as it was for the gangs of little boys revelling in the 'freedom' of the bush between alarm bells. Later, Eric grasped the sad irony that the trackers were as much captives of the settlement system as the inmates they policed. It struck him, for example, that the straps they carried were an emblem of servitude, not sadism. 'I used to find that sad', he remembers. 'I don't think they wanted to do it, but they were like us. They had to be disciplined, and that was their job: to pull us into gear.'

133

The idea of using black trackers was obviously inspired by the 'trusty' system of prison management — a system with a long pedigree in the annals of punishment history. Like its antecedent, the genius of the tracker system lay in the illusion of self-discipline it fostered: that blackfella justice was being served because it was blackfellas who were serving it. By deflecting resentment away from white administrators, the tracker system was also calculated to encourage tension and division within the ranks. But somehow or other, things never quite worked out that way.

The reason probably has a lot to do with differences between Aboriginal and European responses to power. The logic of the trusty system assumes that the privileged prisoner will become slightly power-drunk. The more completely he comes to accept the illusion of his own omnipotence — the more he struts and swaggers — the more deeply resentment will fester. Ultimately, it is the trusty himself who is scapegoated and despised. In the meantime, the true gaoler, safely hidden behind the scenes, continues to pull all the strings. But at Moore River, no one except the children ever took the trackers particularly seriously — and even they were sometimes aware that their authority was simply a pose. Nor were the trackers themselves terribly concerned with winning power games. It was simply not part of their cultural orientation even to try.

Doreen Dalgety remembers that on the odd occasion when the trackers would try to swagger, they'd simply look ridiculous. She remembers one old tracker who used to like to stand around with his thumbs in the lapel of his jacket as if to tell the world, 'Yes, I am a police constable!' But in the eyes of the Aboriginal community, 'they was just men', as Bella Yappo explains. 'They wouldn't hurt a fly, they couldn't hit a bobtail on the head.' Bella recalls that the trackers socialised freely with other Aboriginal staff, with whom they quite obviously identified. She explains, 'When we knocked off work, we used to go around to their place at the back of the boys' dormitory. We'd go around there and sit down and chuck a chop on the coal and join them. It was really good.'

Although seen by some as Uncle Toms, dancing to the tune of their white-collared overseers at the Big House, the trackers obviously saw themselves as Aboriginal first and staff second. There

134

were countless instances of collusion and deal-making with the 'wrongdoers' they were charged with disciplining. Nor did they have qualms about using their comparative freedom to personal advantage. Their loyalty to the Big Bosses, while just firm enough to keep their jobs secure, was always soft around the edges.

In an environment that was so overtly shaped by an either/or mentality, the trackers inhabited a no-man's land of neither/nor. They were neither staff nor inmate, neither exactly one of 'them' nor quite yet one of 'us'. Part whitefella lawman, part ordinary black-fella, the tracker seemed to personify the dilemma of their 'half-caste' charges, who struggled to negotiate equally mixed messages about their own identity.

Even the trackers' uniform spoke of their peculiarly ambivalent status. As Ralph Dalgety relates, they 'never had the full rig out'. On top was a standard policeman's uniform — a jacket, minus decorations or badges, plus a hat. These were discards, supplied gratis by the Police Department. The bottom half of the ensemble, however, was left to the tracker to complete. To the adults in the camps, this quasi-uniform may have suggested a scarecrow more than a constable. But to the children, and to the trackers themselves, it had potent symbolic value. The trackers 'honoured their job' — and they honoured their uniforms too. 'They used to spruce up', Ned Mippy remembers, 'put their coats on and polish their little buttons'.

Ned explains that, as far as the children were concerned, the authority of the trackers was unquestioned. They feared the tall men in the shiny-buttoned coats, but they respected them too. 'When your own colour talks to you', he explains, 'there's a bit of principle in that'. The children firmly believed that it was the trackers — rather than the white administrators who issued their orders and their rations — who were in control. But the illusion, Ned suggests, served an important function. It created powerful and legitimate role models who were Aboriginal. A child could retain some sense of self worth — some dignity — when accepting punishment 'from our own people, own colour'.

> See, if we had a white bloke there we'd get up in arms. 'Oh, who's he going to tell?' or 'What's he tellin' me

135

that for?' 'What's that white man tellin' me to do?'. As soon as the tracker come over, you'd stand to attention. Yes, you'd stand to attention.

Among the boys who grew up in the shadow of the Moore River trackers, there remains a strong sense of valuable lessons 'learned the hard way' and never forgotten. Today, they speak approvingly of the strict discipline they knew as children. The trackers may have been 'a bit rough at times, but there's times when you got to get rough'. Eric Conway recalls one tracker, Jack Mullega, whose fairness made a lifelong impression. 'Every time he strapped you he told you why he did it', Eric explains. 'I always learnt from old Jack.' In later life, Eric would consciously apply these lessons when disciplining his own children.

Ralph Dalgety believes the harsh discipline he endured as a child — including regular smacks from the trackers' ever-present razor strops — was more than justified. 'I didn't like it at the time', he admits with a laugh, 'but after I grew up I used to think about it, you know. Really, it wasn't strict enough there.' Vincent Lambadgee, whose own father was a tracker, also believes the system was fundamentally just.

> When we did wrong we had to stand the punishment for it. I don't think it done us any harm, you know. Well, I've lived to be a better man out of it ... We can't hold that against them.

For Aboriginal girls, on the other hand, settlement discipline often seemed both cruel and pointless. Today, in contrast to their male counterparts, few women betray nostalgia for their childhood home. And, far from feeling gratitude for the discipline they endured there, they have remained indignant and sad. Lizzy Dalgety confides, 'I didn't like the trackers. I thought they were a little bit cruel — and yet they were Aborigines, you know. I just couldn't understand why they would want to do those things like that to their own people.' In later years, Lizzy was able to reason it through. 'Well, they had to do that', she now reflects, 'because they had whites behind them to push them. They had to do it. Otherwise, I reckon, it must have hurt them inside some ways, eh? — to hit an Aborigine kid like that, eh? Because they're black themselves. That's what I often think back.'

But for Lizzy, and for many of the other girls, the memory still stings. 'Some of the kids used to come late to the dormitory', she recalls, 'and they'd get a whack around the leg or around the bottom with a piece of stick. And, see, a lot of the kids used to just cry and put their hands behind their back to save their bottom from getting hit.' Like Lizzy, Hazel Anderson regarded the trackers with suspicion and fear: 'We didn't like 'em. They were too rough.'

Phyllis Mippy, whose father, Frank Narrier, was a tracker, agrees. During Phyllis's childhood, in the late thirties and early forties, Narrier was the only Moore River tracker who actually tracked runaways. The others — Kingy Hill, Bob Allen and 'Bluey' — were responsible for compound discipline. It was probably just as well. Phyllis remembers her father as a violent and unstable man who seemed compelled to single her out for abuse — particularly when Phyllis would sneak down to the camp to see her mum. 'He was very cruel', she remembers. 'I don't know why. I can remember him belting me with this big green stick. He had me by the hand, and I couldn't run away. He held my hand, and he held me and held me and I was ... he was just beltin' me. My old mum just sat down. She couldn't say nothin'.'

Alice Nannup was fourteen when she arrived at the settlement, and was quickly put to work as a domestic for the white staff. Her age and her status as a 'working girl' enabled her to regard the trackers with more equanimity. 'Oh, they were all right', she remembers, 'as long as you kept in your place'. Then again, Alice had a secret weapon. An excellent cook, she soon discovered that trackers were as hungry as any other Aborigine at the settlement. Their silence could easily be bought for the price of a turkey leg or a loaf of bread. Like Jack Davis and Bella Yappo — who also came to the settlement as teenagers — Alice found the trackers 'had more of a nuisance value than anything else', to use Jack's words.

Those who were small children when they first encountered the trackers have found it difficult, even with the benefit of adult hind-

'Bluey' Frank Wallace, 1939.

sight, to be so blasé. For some, the tracker of the imagination remains a terrifyingly powerful figure — a gigantic northerner, as black as a starless night (and about as cheerful), wielding an arsenal of deadly weapons. One person vividly recalls children receiving twenty-seven lashes with a leather cat o' nine tails — and in his childhood nightmares, no doubt they did. Incidents such as these, which are unverified by other informants who were resident at the same time, reveal yet another facet of the complicated reality of settlement discipline.

Floggings

There were numerous, widely verified incidents of floggings, incarcerations and other violence, both physical and emotional. But there are other stories told which appear to be based only thinly on truth. It is possible that stories of fiendishly violent punishments were invented by staff to frighten the children into acquiescence. But it is possible too that some of those stories — which, like all myths, gave substance to emotional realities — were woven by the children themselves in those long, dark dormitory nights.

The problem of identifying the punishment devices used at Moore River provides an interesting case in point. One informant has claimed that Superintendent A J Neal routinely used a stock whip, although there is much wider agreement that a variety of sticks — including blackboy sticks and canes — were used by everyone from the teaching staff to the trackers to the Superintendent. But it is on the much-disputed subject of the cat o' nine tails that accounts begin to diverge dramatically.

Only two informants out of the fifteen or so who commented on the matter recall the use of a conventional cat o' nine tails — described as 'a whip with a very short handle' with 'at least nine to ten to twelve strands of leather going out from it'. One person maintained that this was used by the trackers, the other that it was the preferred weapon of Superintendent Neal. Most of the other Aboriginal informants remember the settlement cat o' nine tails as an entirely different instrument — although again recollections vary significantly. Some describe an implement resembling a riding crop; others, something more like a stiffened bamboo cane. Archival evidence confirms that Neal's arsenal included the handle of a driving whip.

So which version is to be trusted? The answer may well be: all of them. Although a variety of disciplinary weapons were in use over Moore River's three decades of operation, the same term — 'cat o' nine tails' — was employed to describe a number of them. The fact that this term has a distinct meaning in non-Aboriginal Australian English has only added to the confusion. It is probable that a few informants, who were lucky enough to be spared firsthand knowledge of it, simply assumed the cat o' nine tails to be the conventional leather-thonged weapon.

This would help explain denials by reliable European informants about the existence of the cat o' nine tails. A O Neville himself testified emphatically before the Moseley Commission that 'there is no such thing as a cat o' nine tails at the mission', although he readily admittedly to other examples of institutional cruelty. Over the years, other white staff have corroborated this, including people like Sister Eileen Heath, whose sympathies were definitely on the side of the inmates. These denials have unfortunately tended to undermine the credibility of Aboriginal informants. To set the record straight: the weight of oral evidence suggests that a conventional cat o' nine tails was never employed at Moore River. But two or three other instruments which were called cat o' nine tails — and which were painful and much feared — were in quite frequent use, including Neal's infamous whip handle.

As far as the children were concerned, day-to-day discipline was largely a matter of accountability: turning up at the right place at the right time. As Eric Conway explains: 'You had to jump to attention of two bells. One was to get you ready and the second bell was, for argument's sake, line up at the dining room. When the second bell went, the doors were opened and you were let in, and the doors were shut behind you. So if you came a minute late or anything like that, you weren't let in.' The children would be asked the reason for their tardiness, but this was just a formality. Eric recalls, 'I've never really actually seen a Superintendent or one of the trackers accept anybody's excuse for being late. You still got the strap — always — in front of everybody.'

The Superintendents

More serious offences called for more serious measures, and a tracker would haul off the offending child to the Superintendent's office. On this, agreement is universal. But precisely what transpired once inside that office door is open to some conjecture. Naturally, different Superintendents had very different disciplinary styles —

140

The Superintendent's residence, known to the inmates as the 'Big House'.

and over its lifetime as a state institution, Moore River saw no fewer than twenty-two Superintendents and acting Superintendents, and as many deputies.

By far the longest-serving of these was Arthur J Neal, who followed Brodie in 1927 and served there, with his wife as Matron, until 1939. It is hardly surprising that Neal is Moore River's most vividly remembered Superintendent among the former compound children. Like his employees, the trackers — and like his boss, the elusive A O Neville — Neal has assumed the dimensions of an icon, a figure heavily laden with symbolic baggage. Today, he symbolises a great deal more in the history of Moore River than his achievements, for good or ill, actually warrant.

For some people, the remembered Neal has become a composite of all the worst of Moore River's many bad administrators. There are those who remember him as a foul-mouthed, habitual drunk, for example, although the weight of evidence strongly disputes this.

Arthur J Neal, Superintendent (1927-1939), front row centre. Today, he has assumed the dimensions of an icon: a composite of all the worst of Moore River's many bad adminstrators.

Neal was scrupulous about appearances. It seems that when he did drink — and he clearly did — it was done in the discreet shelter of the Mogumber Hotel. However, there were other Superintendents who do fit this description. Phil Leeming, for example, who was appointed in August 1943 and lasted hardly a year, was probably an alcoholic. Paget, Neal's deputy and immediate successor, was known to have had a particularly vicious temper and a tongue to match.

Others have alleged that Neal always carried a revolver, and that he routinely used his power to seduce and/or coerce young girls to have sex with him. In fact, it was a Superintendent of the mid-1940s, Mark Knight, who always carried a revolver with him. And it was Knight's deputy, William Sutherland, who once punished a tipsy teenaged inmate by shooting him in the leg. (For a full account of

*Deputy Superintendent Paget, 1937. Later Neal's successor, Paget is
remembered for his vicious temper.*

the shooting of Ernest Colbung, see Chapter Five.)

The charges of sexual abuse are much more difficult either to
substantiate or to refute. This is, of course, in the nature of sexual
offences, especially those that occur within institutions. The victim's
sense of shame, coupled with a very real threat of reprisal, often
creates an airtight immunity for abusers.

There are some — including Jack McPhee, in Sally Morgan's
Wanamurraganya — who allege that Neal considered sexual access
to Aboriginal females a perk of office. His usual victims, it has been
claimed, were young women seeking permission to marry. Others,
both Aboriginal and non-Aboriginal, have disputed this charge, and
— perhaps inevitably — there have been no firsthand accounts to
settle the matter.

On the other hand, one informant distinctly recalls that, as a child of eleven or twelve, she narrowly escaped being molested by Deputy Superintendent Tanner. Paget's second in command, Tanner had a long career as a settlement staffer and even acted as Superintendent for a period in 1941. His reputation for inveigling young girls to 'come for a ride in his truck' to remote destinations was well known. While it is certain that sexual abuse did occur at Moore River, the extent of Neal's personal involvement must remain speculative.

Disentangling the real Arthur Neal from the powerfully symbolic figure of memory is a tricky task. We know for certain that Neal was a small man, and probably rather vain. Eileen Heath remembers him basking in the admiration of the younger female staff, and photographs reveal that he was partial to self-consciously dapper suits, set off by an enormous waxed moustache. His relationship with the much-loved but undeniably plain Matron, his second wife and former housekeeper, was perfunctory. It was clearly a marriage of convenience. The widowed Neal needed a permanent housekeeper and nanny for his four young children; Jane Sarah Edmunds, a Welsh migrant and trained nurse, needed a permanent position. Well beyond her own childbearing years, she would prove an extraordinary step-mother. 'Aunty' won the devotion not only of her husband's children, but of the literally hundreds of others she cared for and worried over during a legendary twelve-year tenure as Matron of Moore River.

They were an unlikely pair: the compact, dandified disciplinarian and the ungainly earthmother, ubiquitous in her starched white uniform and spotless veil. Yet they proved oddly effective as a team. He got things moving — even those who despised him admit that he was a tireless worker and an astute administrator — but it was she who gave the place its breath of life. Left to his own devices, Neal, the Boer War veteran, would probably have turned Moore River into an efficiently run work camp. His daughter Eileen remembers him as a strict and rather distant figure, who was accustomed to issuing orders. He had little tolerance for 'cheek' — whether from his own children, the natives, or even his bosses at Head Office.

Often brusque to the point of rudeness, Neal prided himself on being a man of action. Equally, however, he was no sadist. Unlike his predecessor Brodie, for example, he was never given to fits of unprovoked rage. Nor did he inflict punishment for its own sake. His style as a disciplinarian was harsh but rarely vicious; and, despite an explosive temper, he was generally master of his own emotions. Jack Davis remembers that the kids regarded Neal's waxed moustache as a barometer of his anger: 'All the kids knew that once that moustache started to tremble at the ends, you got out of his road quickly because he was becoming angry'.

In his disciplinary style as much as in his drinking and his alleged extra-marital 'romances', Neal was extraordinarily discreet. It is easy to believe Eileen Isbister when she says, 'I never ever saw him punish anybody. He might have reprimanded them. He might have threatened them. But I never ever saw him punish anybody.' Marj Bandy, who as a young and vivacious staff member was an important member of the Neals' social circle, agrees. 'I've read about how sometimes the children have been punished', she admits, 'but not while I was there'.

The fact is, Neal's punishments were always meted out behind closed doors in his office, away from the uncomfortably inquiring eyes of missionaries, matrons and schoolmarms. Most of the time, to be fair, there would probably have been nothing more sinister to see than the sight of Neal glowering down his glasses at a group of ragged children. If the children were small girls, they would rarely receive a worse punishment than what was considered standard for those harsher times — a few hard whacks with a stick on the palm of the hand. Hazel Anderson recalls a typical encounter:

> When we go into the office to get punished he'd look over his glasses at us, like that [demonstrating]. We never used to like that look! This is how he used to talk [puts on deep voice]: 'What are you girls in here for?' 'Oh, we was stealing some carrots' or something you know like that. 'You know I tell you not to go down there.' 'Yeah, Mr Neal.' 'Come on' — he'll jump up off the chair — 'come on now'. There was one girl — she was older than us — we used to put her in the front, 'cause she was the oldest. She'd get a go first [laughter]. 'Put your hand out, put your hand out.' We put our hand out [makes hitting sound]. Other side, two cuts. 'Go. Next one.' He used to do that to all of us.

Although the cuts were given hard enough to raise welts, there were never any hard feelings afterward, says Hazel. 'We still liked him, never mind', she explains, '''cause we thought, well, we do wrong we got to put up with it, see'. Most of the other Aboriginal people interviewed expressed similar feelings about Neal. As Doreen Dalgety put it, 'There was a method in his madness. He could be very bad — but he could be very just.'

Neal rarely let the boys off so easily, yet they too express surprisingly positive feelings about him. Even Jack Davis, whose *No Sugar* portrayed Neal as a lascivious, drunken bully, admits to a grudging respect for him. 'I think lesser men than Neal would have succumbed and thrown the job in', he says. 'But he was a tough man and he had a pretty tough situation at the time.'

There is general agreement that Neal's usual punishment routine was to drag the boys off to the storeroom — which conveniently adjoined his office — where they would be ordered to drop their trousers and bend over a pile of flour sacks. Neal would then thrash them with a device that seems to have been his own personal property. It has been described by informants who knew it intimately as a stout, sixty- to ninety-centimetre stick, covered in leather or rubber, with a stiff wire inside. Doubtless this is the same instrument witnesses identified as 'the handle of a driving whip'.

Like many of the boys who grew up at Moore River in the 1930s, Vincent Lambadgee became something of a veteran of Neal's thrashings — and the years have not dimmed his memory of the pain. Yet he is now convinced that 'It was a hidin' for the wrong to make a right man out of us'. After all, he explains philosophically, 'if I didn't get it from the superintendent, I'd get it from me mother just the same'.

Eric Conway appreciates the lessons that were sometimes 'forced down his throat' at Moore River — like 'teaching of manners, learning to be punctual and to be responsible for things'. But he remains ambivalent about the extent of physical abuse the children were made to endure. 'They seemed to be very keen on trying to thrash everybody all the time', he observes drily. 'There were thrashings every day.' Yet the effectiveness of all this discipline was questionable. 'There were some boys', Eric recalls, 'who would never, never toe the line. It was just in them to be naughty, being typical boys. No matter how hard you flog them and carry on and yell and scream, they'll still go and do something silly the next day.' There were others, more sensitive, who would emerge 'touchy and scared. Then we'd do the right thing for awhile.'

Adult Discipline

More controversial by far, however, were the punishments inflicted on Moore River's adult population. Although the present study is concerned mainly with the experience of children, there are two reasons for examining these practices. One is the fact that adult discipline had a powerful impact on the children who witnessed or heard about it. As such, it was a significant factor in shaping their ideas about Aboriginal-European relations. But it is also important to remember that, at Moore River, the boundary between 'childhood' and 'adulthood' was both problematic and permeable.

At institutions like Moore River — and in the wider Australian culture which supported them — Aboriginal adults were regarded as fractious, overgrown children and treated accordingly. The language of policy makers, churchmen and others concerned with native welfare was peppered with pious references to Australia's 'child race'. Indeed, as we shall see in more detail in Chapter Seven, it was on the basis of such rhetoric that children were removed to government institutions like Moore River in the first place.

Aboriginal men and women, it was widely believed, were biologically capable of producing children but morally, socially and intellectually incompetent to rear them. The rationale for government-supported institutions like Moore River was the assumption that native children needed to be quite literally protected from native adults. And native adults, the logic ran, needed to be protected from themselves — as well as from the possible abuses of the white community. These were the responsibilities of the aptly named Chief Protector of Aborigines.

The most devastating result of this protectionist propaganda was that many Aboriginal children grew up believing it. Settlement life

147

systematically deprived them of any evidence to the contrary. The dormitories were full of children who had been literally kidnapped by 'protectors' in officially sanctioned raids. Many of the compound kids were too young to retain even a dim memory of their mothers and fathers. Furthermore, it was settlement policy to keep contact between the children and adults, whether family or not, to an absolute minimum. Families who arrived at the settlement voluntarily were shocked to discover that, in order to obtain a camp cottage, they were expected to surrender their children to the care of compound staff.

For various reasons, however, effective segregation proved impossible. For one thing, there was always a lack of accommodation: too little room and not enough beds. Some of Moore River's more incompetent Superintendents simply couldn't be bothered to enforce the policy. Others started out gung-ho but were finally beaten by the sheer persistence with which the boundaries were violated. The children of Moore River owe a debt of gratitude to this administrative failure. Because it was thanks solely to their contact with camp life that so many were able to retain a sense of their Aboriginality — despite insistent institutional messages to the contrary.

But it was not only in regard to parenting that Aboriginal adults were treated as helpless children. The price for the 'protection' of settlement life was higher still. It entailed complete submission to settlement authority (or at least the appearance of complete submission) in virtually every sphere of adult life — from work and leisure to sex and spirituality. People were not even trusted to prepare their own food from rations. Instead, their meals were doled out through a window — barely edible, it is true, but ready-made.

Adult recreation was monitored almost more closely than the children's. Two-up was tolerated, for example, but alcohol was strictly forbidden. Pre- and extra-marital sex, while frowned upon, was hard for even the Chief Protector to police. But adults were still required to obtain the Superintendent's permission to be married. Having received this, they would then be appropriately costumed for the occasion, down to veils, hats and wedding rings supplied gratis by Head Office.

As we have already seen, the most destructive form of discipline inflicted upon adults at Moore River was a web of protectionist policy designed to subvert personal choice and authority or, to put it more simply, to turn adults into children. But adults at Moore River were also punished in more specific ways. For instance, there have been numerous reports of adult floggings — including women. One of the first of these to receive official attention appeared as evidence before the 1934 Moseley Commission. Mrs Annie Morrison (Stack), a mother of six, testified that she heard 'some girls [young women] screaming in the office and the trackers said two trackers held the girls' hands and feet over a sack of flour and Mr Neal gave them a hiding until they wet themselves. We had to eat the flour after.' Some of the details of this horrific incident — which is also related in Jack Davis's *A Boy's Life* — do run contrary to information provided by contemporary Aboriginal informants. They have stressed, for example, that Neal never worked with the trackers as a team. On the other hand, it is dangerous to allow contentious details to obscure obvious truths. Grown-up people were definitely flogged at Moore River, and the children were aware of this.

Undoubtedly, however, the most notorious adult punishments were those which inflicted not pain, but humiliation. The most infamous of these occurred in 1926, when a young man named Norman Gidgup — accused of stealing a packet of cigarettes — was tarred, feathered and paraded through the compound. The Superintendent in charge was John Brodie. Neville himself wrote about the incident in his book *Australia's Coloured Minority:*

> One Superintendent I had, because he suspected him of some moral lapse, tarred and feathered a native, and he did the job thoroughly, calling the staff to see the rare bird he had captured ... He had to be larded and rubbed for days to be rid of the tar and feathers with which the Superintendent had plastered him from head to foot.

Ned Mippy, who was seven years old at the time, was among the stunned crowd of Aboriginal children and adults who witnessed the scene. 'He ran out naked and he looked like a feathery bird, all this

149

stuff on him', Ned recalls. As an eight-year-old, Hazel Anderson looked on in rapt bewilderment. 'All the little kids was watching it', she remembers, 'and the older girls, they ran and hid, they hid their faces ... We was wondering what they did it for.' Yet even children as young as Ned and Hazel knew better than to ask questions. As Ned explains, 'Whatever you'd think you had to keep it to yourself. Otherwise you'd be in it.' One can only speculate on the impact such incidents would have had for those children, and how they helped to shape later assumptions about Aboriginality, authority and adulthood.

The tarring and feathering of Norman Gidgup was an extreme and isolated case — which is one reason it is so vividly remembered. Indeed, far from receiving official sanction, Chief Protector Neville deplored such punishment. He wasted no time in sacking Brodie, who afterward 'fled the State just in time to avoid being prosecuted for assault'. (The bible-bashing Brodie later resurfaced in Western Australia, where he was seen peddling 'religious literature of the Jehovah Witness type' door to door.)

But routine humiliations and what might be described as casual contempt were part of the very fabric of settlement life. These everyday structures of discipline would have had an enormous impact on children struggling to work out the roles, rules and relationships in their strange new home.

Runaways

If settlement discipline was all about the maintenance of boundaries, it is hardly surprising that the most persistent misdemeanour was attempted escape. Runaways from Moore River were drawn almost exclusively from a segment of the population who dwelt uncomfortably in the borderland between childhood and adulthood. These were the so-called 'big girls' — those who had passed the school leaving age of fourteen, but who had not yet been sent out to work or marriage.

The evidence is very clear that it was these adolescent girls — and only rarely their male counterparts — who persistently absconded. It's not hard to understand why. Of all settlement inmates, they were the most vulnerable to abuse and the least able to sustain the illusion of freedom. By contrast, most men and many of the women informants have quite happy memories of their school days. As Hazel Anderson explains, 'My school days were the best days for me, 'cause I never ever got in trouble much, only just stealing a bit from the garden'. It was only later that everything went sour, when she left school and found herself without an occupation, a social life or any foreseeable future outside the compound fence. 'I used to run away when I grew up', she relates. Eric Conway has pointed out that few of the smaller children ever tried to run away for the simple reason that 'we just didn't have an idea of where our home was'.

Boys who had left school were either put to work on the compound, sent to the farm, or went out to work for pastoralists. Others, who could not or would not find employment, simply drifted away — usually only down to the camps to join family or friends. During Neville's early years as Chief Protector, young men were still largely subject to 'Mr Devil's' jurisdiction, and it could prove extremely difficult to secure a legal release. Accordingly, in 1932, the annual report of the Aborigines Department records that ten males and eighteen females had decamped, 'practically all adolescent youths and girls.' But as the Depression deepened, Neville was forced to loosen his grasp somewhat, and by the forties young men who wished to leave the settlement had little trouble obtaining permission through the proper channels. Not surprisingly, young males who did abscond rarely cited a lack of freedom as the reason. Quite simply, most of them only ran away because they were hungry.

For adolescent girls, on the other hand, Moore River was a virtual prison. Apart from the dozen or so women who laboured in the sewing room, the girls were not generally overworked. Most were given jobs around the settlement, but these would consume only a few hours each day. And there were some who, rather mysteriously, were never assigned any work at all. Instead, they passed their days wandering listlessly about the compound or down to the camps, gambling their hairpins at two-up or listening to the latest gossip. There were no opportunities for outside social contacts or for vocational training. There wasn't even anything to read. Sewing was

151

virtually the only skill which girls were encouraged to cultivate and, while some were motivated enough to produce prize-winning embroidery, many others must have considered it pointless drudgery.

Perhaps most importantly of all, there was never more than a handful of single young men on the premises. Indeed, after a time it became departmental policy to endeavour to ban them outright. While this was never entirely successful in practice, young men remained a scarce commodity, and demand definitely outstripped supply.

Although some girls ran away because they were hungry, most were simply bored out of their minds. Although experience had shown that few escapes lasted longer than a day or two, they could at least experience a change of scene, the thrill of high adventure and a few moments in the local spotlight on their return. As Sister Eileen explains:

> The girls knew they'd be brought back sooner or later —
> they knew that. But it was a bit of excitement to get away
> ... I think mostly that the trackers knew which way to go
> to look for them, and I think it was just, well, boredom
> — just to get away from the place.

The runaway also achieved a certain social standing. 'You just hadn't arrived until you had run away a few times', Sister Eileen recalls. This was all too subtle for Chief Protector Neville, who in his 1935 annual report expressed dismay over the growing legion of runaway girls:

> The elder girls, some of whom have proved unemploy-
> able outside the settlement, have given a lot of trouble by
> decamping from time to time, and it is difficult to know
> what to do in some cases. They can supply no valid
> reason for their actions, unless it be the desire for a
> change of surrounds.

Eileen Neal Isbister was not puzzled at all: 'Every week there

152

would be two or three girls run away to meet their boyfriends up the river or up Moora somewhere. It was a natural thing, but they weren't allowed.' In fact, the Superintendent's daughter once ran away herself. It was during the school holidays (Eileen was a boarder at Perth College) and Neal had gone down to the camps to settle a fight. Frightened by all the commotion, Eileen walked straight out of the Big House and headed for town. 'I said, "Well, I can't bear it". I was scared stiff ... I walked down the main road and I kept going [laughter]. I was scared, but I had no need to be. When I came home I got into hot water. Father came to pick me up. He was really cross with me.'

Most of the older girls who ran away from Moore River set out either to join boyfriends, or to seek them. One popular destination was the Benedictine mission at New Norcia, about twenty kilometres north-east of Mogumber. The New Norcia football team, the Moore River boys' arch-rivals, made regular visits to the settlement and provided one of the few opportunities for socialising with outsiders. Another favourite spot was Walebing, about forty kilometres distant. Here there was a large Aboriginal reserve where runaways could always find a friend or relative, a decent feed and a few hours of freedom. Bella Yappo — whose husband (not at all coincidentally) came from Walebing — recalls that Walebing boys would also 'come out for football, and of course they'd tee up from there, and few days after they'd have some girls missing'. Ralph Dalgety remembers that at Walebing, 'there were hundreds of men. They must have picked their own boyfriends, see.'

After she left school, Hazel Anderson ran away to Walebing regularly, where she discovered she had a cousin. The first few times, she went with a mob of five friends. 'Then, after I got used to that road, I used to run away by myself.' It was no wonder the trackers usually experienced little difficulty finding the girls. By all accounts, they themselves looked on a breakout as a welcome opportunity for a change of scene. Hazel remembers that Frank Narrier, Phyllis Mippy's father, was a particularly skilled tracker. But 'Uncle Frank' was in no hurry to return to the settlement and would often allow the girls to reach their destination before making an appearance. Other times, he'd strike a deal:

If he catch us, he'd let us go, as long as we don't run
away when he's ready to go back home. He'd say, 'I let
you girls stay, but don't run away from here. Don't leave
Walebing, and I'll let you know when I go back, see.' I
think he wanted to get away from the settlement, too, in a
way. All his people was there too in Walebing.

Phyllis Mippy confirms that her father was rarely harsh with the
runaways he was paid to track. But when it came to his own
daughter, he was capable of extreme violence. When Phyllis ran
away as a fourteen-year-old with her mates Blanche Quartermaine,
Rosie Conway, Theresa Jackamarra and Daphne Lyon, Narrier was
outraged. 'When he found me he gave me a good hidin' with a
stick', Phyllis relates. 'He just broke a green stick and gave it to me.
I had no choice, but the other girls, they was frightened. Then he
made us walk all along the river going back to the settlement.'
Narrier had no compunction about handing over his daughter and
her friends to gun-toting Superintendent Mark Knight.

In some cases, the job of tracking runaways was actually quite
difficult. But the Moore River trackers had a remarkable success rate
— so much so that no runaway seems to have seriously entertained
the hope of getting away for good. According to Eric Conway, the
trackers had highly developed analytical skills, as well as the
uncanny ability to read the signs of flight:

They'd go on what that person would be thinking. They
could work on your mind ... If they'd miss your tracks
sometimes they'd know where you were going to try and
dodge so that you wouldn't leave clear signs behind.

Running away was an important 'coming of age' ritual at the
Moore River Native Settlement, and girls would usually make their
maiden journey at around puberty, often in the company of friends.
Olive Hart recalls running away at around this age after a fight with
two of her mates. 'Me and another girl took off', she remembers.
'We got caught way out, goin' towards Perth.' The girls made the

154

mistake of stopping at a farmhouse to have their water bottle filled. In their ragged Tuffnut dresses and bare feet, they were instantly recognised. 'I said, "Listen, she's ringin' the settlement. She's tellin' them we here now. We're goin' to get caught. Let's go!" "She couldn't be!"' Hauled before Superintendent Neal, the girls told him, 'We went for berries, but didn't think we walked so far'. Olive somehow escaped a thrashing but her friend didn't. 'She got two cuts — I heard her screaming.'

The Boob

By age fourteen or so, the standard punishment for runaways was a term in the settlement prison, known by both inmates and administration alike as the 'boob'. As Alice Nannup recalls, 'They put them in the boob if they're naughty — that's a little gaol they got up there. Bread and water for about three or four days. You go in there round and rosy, you come out drawn and a few pounds less!'

The original structure, about the size and shape of a dunny, was designed for solitary confinement. With sides and roof of galvanised iron, the boob in summer was a virtual oven. There was just enough room on the dirt floor to sit; lying down was impossible. Bread was brought by the trackers three times a day — sometimes with water. Alice Nannup recalls, 'You could bang on the wall and ask for water, and they'll make you wait until you nearly famished, then they'll bring you a drink'. Olive Hart spent only one day in the boob, but she was given no water at all. 'They didn't give me no water, nothing', she remembers. 'Just food, give me no water to drink. Dear, I was thirsty!'

The trackers would also stand watch as the prisoner carried out her sanitary bin, dug a hole alongside the wall and buried the contents. According to the Royal Commissioner who observed these practices in 1934, 'No disinfectant is provided, but the girls throw sand in'.

Sister Eileen recalls that the prisoners would gouge little peepholes in the iron sides to let in a bit of light and 'so that their friends could come and talk to them and tell them the settlement news'. She also remembers the sound of the caged girls singing. 'And their

155

The 'Boob' (right foreground).
'They put them in the boob if they're naughty — that's a little gaol they got
up there. Bread and water for about three or four days. You go in there
round and rosy, you come out drawn and a few pounds less!'

favourite song was "You are my sunshine, my only sunshine".' Yet
even on the brightest day, the interior of the boob remained dark
enough to cause temporary blindness. Lizzy Dalgety remembers this
happening to a friend of hers, and the incident terrified her:

> This Jean Kelly, she ran away from Mogumber and when
> they caught up on her they put her in the boob. She was
> there for two weeks, and the poor girl, when she came
> out, she couldn't see a thing. She had to hold her hand
> over her eye ... And I always said, 'I'm never going in
> there', and I never ever been in there. Tell you the truth,
> that learnt me a lesson that I never went in that boob. But
> I seen a lot of girls go in there.

In testimony before the Moseley Commission, Superintendent
Neal defended the practice of sentencing runaways to solitary confinement in the boob. And in fact, as a duly designated 'protector of

156

Aborigines', he had a perfect legal right to do so. The Aborigines Act and Regulations provided that a protector was empowered to 'inflict summary punishment by way of confinement for not exceeding fourteen days upon an inmate guilty of misconduct, neglect of duty, insubordination, or breach of regulation'. Nevertheless, Neal carefully recorded each incarceration in duplicate, in a 'punishment book' that has since vanished from the Moore River archives.

Neville was equivocal on the subject of the boob. The idea of incarcerating young women seems to have offended his Christian sensibilities. But as an administrator with limited resources he opted to let 'the end justify the means', as he commented elsewhere. After all, he pointed out to the Royal Commission, the boob was tame stuff compared with some of the legal alternatives:

> I have said before, and I repeat, that I do not like sending women and girls to Fremantle Gaol, and I feel sure that they would infinitely prefer to serve a few days of imprisonment in the lock-up at Moore River.

Judging by the testimony of people who actually spent time in the boob, however, this assertion is questionable. The combination of solitary confinement, pitch darkness and insufficient water or sanitary conveniences created conditions far harsher than in any conventional lock-up — including the notorious Fremantle Gaol. Neville continued, in obvious discomfort:

> When funds permit, more suitable provision will be made in this direction, but if anyone can tell me how otherwise these recalcitrant inmates can be dealt with, I for one should be ever grateful.

Men were also imprisoned in the boob, of course — although Neville had far fewer compunctions about bundling male offenders off to gaol. Jack Davis explains that if a boy and girl ran away together, the boy would often receive an automatic sentence of six months in gaol:

He would be taken to a court in the town where he was picked up. And because Aboriginal people were not allowed to plead guilty or not guilty in those days, the Police was prosecutor as well as lawyer for the Aboriginal person who would be in the dock. So he would just say, 'This man absconded from Moore River settlement with a girl' and bang! automatically he was sentenced.

As Jack points out, the irony was that, more often than not, 'the young man would return to the settlement and then marry that girl'.

Escapes from the boob were uncommon but not unheard of. Occasionally a prisoner would actually manage to dig his way out. Olive Hart remembers that Norman Gidgup — the same man whom Brodie tarred and feathered — was renowned for his Houdini-like skill in eluding his captors: 'They locked him up in there and he dug out. They take his breakfast next morning, unlock the door, he wasn't there. When he got out he threw all the sand back, and he was off. Perth or further.' It's no wonder Gidgup had a reputation as a magic man. The children were convinced he could make himself disappear at will, and were desperate to learn his secret. 'We used to ask him over and over. He wouldn't tell.'

Although casual incarceration of 'recalcitrant natives' under the age of sixteen was illegal, under certain Superintendents it became fairly standard practice at Moore River. Ned Mippy remembers that 'for a couple of hours kiddies'd be put in there, no doubt of it. Yeah, just to know that if they do it again they'd go back in there.' Ned recalls that sometimes the children were given a choice between imprisonment or a thrashing. 'It's a toss between that boob or the cat o' nine tails, so you had to think quick.'

Eric Conway grew up at Moore River during the 1940s, a turbulent decade which saw nineteen administrators come and go. He also remembers school-aged children locked up in the boob, where their meals consisted of the standard prison ration of bread and water. By this time, however, the original boob had been replaced by a much bigger and more permanent 'detention block'. 'I think dynamite would have some problem moving it', Eric Conway observes. This concrete structure, which still stands today, was built by inmates — Ralph Dalgety was one of them — under Paget's administration in the early 1940s. There was one side for men and another for women.

But quarters were still cramped, dark and unsanitary — particularly during mass lock-ups. Hazel Anderson recalls one occasion when she was locked into a cell with a dozen other girls. It was a hot summer night, and conditions in the sealed dormitory had simply become unbearable: 'We just wanted to get out of the dormitory 'cause it was too stuffy. So we said, "Come on, girls. Who's coming down the football ground to play?"' Before long, the girls were caught and herded together into the boob, 'all squashing one another'. Even as a lone prisoner, Hazel remembers, it was 'filthy and frightening in there'.

Phyllis Mippy and three of her teenaged mates actually enjoyed a night spent at the Roe Street lock-up in East Perth, where the accommodation seemed almost luxurious compared to what they were used to at Moore River. The girls had jumped the train from Mogumber but got no further than Midland, where a policeman was waiting at the station. 'Took us to the lock-up, and we was all in the cell together. We was all talkin' and laughin'', she remembers. The next morning Deputy Superintendent Tanner arrived in his infamous truck to take them home. The girls didn't know which to fear most: going straight back to face the Superintendent's wrath or accepting Tanner's suspiciously solicitous offer of a drink. 'We was frightened', Phyllis remembers. 'We said, "No, we don't want nothing. Take us home", we said.' Back at the settlement, the girls were thrown in the boob for three days and three nights. They were given one rug, and no mattress, and the usual bread and water ration.

Yet the dungeon-like conditions of the boob proved totally ineffective as a deterrent to runaways. Quite simply, the hunger for freedom and variety — even if only for a few brief hours — was stronger than the fear of pain and imprisonment. 'By gee, those kids used to get a good hiding, but it never learn 'em', Olive Hart recalls. 'No, as soon as they out they gone again.' Like many, many other young women at Moore River, Phyllis Mippy ran away more times than she can remember.

For young Aboriginal women of spirit, escaping from Moore

River was almost an imperative. For this most powerless segment of the settlement population, running away presented a rare opportunity to think purposefully about the future: to make plans (however short-term), to carry them out and to accept the consequences. Among the older girls, one of the most common consequences was an out-of-wedlock child. In 1932, Neville reported sixteen such births at Moore River, half of them fathered by white men. Young women who looked to the birth of a child to achieve status as an adult — or even simply to find love — were soon disillusioned. They looked on helplessly as their babies were simply absorbed into the settlement system: appropriated by the white 'professionals' who delivered them, named them and — in many cases — eventually removed them to other institutions. There have also been allegations of infanticide: that white staff routinely 'disposed of' the babies of single mothers, particularly very dark babies, burying their bodies in the pine plantation. These charges have been vehemently denied by many reliable informants, and it seems unlikely that such practices could have been successfully hushed-up over succeeding decades. Yet it would be naive to reject the possibility that isolated incidents of infanticide may have occurred. There is little in the history of discipline at Moore River to encourage optimism on this or any other score.

For young women at Moore River, the only truly effective avenue of escape was marriage. Any marriage, even a bad marriage, would do. As Doreen Dalgety explains, 'I think a lot of us just went headlong into marriage. Well, it couldn't have been love. It was just to get away from Moore River.' Doreen herself used an early marriage as a ticket-of-leave from settlement life. When the relationship broke down and she found employment in service, she experienced freedom for the first time in her life.

Lizzy Dalgety was more fortunate in the choice of a partner. She and Ralph met as teenagers at Moore River and married in 1943. In 1992, they were still together. Lizzy remembers:

> Well, a lot of girls used to say, 'The only way you get out of this mission, you have to marry. Then you can go out with your husband. Otherwise, you got to stay in here all your life', they used to say to us, the older ones.

160

Bella Ashwin (Yappo), Deaconess Heath, Gladys Onslow, Veronica Kalin. Front: Ursula Kalin, Mrs Campbell, 1940. Young women who looked to the birth of a child to achieve adult status were soon disillusioned. Their babies were simply absorbed into the settlement system: appropriated by the white 'professionals' who delivered them, named them and — in many cases — eventually removed them to other institutions.

Although Lizzy had borne three children by the time she and Ralph finally left the settlement, she recalls, 'By gee, I tell you I was glad to get out of there'.

*

As Sister Eileen has observed, 'Mogumber was its own little world'. Keeping safe the boundaries of that world — and making

Mick Dalgety (Wadaby), Doreen Thompson. Like many young women at Moore River, Doreen used an early marriage as a ticket of leave from settlement life. When the relationship broke down and she found employment in service, she experienced freedom for the first time in her life.

certain that the natives learnt their place within it — was the primary object of settlement discipline. It never really succeeded. One way or another, the Aboriginal inmates of Moore River defied containment. They persistently violated the institution's heavily guarded boundaries in time and space — the schedules and rosters, the cells and the fences, the 'long trail a-winding' that lay between the settlement and town.

Nevertheless, for the children — for whom intelligible boundaries are almost always better than none at all — the harsh discipline endured at Moore River had a positive side. Especially among the men, many of those who survived the system are justly proud. Imbued with a strong sense of right and wrong, they feel now, in the hindsight of adulthood, that it was all worthwhile. For many of the women, on the other hand, the boundaries so zealously guarded by settlement discipline often seemed arbitrary, and the punishments too brutally painful to enlighten or educate.

Everyday life at Moore River was as complexly textured as everyday life anywhere else. Floggings, scoldings and incarcerations — as common as they were — constituted only a small part of that life. They were the worst of times for the children of Moore River. Next, we examine the best of times: the games, sport and special events organised by the institution itself, as well as the informal and often covert opportunities to participate in and express Aboriginality. It was these breaks from the normal institutional routine that helped make Moore River a bearable and, for brief moments, even a glorious place for the children who called it home.

chapter 4

When We Were Good

The children of Moore River dwelt uneasily amid three competing cultures. Each of these worlds — the outlaw culture of their Aboriginal elders, the improvised culture of their peers and the official culture of their overseers — offered the compound kids a singular version of the 'good life'. This chapter examines each of them in turn.

Aboriginal culture belonged to the children by right and by tradition, yet the 'home' in which they found themselves was formally dedicated to its extinction. In fact, despite the best attempts of its administrators, Aboriginality was not destroyed at Moore River, it was simply forced underground. The physical centre of this subversive culture was down the hill from the compound, in the cottages and humpies of the camp. But its spiritual centre was the bush, where Aboriginality could be freely expressed and nurtured. Despite the barriers erected between compound and camp, aspects of traditional Aboriginal culture survived in the form of cherished special events — from weekend camping expeditions to moonlit corroborees. Equally important were the everyday pleasures of being Aboriginal: savouring short snatches of freedom from rules and bells, seizing opportunities to learn by doing, luxuriating in the unconditional acceptance of family and friends. But according to the dictates of settlement policy, Aboriginality remained an outlaw culture. As a result, its expression at Moore River was stunted and incomplete.

The second, and in some ways the strongest, culture at Moore River was one that the children devised for themselves. This impro-

'Some of the kids who grew up in Mogumber, they thought it'd be a shame to be jumping around corroboring like that. That's how good a job they did.'

vised culture of childhood had its own ritual and romance, its own rules and roles, and its own undisputed relevance to compound life. The adults in authority never bothered to interfere with it, because they never realised it existed. The culture of childhood that grew up at Moore River was distinctively Aboriginal yet utterly non-traditional in orientation. A culture of the here and now, it exalted the values of resourcefulness, of group solidarity and of survival against all odds. Its delights were many — from simple games of chance to complex rites of passage. Part inheritance, part loan, part pure invention, this brilliant patchwork quilt of a culture transformed Moore River from a state-run compound for undesirables to 'sort of a place like home'.

Finally, there was the official culture of settlement life — the one designed by Head Office, implemented by the Superintendents and minutely documented in each year's annual report. Above all else, this culture stressed the virtues of obedience, rewarding those who remembered their place and who did as they were told. The official culture of the compound offered the children a limited range of 'legitimate pleasures', as one newspaper account delicately phrased it — institutionally sanctioned outlets for youthful native energies. Not surprisingly, these tended to be centrally organised and distinctly hierarchical in structure, with activities like scouting, cricket and church involvements taking pride of place.

Aboriginality

Nobody taught us anything like that. No, when I went back to Kalgoorlie and met my old Aunty, then I seen some of these old people walking around with a spear and a red band on and I used to ask her, 'What's he doing with that on his head?'... They learn all these things now because kids have been brought up with their parents and we weren't. See, we was chucked down to the mission. All of us reared up with white people down there, see, and we don't know nothing.

Elizabeth Dalgety

Some of the full-blood kids who grew up in Mogumber, they thought it'd be a shame to be jumping around corroboring like that. That's how good a job they did.

Eric Conway

The official culture at Moore River regarded Aboriginality as a kind of communicable disease, spread by contact. The settlement was designed to function as an isolation ward, cordoning off the infected from the wider community. But institutional policy also acknowledged degrees of infection. There were the terminal cases — that is to say, the older youths and adults who inhabited the humpies and

167

sheds of the camps. But there were others who were regarded merely as 'carriers'. These were the compound children, especially those who had been snatched from their families at a tender age. Their exposure to the disease of Aboriginality had been minimal; their prognosis was therefore excellent. It was believed that, under proper conditions of quarantine and rehabilitation, they might even survive to lead productive, European-style lives.

Officially, the Moore River Native Settlement was dedicated to 'containing' Aboriginality among the adult population and to eradicating it among the children. Strict segregation of the children from their Aboriginal elders was considered essential to these aims. Fortunately, however, the policy was never successfully translated into practice. For one thing, there were never enough staff to enforce it, even if they'd wanted to — and there were clearly those who did not want to. Among the rest, many were simply grateful for a break, and if that meant the children spent more time in the bush than they did in school, then so be it. There was also the continual problem of overcrowding, which meant that children were often permitted to lodge wherever they could find a bed.

But there was another factor which the bureaucrats in Head Office had failed to take into account, and that was the sheer persistence with which Aboriginal people, both young and old, sought each other's company. The institution was capable of limiting the quantity of that contact, but never its powerfully enduring quality.

Ralph Dalgety cannot recall learning anything about his own culture at Moore River — not even from the old people he would sometimes visit down at the camps. 'Nobody there would teach us', he says. 'Nobody was interested in them things down there.' Yet his memories of settlement life make it clear that, even as a young boy, he had somehow acquired a broad stock of traditional knowledge. He knew not only how to hunt a kangaroo, but how to clean it and roast it in ashes. He could also fashion a shanghai or a spear, catch rabbits and identify the local bush tucker. Practical lessons like these — unlike the abstractions so many children struggled with at school — were absorbed effortlessly. Like many other compound kids, Ralph learned them without even being aware of it.

Weekend camping expeditions, carried out under the supervision of Aboriginal adults, provided the ideal classroom for this traditional instruction. The children learned naturally, by example — watching and doing and having fun all at the same time. And they learned from each other, too. Jim and Myrtle Brennan remember the Nyoongah kids showing the nor'westers how to find the local bush tucker, for example. Angus Wallam can't remember exactly how his mates learned to make fishing spears; somehow they just knew.

Despite settlement policy to the contrary, many of the compound children managed to see their parents or other relatives on a regular basis. Ken Colbung was a compound kid in name only — he remembers he practically lived at the camps. Ken was born at Moore River, although his mother died when he was only a few months old. But there were plenty of other Colbungs on hand to keep an eye on young Ken — including his Aunty, Hazel Anderson, who was already married at this stage and living in the camps. Ned Mippy was in the unusual position of having both parents working on the compound. His mother, Clara Leyland, was the girls' dormitory attendant, and his father was in charge of the bakehouse. As trusted employees, they were granted the special privilege of having relatively open access to their son. Even so, Ned's father was required to obtain the Superintendent's permission before taking his son on a camping trip. 'Dad'd go down and say, "I want to take me son out"', Ned remembers. '"All right", Mr. Neal would say.' Ned proudly remembers that his dad always made a special effort to 'adopt' some of the compound orphans, teaching them bush skills and Nyoongah language. Decades later, Ned would carry on that tradition, teaching Aboriginal culture to children in the Moora schools.

But it wasn't only the boys who looked forward to camping trips. Like her future husband Ned, Phyllis Narrier also had both parents resident in the camps. On their expeditions into the bush, the Narriers travelled light, Phyllis recalls, often taking only a kangaroo dog and a frypan. Whatever else they needed, the bush would provide. This must have appealed to Phyllis's independent spirit, and she still remembers her amazement the first time her dad showed her how to get water from a paperbark tree:

> We come to a big paperbark tree. He says, 'I'll show you

where water come out now'. So he hit this paperbark tree, pulled the barks off, hit it, next thing the water is just running out there. And I wouldn't believe it. I would be a good-sized girl, and I said, 'Oh yeah!' He said, 'Taste that water.' So we drank that water. It was all right!

Hazel Colbung Anderson — herself the mother of twelve daughters — comes from a long line of strong Aboriginal women. She was fortunate enough to have some of them with her during her childhood at Moore River. Hazel and her sister Eva lived in the dormitory during the week. But they were allowed to take turns being with their mum and aunty on weekend camping trips, leaving Saturday after the girls' weekly bath and returning the next morning in time for Sunday School. The two older women would supplement their usual rations with fish and turtles caught in the Moore River. 'They were two good old fisherwomen, them two old sisters', Hazel remembers proudly. After sleeping all week in the stuffy, bug-infested dormitory the girls used to revel in the freshness of their open-air shelters. Hazel remembers learning to make a 'break up' out of bushes and sticks piled up against the wind. For beds, the women would gather soft bushes, which would then be piled along the inside of the break and covered with a 'wogga' — a kind of bedspread made from wheat bags stitched together.

Like Ned Mippy's father, Hazel's mother felt a special responsibility toward the compound orphans — so much so that Hazel herself was often jealous:

'Oh, mum, why you got to bring them fellas from up the north? We don't know 'em.' 'Look, Hazel', she say to me, 'you must learn to love, you know, 'cause they got nobody. You got me', she'd say. 'You got me here, you got your mum. They got no mum ...' Oh, there was a lot of them like that. I don't think they know who their mother is from that day to this now.

Today, Hazel recognises that she was given a great gift. She not only knew her mother, but, thanks to that woman's extraordinary strength and skill, she came to know something of her mother's culture, too.

Angus Wallam had a huge extended family at Moore River with whom he managed to maintain regular contact. But the official culture he was absorbing as a compound kid proved strong enough to alienate him from his own tradition. 'I wasn't interested, you know', he admits. Today, he regrets those lost opportunities. 'My old grandfather used to sit down and tell us a yarn. He'd sing the blackfella song, too. Then I wasn't quick enough to catch onto it, see, and I lay down and think some nights, how silly.'

Doris Pilkington (Nugi Garimara), today a noted Aboriginal historian and novelist, was forcibly removed to Moore River at the age of four. Although Doris was accompanied by her mother, the two were separated upon arrival, and never lived together again. Doris's early years at Moore River were spent ` he hothouse environment of the kindergarten, which was strictly segregated, not only from the campies but even from the older children in the dormitories. The little ones quickly absorbed the subtle and not-so-subtle messages of compound culture. Doris writes:

> On arrival at the Settlement the newcomers were told that speaking 'native language' was forbidden. Those who misunderstood or knowingly disobeyed the instruction (which had become an unwritten law) and continued to communicate in their traditional language were intimidated and victimised by others. Foreign and colonial words such as 'uncivilised,' 'primitive' and 'savages' were bandied about in the compound and the school playground.

It is hardly surprising that children subject to such indoctrination sometimes found themselves, like the young Angus Wallam, resistant to traditional teaching. In extreme cases, as Doris points out, the culture of the compound 'gave birth to one of the damaging concepts in this so-called new Aboriginal society — discrimination against their own people'.

Fortunately, the settlement system of segregation was not only poorly policed, it was riddled with loopholes. Even those children who were never given the opportunity to mix with their elders in the camps had daily contact with adult Aboriginal staff. As Doris Pilkington points out, not only were there Aboriginal nursemaids, cooks and laundresses but 'breastfeeding motherless babies was a common practice amongst nursing mothers'. These surrogate mothers — although forbidden to participate in traditional rites and ceremonies — would nevertheless find opportunities for passing on the wisdom of Aboriginal myths and legends. These 'forbidden topics', Doris writes, 'were whispered in hushed tones in the privacy of the dormitory in the evenings, or discussed on the grassy banks near the river under the shade of the huge river gum'.

For the boys, as we have already seen, the trackers — some of whom were full-bloods — were particularly important cultural links. Vincent Lambadgee has vivid memories of kangaroo hunting with a gang of five or six mates, led by tracker Arthur Morrison. The experience of freedom was intoxicating. But it was more than that — it was the strange and wonderful realisation that in learning about the bush you were really learning about yourself. This was powerful knowledge. Vincent remembers, 'When one of us was thirsty, old Morrison would make us drink the blood of the kangaroo. It was natural to us, something like nature [laughter]. Never felt thirsty, no.'

The example and influence of the trackers were also important for Eric Conway, who had no adult kin at all at Moore River. Eric arrived at the settlement at the age of six, speaking the language of the Marble Bar area. Yet, he remembers, 'all my culture was taken away from me whilst we were in Mogumber'. It was not until he left Moore River and went out to work among Aborigines that Eric began to recapture what had been lost: 'That's when I started to really get the gist of things. And I thought, "Now all that I missed, see, because I learnt part of the white man's world (which isn't too bad) but what happened to our world? Why was that taken?" I started to feel, not resentful — disappointed.'

Although Eric's contacts with Aboriginal adults at Moore River were rare, each encounter was relived over and over again in memory. Among Eric's 'surrogate fathers' was a blind, crippled

Jack Spear with Jim Kelly and Lucy Milly Milly. Spear was one of the few individuals revered by both blacks and whites at Moore River. He shared his wisdom with several generations of compound kids.

Aboriginal man named Jack Spear. Spear was one of the few individuals revered by both blacks and whites at Moore River. Sister Eileen, who was always a regular visitor to the camps, came often for a chat or to read him the newspaper, and at one point the institution even purchased a special bed for him. By the time Eric came to know him, Jack had already shared his wisdom with several generations of compound kids. Although he had lived among whites his whole life — having himself been reared on a mission — Jack was a potent reminder to the children that Aboriginal authority was worth listening to, too. As Eric Conway recalls, 'He spoke well. He used to teach us kids a lot of things about his history and background. It was never a fully tribal sort of thing ... but it was still interesting to us how they battled.'

Eric caught other glimpses of his heritage during his compound childhood, and there are images he recalls with great clarity — of the trackers telling yarns around the campfire, for example, or of the delicious taste of properly cooked kangaroo meat. ('Maybe the culture was pushing us in the right direction there, 'cause as much as we liked a bit of beef and mutton we still wanted to go for the wild stuff.') At such moments, it was almost as if he had glimpsed himself unexpectedly in a mirror.

Eric's introduction to the corroboree was one such occasion, and forty years later he remembers it with astonishing accuracy. The participants, ironically enough, were a group of twelve Wyndham men remanded to Moore River in connection with a murder trial, 'just until they sorted out the court case and things'.

> Well, they were fantastic. They brought the corroboree back alive. We used to beg to get permission to go and watch it, and at first the Superintendent was a bit against it, but he thought, well he liked it too, so everybody was allowed to go up and have an hour and just sit around a big campfire and watch these fellows do their corroboree. It was fantastic. It wasn't long that some of the kids wanted to do it. So that brought it back, a bit of it. But they were only there for a couple of weeks and they disappeared — they went back up to Wyndham again. But it stayed in some of the boys.

In fact, the performance of corroborees was a rare exception to the ban on traditional activities. The reason for this, Jim Brennan explains, was simply that the corroborees were considered good public relations. He remembers Neal trying to get the men to hold

174

corroborees whenever important visitors were due. Various press accounts over the years confirm this. Journalists 'investigating' conditions at Moore River were invariably impressed by the colourful spectacle of a staged corroboree. These command performances often formed part of a lengthy concert programme of skits, songs and dances. In such a setting, the ages-old ritual was stripped of its power and dignity, becoming just another amusing item in a native minstrel show. As Jim Brennan remembers, it wasn't long before the performers caught on to what was happening.

> Now and again Neal, he might say, 'There's a big mob of white people comin' up here today. You better put a corroboree on.' ... We said, 'Oh, no. No corroboree. We not corroboring tonight. We might corroboree next week. ... They wouldn't put the concert on so that he can prove to the whites that everybody's happy, you understand? They're not happy.

The real corroborees were the ones that happened out of sight of prying European eyes. Vincent Lambadgee, who lived with his parents in the camps before becoming absorbed into the culture of the compound, remembers the old people staging corroborees on the old football ground. Although the little ones were forbidden to watch the adult rituals, they were taught special children's corroborees, using local chalk to paint their faces. It all happened so naturally, Vincent remembers, that the children were hardly aware that they were learning — let alone why they were learning it. 'Well, there was a special way of doing it', Vincent recalls, 'but it didn't really mean anything for us, you know. We just took it as a sport and thought it was great for us to be there. At the same time, we were learning something — but what that something was we didn't know.' The compound children knew even less, of course; most had no access at all to such rich cultural experiences.

Jack Davis was a young man of sixteen when he arrived at Moore River with his brother in 1932, at the height of the Depression. The boys had been sent by their father at Neville's personal invitation, on the understanding that they would receive training in farming

175

skills. As it happened, they would learn nothing at all about farming
— but they received an impressive education all the same. They
learned to hate bread and scrape, Jack recalls, and they learned to
stab acres and acres of zamia palms. They learned to keep clear of
Mr. Neal when his moustache started to twitch, and how to gamble
their tobacco ration for black market meat. But they also learned —
despite the most strenuous institutional imperatives to the contrary
— a sense of acceptance and belonging as Aborigines.

The Davis boys came from a family of ten children, the sole
Aboriginal family in the small timber town of Yarloop. It was no
wonder they had grown up with little conscious sense of their own
Aboriginality. Arriving by train at Mogumber, Jack was completely
unprepared for the sight of mobs of people who looked just like him.
In his autobiography, *A Boy's Life*, Jack confesses he was
'somewhat bemused by the scene. I had never seen so many
Aboriginal people before in my life'. Over the next few months, the
Davis boys would discover to their delight that, as far as the inmates
of Moore River were concerned, their dark skin was neither a stigma
nor an accident but 'a passport. We were black like everybody else.'

By contrast, the presence of European children on the settlement
was rare indeed. Staff couples tended to be well past their child-
rearing years, and the few who did have young children invariably
sent them away to school in Perth. When they returned to the settlement for holidays, their interaction with the native kids was closely
monitored. 'They had to keep a tight rein and watch them', Eric
Conway recalls, 'because the white children, they were keen, they
wanted to play with the Aboriginal children. You know, kids are
kids. They don't make no distinctions and things like that, unless the
parents are putting it in their heads.' All of this would have come as
a shock to the Davis boys, however, who had mixed freely and
unselfconsciously with white families all their lives.

But it was not white culture that intrigued them; it was their own
people and traditions they were avid for. Ironically, Moore River
gave them this exposure, including firsthand experience with corroborees. Jack vividly recalls the clandestine corroborees performed
by the nor'westers in the settlement pine plantation. Although only
the men and older boys were allowed, 'there used to be quite a good

turn-up'. He remembers that the experienced older men, including some of the trackers, got 'us boys up and teach us and show us how to dance. They had the didgeridoo there in those days also, which was not really well known in those days, but somehow one of them got to Moore River.' The sights and sounds of that first corroboree fired the imagination of the sensitive young man.

> I thought it was wonderful, it was wonderful, you know: the firelight and the starlight, and these men used to really dress themselves up, paint themselves up (because there was plenty of white clay in the river) ... I've never seen it since being so startlingly beautiful as it was, because those people were natural, just natural dancers.

Because Jack and his brother were past school age, they were permitted to live for a time in the camps, where they were adopted by 'Aunty' Lucy Movell. It was there that Jack met an old Kimberley couple whose tribal songs and stories still echo in his writer's memory. Fred and Gummoo were blind and they relied on Jack to cart wood and water for them. But they repaid their young friend with a gift he has never forgotten:

> Sometimes they would sing, and to hear their two voices mingle and sing songs of their country in their own language was to me pure magic. Sometimes when Gummoo would be resting, Fred and I, the old and the young, would just sit staring into the fire. Sometimes my heart used to ache for him, though I didn't really know enough about my own feelings to know why.

For most of the children of Moore River, expressions of Aboriginality — however furtive and incomplete they may have been — remain among the most vividly remembered experiences of childhood. What the institution regarded as a disease, even the smallest inmates recognised as a source of life and health. Like plants in a darkened room, they turned instinctively toward this light. In some, a strong sense of Aboriginal identity managed to flourish in spite of the institution. In others, that identity was so repressed, so early, that it never took root at all. For most, the process of fully reclaiming their Aboriginality would take years of searching and struggle, of learning and unlearning. The lessons of the compound culture died hard. But the lessons of the forbidden culture — the one that stretched so far behind the past and beyond the future that it transcended both — these lessons were written on the heart.

The Culture of Childhood

With the contact between Aboriginal young and old so painfully constricted, the compound kids were forced back on their own resources. In many ways, this peculiar freedom proved a great asset. Like boys and girls everywhere, the children of Moore River were happiest among their own kind — that is, in the company of other children. Cut adrift from their families and their traditions, the compound kids had a unique opportunity to develop a culture all their own. This childhood culture was strongly Aboriginal in flavour, but it also had its own rites and rituals, myths and games.

The compound kids looked after each other, and new arrivals were swiftly adopted by older kids who showed them the ropes and initiated them into the mysteries of settlement life. Jack Davis relates:

> We used to all help look after the younger kids ... I mean, we had children in our dormitory as young as eight years of age. Well, we used to look after those kids. You know what I mean, see that they got to bed properly, they had a wash, they got up in time to go and have their breakfast, that they combed their hair ... We sort of adopted each other.

Not surprisingly, siblings tended to stick closely together. Olive Hart never trusted the busy settlement staff to look after her baby brother, and during the day she took complete responsibility for his care. She always saved some bread from breakfast for his morning tea and, when it was time for her to go to school, Olive would settle

With the contact between Aboriginal young and old so painfully constricted, the compound kids were forced back on their own resources. Here, two enterprising lads demonstrate their 'sand car'.

the toddler in a makeshift shelter she could watch from the class-room window. 'He sit down there and make a cubby out of sand there, and go to sleep. When he wake up he got his bread and he's right. He stops there all day till I finish school. Wash his hands and face and take him to dinner.'

Olive remembers that she was 'frightened he might go to the river, 'cause it was high, real high. Kids might get drowned.' She had good reason to worry, for at least one child did die in the flood-swollen Moore River. It was remarkable that there weren't more such deaths. Particularly treacherous was the old spring bridge the kids used to dare each other to swing on. 'When you get a swing in it, and it gets goin', it'll go all the time', Olive remembers. 'I don't

Girls in the river at the Elbow.

know what they have it there for, don't know what they put it there for, it's stupid.'

Although the bridge was finally pulled down, the river itself provided the children with a unique and beautiful playground. Unlike Olive, most kids never gave a thought to the potential dangers. They were strong, they learned quickly — and they were usually having far too good a time to stop and worry.

Phyllis Narrier, who tended to be fearless anyway, remembers that flood time made swimming in the Moore River even more fun. 'Used to have a good time when that big flood come', she recalls. 'We used to go and swim in the big flood, and we used to climb these trees and jump in the water. We didn't care because we didn't know anything different. Had a good old time in the flood.' The little girls used to swim naked, while the older ones modestly kept their bloomers on. Like adolescents everywhere, the girls were naturally curious about their developing bodies. 'We'd say, "Look at your meemee gettin' big" — you know, that's what we called our titties. And "Yours too", they'd say.'

The girls and boys of the compound went to school together and often participated side by side in organised events. But when left to their own devices, the girls chose to play with the girls and the boys with the boys. Each group had its own favourite swimming hole, which were given names like 'Long Pool', 'Hell Bound' and 'Rainwater Pool'. One of the favourite riverside sports for girls was mudskating, which for obvious reasons was also practised naked. The boys would sometimes make a surprise attack, Phyllis Narrier remembers. 'Someone would say, "the boys are coming!" Oh, we was all muddy, and we'd just slip our clothes on, and we would run and hide, yeah, from the boys. We said, "Let the boys skate. We'll go now."'

The children found plenty of uses for the rich river mud and white clay. In fact, the kaolin from the banks of the Moore River was so pure it was much sought after by Perth artisans. The young people used to paint their faces with it, and so would the adult corroboree performers. Ironically, the lighter skinned kids would sometimes paint themselves black with mud, in a touching effort to identify more closely with the group. Ned Mippy remembers the boys would make their own mudslides by throwing water down the hill from the Big House. It was a bit like high-speed skateboarding, only it required no special equipment.

The bush surrounding the river provided plenty of drier diversions for the children. Lizzy Dalgety remembers the girls used to head for the bush to practice the dancing they had learned in school. They would weave bracelets and necklaces from dandelions, and even fashion special skirts out of bark. After endless months in the same drab, Tuffnut dresses, the opportunity to play 'dress up' sent the girls practically delirious with joy, and they spun around the bush like tiny dervishes in their finery. Another springtime ritual was gathering the wildflowers which grew in abundant and bewildering variety — including a number of rare species that grew nowhere else on earth except the unlikely sandplain surrounding Mogumber. Sister Eileen used to go roaming through the bush with the girls to find them, although 'you'd only just go out the back door

181

*In the hothouse environment of the kindergarten, children were strictly
segregated not only from the campies but from the older dormitory kids.*

and you could pick leschenaultia and kangaroo paws and spider orchids, beautiful spider orchids, and donkey orchids'. This was one pursuit the boys found rather pointless. 'I think we could have picked them if we wanted to', Vincent Lambadgee remembers, 'but there wasn't any place for us to put it, a flower'.

The settlement provided few recreational facilities for the children, with the single but spectacular exception of the kindergarten, which for a few short years in the late thirties was furnished quite lavishly with toys, books, playground equipment and even a piano. The kindergarten functioned as an institution within an institution — with its own dormitories, dining hall and sanitary facilities.

A daring and quite blatant experiment in total social engineering, the kindergarten was designed to function as a kind of hatchery for European culture. The hatchlings were half-caste children from the ages of two to six who had been orphaned by circumstance or by force. Kept in quarantine behind the kindergarten fence, these little ones inhabited a universe as far removed from dormitory life as bacon and eggs is from bread and scrape. They had their own dining room, their own dormitory and even their own Christmas tree at Christmas time. As the scheme was originally envisioned — and A O Neville remained its greatest champion — the kindergarten kids would continue to enjoy a splendid isolation from their peers as they grew to school age, using totally separate (and completely unequal) facilities.

With Neville's retirement from Native Affairs in 1940, however, financial commitment to the costly scheme eventually foundered, and the former kindergarten kids found themselves thrust abruptly into the unaccustomed rigours of dormitory life. Their white cotton quilts and pretty enamelled cots were replaced by bug-infested mattresses, and as the rather stunned children began to get their bearings and run wild, the staff wrung their hands to see all their hard work undone.

But the compound kids were nothing if not resourceful, and they never allowed a lack of facilities to ruin their fun. If there was a game or activity that required special equipment, they simply made it themselves. Ned Mippy remembers fashioning serviceable little kylies, or boomerangs, out of scrap tin. Along with many others, he

At Dongara, March 1940: The official culture of Moore River provided a limited reward system that included occasional treats and outings for deserving inmates.

also learned to make his own hockey sticks out of wattle. Phyllis Narrier explains: 'We used to cut that, and we used to go and burn them for a while. And when they were soft, we just wrap 'em round a tree like that, wrap 'em around the fork of a tree. We used to leave 'em overnight and next day we all rush for our hockey stick.' Although they used an ordinary tennis ball, the kids preferred Aboriginal-style hockey to the European version, Ned recalls. 'No, no, there was none of this blowin' the whistle and gettin' in front. The strongest survived, the fittest survived.'

One of those who didn't survive was Alice Nannup. She failed to find the rough and tumble play amusing: 'I got smacked across the knuckles and that was it, I wouldn't play no more'. Hazel Anderson and her gang also shied away from games involving boys. They preferred more sedate games like 'kitty kitty', which was a bit like dodge ball. Hazel also remembers her girlfriends teaching her a version of charades. 'We all gotta act something', Hazel recalls, 'no

talking, but just doing the actions, and they gotta guess them.' The
game would always start the same way:

> We used to say, 'Here we come'. And the ones standing over
> there, they say, 'Where from?' We say, 'New York' and
> they'd say, 'What's your trade?' We'd say, 'Doing tricks'.
> And, 'Well, show us one'. Then we got to start acting.

The girls learned other European games, too, including hop-
scotch, marbles (whenever anybody had some) and knucklebones,
played with actual sheep knuckles dyed red with ink. As they grew
older, the settlement girls graduated to more adult versions of these
games, playing two-up for safety pins, marbles and the bangles and
combs they would receive for Christmas presents.

Rounders, played with a tennis ball and a wattle bat, was one of
the few games that pitted boys against girls. Matches were held after
tea in the pine plantation, or in the big sand patch behind the girls'
dormitory. Like Alice, Phyllis Narrier remembers that the boys
played far too roughly. But despite that — or maybe even because of
it — the girls enjoyed themselves hugely:

> When we were running, they hit us cruel, anywhere —
> head and all, back and all. We thought it was fun, but.
> Yeah, we used to have some good fun. And when it's
> gettin' a bit dark, see, the two trackers comin', blowin'
> the whistle. All up the compound, into the dormitory —
> lock us up, that's it.

Amusing the Natives: The Culture of the Compound

The official culture of Moore River — the white one — provided a
limited reward system that included occasional treats and outings for
deserving inmates. In addition, it provided a range of more regular
amusements in the form of dances and games, sports and holidays.
These were often seen as necessary outlets for native energy that
might otherwise 'erupt'.

Compared with the richness of Aboriginal culture and the good

185

The culture of the compound: Visit of the YAL Band, 1940.

times invented by the kids themselves, the recreational outlets sponsored by the official culture were few and dull. Fun was never a high priority for settlement administrators, who as a group suffered from an acute lack of imagination. The amusements they organised tended to reflect this. Luckily, however, there were a handful of staff members with enough creativity and commitment to challenge the prevailing institutional torpor. From the mid-thirties to the early forties, the clubs, outings and special events they organised made a real difference to everyday life on the compound.

As we have already observed, settlement routine was overwhelmingly concerned with maintenance. Considerable care was taken to ensure that the children's survival needs were met — that they had just enough food and shelter to keep them from dying of starvation or exposure. The institution also supplied a kind of survival schooling — enough reading, writing and figuring to make them useful to white employers. Settlement administrators prided themselves on

186

their practical, no-frills approach to these responsibilities. Always wary of 'spoiling the natives', they tended to view with suspicion any deviation from established routine.

In this, Moore River was not much different from any other children's institution of its time, whether hospital, orphanage or boarding school. The idea that children had any real needs apart from purely physical ones would have been considered most avant-garde to the average Western Australian in the 1920s and 1930s. psychological experiments showing that institutionalised babies could actually die from want of 'love' — that is, social and physical contact with their caretakers — did not begin to make headlines until the 1940s, and changes in practice lagged even further behind changes in theory.

But they lagged even further for the small inmates at institutions like Moore River. It is quite true that in Australian society at large, there was scant acknowledgment that any children had special needs. But half-caste boys and girls — the children of the 'child race' — suffered a double handicap. If white children needed little to survive, Aboriginal children must need next to nothing. And that, more or less, is exactly what they were given.

Given the priorities of the institution itself — and the assumptions about the nature of childhood in the wider Australian society — it is easy to see why organised recreation at Moore River was so limited. The activities that were available — from dances and lantern lectures to scouting and comic books — were frequently organised in spite of the institution, by a handful of dedicated staff who gave freely of their time and talents.

This is not to suggest that there was always outright opposition to such activities at the administrative level. Most Superintendents tended to be agreeable to staff initiatives, so long as they didn't require any extra work or money. At Head Office, Neville took an active, if rather narrow, interest in the children's intellectual and spiritual development. But with the budgetary odds so dauntingly against him, he chose to concentrate resources on outfitting the kindergarten, leaving the older children to go begging. Bray's interest in the natives' social and recreational activities was purely pragmatic. If it kept the natives from getting restless, and it didn't cost anything extra, he was all for it.

In this, as in so many other areas of settlement life, sheer administrative incompetence was often the greatest obstacle to achievement. The matter of the settlement library — which took twenty-six years to establish — is a good case in point. As early as 1920, Neville was seeking permission to establish a library of 'simple and childish' books and periodicals. Shrewdly, his sales pitch centred on the need to keep idle hands and minds occupied. 'The people have at different times applied to me for literature', he explained, 'and it is most desirable that we should endeavour to keep them employed in every possible way'. Neville's request to hold a public appeal for suitable donations was duly granted. Nevertheless, no library was formed — whether from lack of donations or from lack of commitment to the project, it is impossible to say for certain.

Thirteen years later, Neville proposed purchasing a number of storybooks suitable for the older children 'out of the fund we are holding for educational purposes'. But he was informed that there was no such fund available. A 1941 Education Department report on the settlement noted, with ill-concealed disgust, 'Children are taught to read, but no library is provided'.

Another four years would pass before the idea of a settlement library was again mooted. From his armchair at Head Office, Commissioner Bray envisioned a collection of five hundred books plus a supply of comic papers. But back in the real world of Moore River, Teacher Holland was willing to settle for an empty room — any place where the children could read under supervision outside of school hours. Although by this time there would have been ample Child Endowment funding for such an initiative, Head Office persisted in finding excuses not to act. 'Even if I approve the provision of a Reading room, labour is not available', one officer pointed out, almost smugly.

Although the reading room never did materialise, Miss Holland finally succeeded in securing some books. It is unclear who made the selections — it may have been Bray himself — but they reflect the usual bias of the day toward the sturdy classics of 'Home'. A volume of Mother Goose may well have been appreciated, but the compound kids failed to work up much enthusiasm for novels like *Silas Marner, Cranford* or *A Tale of Two Cities*.

In 1939, the compound kids began to receive monthly parcels of comics from Perth distributors Gordon & Gotch. Again, it was Neville's idea, and he made the arrangements personally. He instructed Neal to 'see that the comics are evenly divided between the children, and passed from one to another as far as possible'. But wartime shortages intervened ('international troubles have made our supply of Comic Papers extremely scarce', the distributors solemnly explained), and the service was discontinued from 1941 until the end of the war.

By 1945, Head Office was supplementing the children's reading matter with a suspiciously adult selection of magazines and tabloids, including *Pix, Picture Post, World's News, Woman's Mirror* and *New Idea*. The Acting Commissioner of Native Affairs, who had chosen the publications himself, hoped they might prove compelling enough to keep the big girls safely in their beds of an evening. He wrote, 'It is felt by me that natives in the dormitories may display a great deal of interest in the magazines I have chosen for their entertainment and it is possible that with these amenities at their disposal it may lessen the desire of a certain [sic] to abscond from the dormitories'.

Although this was a bit overly optimistic, the theory that having something to do at night might keep the children out of mischief was eminently sensible. It was also painfully obvious. The fact that the settlement was in operation for more than two decades before anyone thought of it is therefore rather puzzling. Again, the answer probably has a lot to do with the way white policy makers construed the matter of 'needs'. The children had been fed, they each (more or less) had a bed to sleep in and a rug to cover themselves with. What else could they need? Challenging those assumptions proved an impossible task, even for those rare administrators who suspected there was something illogical about them. One of those was Bray's Deputy Commissioner who in 1943 ventured to speak his mind on the matter of locking the children in the dormitories every evening with nothing to occupy them. 'If we attempted to apply the same conditions to children in our own homes', he wrote, 'I think the outcome would be disastrous and result in the rearing of children with a generally depressed outlook, and this is difficult to manage'.

In 1943, Bray went so far as to consider employing a 'Welfare and Playtime Officer' to lead the children in games and pastimes between tea and bedtime. But Matron Leeming (whose husband, Phil, was one of Moore River's least competent administrators) pointed out that unless this person also supervised evening bathing, regular staff would need to be on call until much later than presently — a situation, it was hinted darkly, that might well spark mass mutiny. Bray seems to have got the message. He never mentioned it again.

By contrast, the idea of furnishing the dormitories with a few cheap weeklies seemed an ideal solution. The following year, Head Office inspectors spoke of a 'hunger for literature by the natives' and recommended doubling the number of subscriptions. A few months later, however, it became apparent that those curiously adult publications — which were nevertheless being charged to Child Endowment — were failing to reach their intended audience. 'Upon enquiring regarding periodical and comics', a Head Office inspector confided to the Deputy Commissioner, 'I ascertained that the white staff have first use of these periodicals and then send them to the native dormitories for the use of the children. I intimated that you would be most dissatisfied with the procedure as there was a doubt in the fact that the natives did ultimately receive the periodicals.'

Although the question of what 'the natives did ultimately receive' remains a matter for speculation, the evidence suggests that it was almost always significantly less than it should have been — and this was as true for provisions like butter and fresh vegetables as it was for the supply of newspapers and magazines. The diversion of stocks and supplies intended for the inmates appears to have been established settlement practice. It was, perhaps, one of the ways in which Moore River's underpaid, overworked white staff attempted to establish a rough justice — avenging themselves at one stroke against their employers and their charges. Many of these people, it must be remembered, saw themselves as the true victims of the settlement system. After all, it was they who were expected to work unconscionably long hours and to endure conditions both deprived and isolated. The natives, from their point of view, simply hung about playing two-up and waiting for their next meal to appear.

Before the mid-1930s, organised amusements at Moore River were rare, and the annual report of 1934 is the first to contain the heading 'Amusements, Etc.'. The following year, Sister Eileen Heath came on board as Anglican Missionary, and most of the recreational activities offered throughout Neal's administration were a direct result of her personal initiative. Neal was able to boast that 'With the exception of Saturday night, there is some form of entertainment or religious instruction every night. Amusements take the form of dances (weekly), gymnastics, plays (natives own make up), lantern lectures, drill and club swinging.' But in fact, with the exception of the dances, Sister Eileen was responsible for every one of these activities. This may explain why Neal tended to regard 'entertainment' and 'religious instruction' as two sides of the same coin.

Eventually, even the bureaucrats in Head Office were forced to reassess the value of such seemingly frivolous offerings. For one thing, they were helping enormously to improve the settlement's public image. But equally, organised amusements were proving an unexpectedly useful technique for controlling the natives. By 1941, even Bray — ordinarily the hard-headed pragmatist — was searching for ways to expand offerings. 'Is there anything further we can do in the way of social evenings and other forms of recreation for the natives?' he inquired of Superintendent Paget, adding — again, most uncharacteristically — that 'any little expenditure along these lines would have my warm approval'.

The only regular 'social evenings' at Moore River were the Saturday night dances — but these were without doubt the highlight of the settlement social calendar. It is unclear precisely when the tradition began, but Hazel Colbung remembers they were in full swing when she was still a schoolgirl in the 1920s. The dances were virtually the only events at which staff and inmates, compound people and campies, mixed freely. They gave people an event to look forward to — something a trifle unexpected in the familiar, humdrum cycle. Perhaps most importantly of all, dance evenings — although sponsored by the institution — were planned and executed

191

Ruby Dalgety and Gracie Comeagain model 'ball gowns' fashioned from crepe paper by Sister Eileen.

by the inmates themselves. Music was generally supplied by Aboriginal musicians, including, at various times, Frank Narrier on the concertina, and Jimmy Anderson or Charlie Neville on the accordion. Other people played mouth organs and fiddles, and some even rattled bones. The Lotteries Commission donated a piano in 1935, although only Teacher Brenchley knew how to play it.

But as far as the girls were concerned, the purpose of a dance was dancing. Olive Hart remembers the girls were so eager to get going they would 'never wait for somebody to get us. Soon as the music started, we started.' After all, there was a strict midnight curfew, and the dances didn't start until seven or eight. They were a precious few hours, and not even the occasional 'mix on' between jealous lovers could slow the action. 'People from the camps used to come up', Bella Yappo recalls. 'Someone would get jealous for somebody

192

else, and there'd be a fight — but while they're fightin' you're still dancin'!' Most of the young people at Moore River learned to dance simply by watching the grown-ups — 'just picked it up as you go, you pick it up', Bella explains. Alice Nannup, who as a teenager became a valued employee at the Big House, remembers Mr Neal teaching her to dance:

> Oh, we used to have some fantastic dances, you know. He used to always call 'em. 'Come on Alice-ooooo!' He talked funny, you know. And we'd spin around there, and we'd do the garden waltz. We'd do the Scottish and the Canadian barn dance and the waltzes, and oh! we used to have some marvellous times!

Although cosmetics and accessories were rare, imagination and ingenuity were always in good supply at Moore River, and the girls looked forward to the opportunity to preen their feathers a bit. Girls who were fortunate enough to procure the fabric were often allowed to make their own party dresses using the settlement sewing machines. Alice — who became a crack operator — was given some special material as a reward for service, and Bella Yappo still has fond memories of the salmon pink evening frock that Mrs Paget helped her to cut out. Myrtle Cordella, who worked as a school monitor, had her evening frocks made especially for her by Biddy Wendy, the Aboriginal forewoman of the sewing room and a legendary needlewoman. The fabric was ordered from Perth by Teacher Perrett, and paid for with money sent by Myrtle's working mother. Other girls simply went 'in their own old little things', sometimes eked out by borrowings from Sister Eileen's special hoard of ornaments and oddments. Affectionately known as 'Sister's Mrs Biss's', after a popular Perth secondhand shop of the day, this was a store-room treasure trove of 'everything from choir robes to fancy dresses to ballroom dresses to wedding gowns to cub clothes and angels' wings and all sorts of things'.

The earliest reference to organised sport at Moore River is a newspaper item from April 1928, reporting a 'sports gathering' in which 'hundreds of well-cared-for, healthy and happy-faced natives,

193

On the local mission circuit, the boys from Moore River were definitely the team to beat.

indulged in races, with a background of hills covered with their homes'. Organised sport at the settlement did not get properly under way until 1933, when a Sports Fund was established with a £26 donation from the Sunday Times Publishing Co. Three years later, Superintendent Neal reported proudly that 'The Fund is now all but exhausted but it has been the means of providing cricket, football, gymnasium and games material generally, much to the benefit and pleasure of the inmates'.

Once the fund was depleted, only the football team appears to have survived. The expenses must have been minimal indeed. The team rarely travelled and — apart from a Head Office order for twenty pairs of football boots in 1947 — there is no evidence that they had any uniforms either. (Even in the case of the boots order, the Acting Commissioner was insistent that 'these boots are not to be retained by the natives after use and I lay emphasis on this

Fairy ring around the pack toadstool, c1939.

point'.) Despite this, the boys from Moore River were definitely the team to beat, and Neal's reports to the Aborigines Department are full of praise for them.

But the superior skill of the Moore River boys didn't stop them feeling intimidated by their arch-rivals from nearby New Norcia. Ned Mippy recalls that the New Norcia boys would arrive by truck about once a month. 'We thought they were good', Ned recalls, 'but we used to beat them'. The Moore River mob were keenly aware of the comparative affluence of the Catholic visitors:

> They had better living and better school in there, and they did see butter on their bread. We used to say 'butter and bread comin' to play bread and scrape' ... They came there with ties on and everything and we didn't know what a tie was.

The behaviour of the settlement girls hardly helped matters. According to Ned, they would invariably barrack for the other side!

'They had a uniform to put on, and they had a scarf around their neck and they had their caps, and they felt they really were somebody when they were dressed up. They were different from that crowd down there.'

Hazel Colbung Anderson confirms this, pointing out that the young people used the New Norcia games to score points in more ways than one: 'That's where some of them, some of them New Norcia boys got in love with the settlement girls and they got married'.

Children were only permitted to enjoy formal sporting events as spectators, however. The only team sports in which they participated were the rounders and hockey matches they organised themselves. On the other hand, as Ken Colbung has pointed out, physical education dominated the school curriculum. 'They had no supplies, no books or anything like that', he explains. 'What else were they going to do with us?' The children would be marched outside at regular intervals for drill and calisthenics, and Ken also recalls being taught to swing Indian clubs. Sister Eileen, who among her many other accomplishments was a trained gymnast and dancer, introduced gymnastics and even managed to procure a mat for the purpose.

A O Neville was a wholehearted supporter of scouting at Moore River, citing 'the excellent disciplinary effect of those movements.'

During the war years, however, labour shortages meant the settlement school was in session only sporadically. Fortunately, at the same time, the institution managed to retain a core of highly dedicated staff. This group, led by the tireless Sister Eileen, introduced a range of scouting and church activities for the children that would have been unthinkable a decade earlier. They did much to brighten the lives of the compound kids during the late thirties and into the early forties. Nevertheless, there remains a bitter irony about the fate of Aboriginal children learning their bushcraft from the Boy Scouts and their spirituality from the Anglican Church.

Scouting troops for boys and girls were established at Moore River in 1939. The Scouting Association itself was a model of administrative efficiency. Commissioners were promptly dispatched from Perth to train the leaders and to meet the children. They reported later that 'the children were naturally shy to talk to the trainers at first but games, Guide camp-fire singing, and singing games soon overcame this and they were particularly quick to grasp what was expected of them'. The association also provided games, textbooks and assorted scouting paraphernalia, including something called a 'Pack Toadstool'.

The leaders continued to ensure that everything was done strictly by the book. Sister Eileen pestered Neville till he obtained ministerial approval to purchase regulation fabric for uniforms, which were run up by the sewing room girls. These carefully detailed uniforms provided many of the compound kids with their first experience of ownership. And compared with the standard clothing issue, the dark grey suits and dresses must have seemed a miracle of fashion. Sister Eileen relates: 'They had a uniform to put on, and they had a scarf around their neck and they had their caps, and they felt they really were somebody when they were dressed up. They were different from that crowd down there.' Phyllis Narrier, who was a Girl Guide, confirms this: 'We all looked nice. We got the badges, and we thought it was great.'

The Girl Guides and Brownies concentrated on bush walking and bushcraft, learning to tie knots and identify wildflowers as well as singing and 'saying our rules of the Girl Guides', Phyllis recalls. Myrtle Cordella looked forward to scout meetings simply because 'it was something different'. The boys had a rather more ambitious program. Sister Eileen recalls leading the Cubs in first aid, tracking and climbing in addition to 'a lot of PT', games, songs and campfires. Picnics were another popular scouting activity, and the kids thought nothing of hiking the thirteen kilometres to Mogumber for a change of scene.

In December 1940, the Moore River Scouts were guests of the association at a Boy Scout camp held at Point Walter, south of Perth. The fourteen boys did their leaders proud. They not only aced the Treasure Hunt, but won prizes in jumping, swimming, diving and roller cycling. Leader Hodgson reported with satisfaction that 'The behaviour and conduct of the boys were all that could be desired, and it is no exaggeration to state that the group was the most popular in the camp'. At the same time, Sister Eileen had obtained permission to take the remainder of the upper school on a holiday in Perth, starting with her troop of eighteen Cubs. Commissioner Bray graciously assented, on the proviso that 'no unusual expenditure except petrol will be necessary'. None was, thanks to Sister Eileen's planning, contacts and ingenuity.

The group camped at a church hall in Cottesloe, and the food they ate was largely donated — including forty loaves of bread from the Swanbourne Bakery. By all accounts, they had the time of their lives. Among other activities, the children went swimming every day (their 'sores responded quickly to the sea bathing'), visited the Zoo, made a trip to Perth for the Parade of Scouts and Guides, visited the Museum and Art Gallery, boarded a special train to attend a picture show at the Ambassadors Theatre (where the management distributed sweets, ices and one shilling to each child), hiked through King's Park and went sightseeing in Fremantle.

As far as their contact with the general public went, there was not only a noticeable lack of discrimination, but people seemed to go out of their way to be helpful. In her report to the Commissioner, Sister Eileen mentioned that the boys swiftly 'made the acquaintance of white children of their own age, playing games and discussing their interests', and they 'received many gifts in the shape of fruit, jam, sweets and ices' from local shopkeepers. In fact, the only sadness of the holiday was back home at Mogumber, where a chicken pox epidemic was in full swing. This proved a bonus to the boys, who were permitted to stay away an extra two weeks, but the girls were forced to forego their holiday.

The previous summer, the epidemic had proved so virulent that giving the children a change of environment became literally a matter of life and death. They were taken in batches to Dongara Beach for two weeks at a time, and according to Superintendent Paget, 'The sea air and the bathing had very beneficial effect'. Phyllis Narrier was one of those children, and she has remembered that one holiday all her life. The kids travelled down on the big settlement truck, she recalls, taking all their own food. They pitched tents on the beach, and went swimming every morning.

The war years took a heavy toll on the children of Moore River, and the scouting movement was one more casualty. From 1941 and

The annual nativity play was a Moore River institution, with Sister Eileen
(centre) as director, producer and occasional guest star.

throughout the administrative chaos of the immediate post-war
years, outings for the children ceased — and the opportunity for
those memorable seaside holidays was never repeated. It is telling
that Aboriginal informants who were resident at Moore River during
this time have no clear memories of any of the ten Superintendents
between Paget, who departed in 1943, and Webb, who took over in
1947. The exception is Mark Knight, whose personal firearms and
exceptional cruelty made him difficult to forget. Apart from Neal,
who inspired mixed feelings in most of the children, Webb is the
only Moore River Superintendent they remember with a degree of
fondness.

Webb attempted to re-establish the tradition of outings begun by
Sister Eileen in the late 1930s. In September 1947, for example,

forty children were taken to the Moora Show and were even given spending money of two shillings each. It was a Moore River first. In October a staff couple chaperoned a train trip to the Gingin Annual Sports Meeting for thirty-one of the compound kids. The following year, the children were taken to the circus at Moora. The modest funding required for such occasions was drawn from the Child Endowment Fund, which the institution had been hoarding since the scheme commenced in 1941.

Sister Eileen had no access to such funds but found it an easy matter to obtain concessions and donations. She also involved the children in fund-raising activities in Perth. These public concerts and plays, performed each November at St George's Cathedral, helped keep the Christmas Cheer Fund afloat for years. (The Lotteries Commission made a donation of about £300 for this purpose each year.) The Heralds of the King, a church youth group involving the upper school girls, would be driven down for the annual November festival in the settlement truck, staying overnight at St Bartholomew's rectory, East Perth. Myrtle Cordella was a member of the Heralds, and remembers that Sister's nativity plays were a great hit with the cathedral congregation. 'I was always the angel Gabriel', she remembers with a laugh.

Leaving aside Guy Fawkes Day (which, in the pre-war years, was sometimes observed with a small fireworks display), Christmas was the only holiday celebrated at Moore River. But it cannot be denied that it was done properly, and with all the trimmings — from carolling and coloured lights to plum puddings and a Christmas tree hung heavy with gifts. The tradition of the settlement Christmas tree seems to have begun during Neal's administration. Even in the leanest years, 'everybody got something', Bella Yappo recalls. 'Even the camp people used to come up to the Christmas tree, and they'd get a new pot or a billy can or something. But everybody got something.' 'We had a decent Christmas', Vincent Lambadgee agrees.

For the convenience of staff, the settlement Christmas tree was usually held a week before Christmas, either in the hall or on the lawn of the Big House. Paget described the event to his Commissioner in 1940:

*By all accounts, Christmas at Moore River was a truly joyous celebration.
Here Mr Paget impersonates Father Christmas. In 1940 he distributed 'toys
and useful articles' to 386 natives.*

The tree was loaded with presents, of toys and useful
articles, every Native getting a present (a total of 386).
Prior to the arrival of Father Xmas, several small items
were put on to entertain the visitors and Natives, i.e.
boxing, singing, percussion band etc. The Boy Scouts
and Girl Guides were in uniform, and the coloured lights
suspended across the lawn helped to make a nice bright
show.

Father Christmas was none other than Paget himself ('He was a good Father Christmas because he could be a bit of a clown', explains Sister Eileen), and he would distribute gifts individually to each man, woman and child. Hazel Colbung conjures up the scene:

> He'll come in with a bag on his back, a lot of balloons, and they all shout when someone will say, 'Well, now, all quiet 'cause Father Christmas is comin' — and then you'd hear the bells — ding a ling. It used to be nice!

Always in attendance at the festivities were official guests from the surrounding districts — Doc Myles from Moora, the constable and members of the local gentry — who listened attentively (even if no one else did) when the Commissioner's Christmas telegram was read aloud. But the ranks were also swelled by Aboriginal visitors — working people and the relatives of inmates drawn back 'home' for the holiday. They added their voices to the concluding events — three cheers for Father Christmas, and the singing of the National Anthem.

Great care was taken to ensure that Christmas day also dawned happily for the compound kids — and their memories shine as brightly today as their faces must have done then. There were usually extra presents that had come in by this time, and Matron and Sister would creep around to the children's dormitories before sunrise, leaving a little something on each bed. 'They might only be just tin whistles or hats or lollies or something or other', but each child received something on Christmas morning.

Church services were held at nine, followed by a generous Christmas dinner that always included roast meat (hot or cold), plum pudding, sweets and soft drinks. The meal was served to the children and compound workers in the dining room, which had been decked out with bunting and fresh flowers. 'Much to the enjoyment of the natives', to use Neal's words, the waiting was done by the entire white staff. In his first Christmas as Superintendent, Paget modestly described the meal as 'a huge success. We killed a sterre [sic], which provided plenty of roast beef. This with boiled new potatoes (from the Farm), pickles, onions and sauce. Fruit salade [sic] with

'Well, we miss the olden days, you know, the days where we were so happy there'.

Custard. Lollies and Cordial Drinks with Nuts to finish up the meal.'

*

In a contest waged by the state of Western Australia, the culture of the compound and the outlaw culture of Aboriginality were locked in a tug of war for the souls of the children of Moore River. Although the odds were heavily rigged in the favour of officialdom, it never came close to achieving victory. Somehow or other, the Aboriginal identity of the children was strong enough to withstand the onslaught. One of the important reasons why may have been the existence of a third culture: the culture of childhood.

As we have seen, settlement life gave the compound kids an astonishing degree of freedom from adult contact of any kind, whether Aboriginal or white. By necessity, children were forced back on their own resources, and they found their security and their nurturing from their own peer group. Although its outlines are much more elusive than the two adult cultures, the memories of the former compound kids suggest that the rich, improvised nature of the culture of childhood was their real mainstay. There is no doubt that it was their life together as mates — playing, eating, learning, laughing — that they remember best. 'Well, we miss the olden days, you know, the days where we were so happy there', Ned Mippy explains. That there were such days at all at Moore River is a testament to the indestructible spirit of childhood.

chapter 5

The Moore River Scrapbook

Istory speaks through as many voices as historians have ears to hear. For the voice of experience, we listen to the oral record, richly textured and bright with detail. Archival sources, the voice of authority, speak in more official accents (and are often more telling in what they omit than in what they reveal). Historical evidence is nothing more or less than the testimony of storytellers. Good history begins when we give them voice, and listen.

What Moore River was like as a place to live, and how it operated as an administrative structure, are relatively straightforward questions. What is not straightforward is why. Why was the tragedy of Moore River allowed to happen in the first place — and to continue to unfold over more than three decades of notorious operation? To begin to address these questions, it is necessary to introduce a new voice in our story — the voice of Moore River's ultimate administrators, the people of Perth. The popular press was their medium, functioning alternately (as do all media) as a mirror and, after its own image, as a moulder of public opinion.

Through an annotated selection of articles, letters and editorials from Western Australian newspapers, this chapter considers the settlement story from the point of view of public knowledge and public accountability. It has been widely alleged that Moore River existed 'out of sight and out of mind' of the wider community. Indeed, ever since the expression was first applied to Moore River in 1944, 'out of sight, out of mind' has become the standard epitaph on the settlement tragedy — with the implied regret that 'if only we'd known', things would have somehow been different.

But really — we did know. And, as this chapter documents, the evidence that we did is overwhelming. From the late 1920s, the Western Australian public had ready and repeated access to accurate, detailed and timely information about settlement life. Its policies, its practices, its politics were all reported surprisingly fully in Perth's dailies. What's more, the *West Australian*, by far the most influential of these papers, not only reported on Moore River in its news columns, it often served as an open advocate of Aboriginal interests on the editorial page.

In the newspapers of the twenties, thirties and forties — just as in the media of today — the creation of news was a delicate balance of description, accusation and innuendo. Moore River provided plenty of fodder for the news machines of its day. The settlement's stark physical realities, all perched weirdly on the lunar-like landscape of the Mogumber plains — coupled with the perceived 'picturesqueness' of its inmates — were a prose poet's dream. Its transient, underpaid staff regularly yielded informants with a variety of interesting axes to grind.

In the wider political forum of Western Australian life, Moore River and to a lesser extent its sister settlement at Carrolup occupied an important symbolic place. Widely (and correctly) seen as A O Neville's baby, the settlement scheme was a regular target for politicians and special interest groups who wished to discredit the unpopular Chief Protector. Some held the settlement up as an example of the department's ineffectual extravagance; others attacked it for its 'concentration camp' austerities. Moore River offered something to offend everyone, which is another way of saying it was pre-eminently newsworthy.

Finally, the settlement at Mogumber became an important focus for two major government-sponsored inquiries, the first in 1934 and again in 1948. Both of these 'exposés' received exhaustive coverage, and they were accompanied by genuine outcries of public concern.

We know beyond a doubt that Moore River's critics were heard. The question remains: why were they not heeded?

During the settlement's first decade of operation, press coverage of any kind was extremely limited, while the few stories that did appear were almost aggressively positive in tone. During these years, Moore River plainly did exist 'out of sight and out of mind' of the Western Australian public. Even later — when local journalism took a much more investigative stance toward Aboriginal affairs — official rebuttals were powerful means of silencing debate.

•

Throughout the decades, whenever, wherever there was criticism voiced about Moore River, there was a Minister, Protector or Superintendent on hand to issue a lengthy disclaimer. In the early years, the official response was always accorded far fuller coverage than the instigating stimulus. In this case, the original criticism remained 'off the record' entirely. Readers were simply reassured that, whatever the mysterious 'detrimental references' may have alleged, they were utterly unfounded.

TRAINING ABORIGINES.
Minister's Reassuring Impressions.

Mr. W. H. Kitson, M.L.C., Minister controlling the Aborigines Department, paid his second visit to the Moore River Native Settlement last week. Thence he proceeded to New Norcia, and inspected the children maintained by the Benedictine Community in the orphanages there.

The Minister, on his return, said that, having heard that several detrimental references had been made of late to the settlement, he was anxious to find out for himself whether there was any truth in the statements. As the result of his inspections he was satisfied that the references were quite without foundation, and that, on the contrary, the Moore River Native Settlement was an institution of which the department had no reason to be ashamed. It was obvious to anyone visiting the place that the inmates were perfectly happy, and it would be hard to find anywhere such a number of bright and happy children as were to be seen attending the school at the settlement. The manager, Mr. A. J. Neal, and his wife, who is the matron, were sucessfully coping with the difficult problem presented by the somewhat heterogeneous mixture of people which the department had found it necessary to bring together on the reserve, and they were ably assisted by Mr. Metcalf, three nurses, the school teacher and the sewing mistress. It struck him that the whole staff were admirably fitted to perform the duties which they were undertaking, and seemed deeply interested in their duties and had the welfare of the inmates at heart. He was particularly pleased to note that the agricultural development decided upon during his last visit was already well under way, some three hundred acres having since then been brought under cultivation, and about nine miles of fencing erected. The immediate erection of a new hospital had been approved, and it was also proposed to proceed with the building of cottages for the married people. He inspected the work of the children in the school, and thought it quite equal to the work of white children of the same age in many of the State schools. He was particularly impressed with the work of the sewing room, in charge of Miss Crosse, where the whole of the garments required by the indigent natives and children throughout the State were being manufactured. He thought it would be a good thing if, instead of criticising the establishment about which very little was known, those so inclined paid a visit and saw for themselves what was being done at the institution for the amelioration of the native race....

West Australian
27 October 1928

*

In the early years, a good deal of ink was spilled to create the impression that Moore River was a kind of Aboriginal Eden, peopled by simple innocents who were as grateful for the Government's bounty as they were obedient to its will. Articles such as the following one encouraged the view that the state was successfully 'cultivating' Aboriginal people as a form of commodity production. The emphasis was on scientific management and productivity, with the inmates regarded as an energy resource to be tapped and harnessed.

FOSTERING THE NATIVE
THE MOGUMBER SETTLEMENT.
Enterprise and Progress.

In their lotus-land at the Moore River Settlement, the natives are a happy, carefree community. They are at liberty, and unburdened with responsibility. The reserve totals 11,600 acres, including 450 acres cleared. Of the clearing, 400 acres have been done in the last eighteen months. The acreage under fallow is 350, mostly sandplain. The 90 acres of crop yielded 50 tons of hay, and the balance, with the stubble, will be fed off by sheep. The scope of the place is being augmented continually under the personal supervision of the super-intendent, who is an experienced farmer and whose one interest in life in making the settlement a success.

There are 305 people in the set-tlement. The latest available statistics are for 1927, when there were only six deaths mostly from senile decay. There were 11 births and seven marriages. The general health of the people has much improved in the last year, thanks to the untiring supervision of the matron and staff. The clothing factory turned out 3,446 garments for the indigent natives all over the State, involving 25,000 yards of cloth. An idea of the consumption of commodities on the settlement is gained from the fact that 26,686lb. of mutton and 400lb. of tobacco were consumed in the twelve months under review. The meat bill was reduced materially, however, by the natives hunting and procuring 9,662lb. of kangaroo. In the bakehouse 16 bags of flour are used every week.

West Australian
28 December 1928

*

An important reason the settlement system failed so resoundingly is that no one was ever quite certain what it was supposed to do. In fact, the ambivalence about Moore River's institutional objectives at times bordered on sheer schizophrenia. In the minds of some offi-cials, the settlement scheme had been erected purely and calculatedly to produce profit for the state. To others — A O Neville among them — their mission was primarily an educative and a 'pro-tective' one. From this point of view, there is a certain metaphoric

Aboriginal people were regarded as a State-owned energy resource to be tapped and harnessed.

aptness about an official visitor — no less than the Chief Secretary Mr Norbert Keenan — getting bogged on the road to Mogumber. Keenan's statements typify the government's irreconcilable demands on the system — that it be regarded as a 'charity' (and therefore subject to the largesse of the government) while at the same time delivering 'value for money'.

Moore River Native Settlement.

The Chief Secretary (Mr. Norbert Keenan), who visited the Moore River Native Settlement on Thursday, said yesterday that the trip was undertaken because he wished to assure himself that the State was getting value for the money spent there, and also to investigate the possibility of reducing the present cost of the establishment. He found that the settlement was very well organised, and in all its details, it was a credit to the department and the officers immediately concerned. The quarters of the numerous children were clean and comfortable, and there was a good school, where among other subjects, sewing was effectively taught, as was shown by the well-made clothing turned out by the pupils. One question which remained in his mind was how far the Government was required to go by its duty to the aborigines, especially as it did not go nearly so far in the case of white children who were orphans or were in distressed circumstances. He did not wish for a moment that the Government should appear niggardly in its duty to the native population, but in existing financial circumstances even the matter of expenditure on charity had to be considered. The trip, which was made by motor car, was an exceedingly rough one owing to portions of the road being hidden by water, and on one occasion the assistance of a passing motorist had to be requisitioned to extricate the car from a bog.

West Australian
5 July 1930

Peter Jackson's abortive escape earned him a place in history as one of Moore River's first popular heroes — and a brief career as a media celebrity. Jackson's case had obvious appeal as a 'human interest story', which partly explains the full and sympathetic coverage it received. It also represents one of the first hints that 'lotus-land' may have fallen somewhat short of paradise.

ESCAPED WITH HIS CHILDREN.
Search for Missing Aborigine.

An inmate of the Moore River Native Settlement, Peter Jackson, an aborigine of more than 60 years of age, escaped from the settlement on June 29, taking with him seven children, four of whom were his own. The Midland Junction and Gingin police are searching for the missing party along the Chittering Valley, in which direction they are supposed to have made, and where they are supposed to be in hiding.

Jackson is armed with a rifle and ammunition, which he was allowed to carry at the settlement for the purpose of kangaroo hunting, but it is considered unlikely that he would become aggressive. When he and his family were apprehended years ago at Kellerberrin, with a view to being sent to the Moore River settlement, he escaped over night from the Kellerberrin lock-up, but was found later and taken to the settlement.

It is understood that since his wife deserted him, years ago, Jackson has exhibited great paternal affection for his children, and dislikes the idea of their having to be confined to the settlement. He is capable of looking after himself and no fears are entertained for his personal safety, but it is thought that the children might suffer as a result of the old man's good intentions.

Mounted Trooper McGuffie, of Midland Junction, is on the lookout for the wanderers and requests any travellers or settlers who should happen to come across them to communicate with the Midland Junction or Gingin police, as a speedy recovery of the party is desired, with a view to having them returned to the settlement.

West Australian
17 July 1930

ESCAPED ABORIGINES.
Police Search Continues.

Discussing the complement of the missing party, the Chief Protector of Aborigines (Mr. A. O. Neville) said yesterday that if Peter Jackson was making for Pinjarra it would not be his first visit there. It was not Jackson's welfare that was causing concern at the moment, but anxiety was felt for the children. The 21-year-old boy was Jackson's son, and four of the seven children were his own by his first wife, who deserted him. The other three were those of his second wife by her former husband. His second wife was working away from the Moore River settlement at present. Jackson, who was under warrant of detention at the settlement so that his children could be cared for as wards of the Chief Protector of Aborigines, had strong affection for his young family. He was at liberty to go wherever he fancied, so long as he left the children at the settlement. He left the settlement on one occasion but returned later.

"I don't know why he took it into his head to do this," said Mr. Neville, "but I do want to find the children for their own sakes, because I am afraid that the treatment they will get in this weather might cause their deaths."

West Australian
22 July 1930

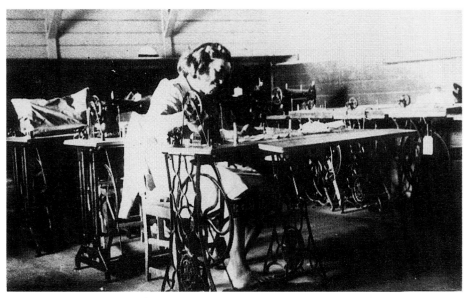

Moore River's founders envisioned the 'lubras' of yesterday as the sweatshop forewomen of tomorrow.

POLICE NEWS.
Escaped Aborigines Captured.

The Fremantle police received a telephone message from Constable Styants, Pinjarra, last night stating that he had recaptured the aboriginal, Jackson, and his family, who absconded from the Moore River settlement recently. The party will be sent to Perth to-day.

West Australian
26 July 1930

215

"TREATMENT NO GOOD."
Peter Jackson's Plea.

While he does not like the Moore River Native Settlement, old Peter Jackson this morning expressed his willingness to return and stay there.

His return will, however, be delayed at least until he has served five months in Fremantle jail. His son, Freddy, will serve one month for having removed seven native children from Moore River. On a similar charge Peter received two months' imprisonment from Mr. A. B. Kidson, P.M., in the City Court this morning; another two for having refused to stay there himself; and one month for having stolen a kangaroo dog from the settlement.

Peter's reply to this charge was naive. He said that the dog did not belong to the settlement in any case, but was the property of one of his pals who lent the animal to him to hunt kangaroos. When leaving the settlement the dog started to accompany him, and he tried to drive it back. Before he had gone half a mile the animal had rejoined him.

"It did not like the place and would not go back," he finished amid laughter.

Four of the children belong to Peter, and repeated efforts have been made to get them away from him since their mother deserted him. They were taken from him two years ago when they were found to be neglected, and were lodged in a receiving house in Perth. During the night Peter got them out and took to the bush. He was arrested with them at Kellerberrin, but broke out of the lock-up, and once again took the children into the bush.

Eventually the family was once again rounded up, and sent to the Moore River Settlement. On June 29 last, Peter, with his son Freddy, aged 20, left the settlement with the rest of the family "in tow', and Jacky, Elsie and Ruby Spratt were also taken.

Peter said that the children did not get enough food or clothing at the reserve, but Arthur J. Neal, superintendent of the settlement, stated that all the children in his care were adequately fed and clothed. Freddy's chief complaint was that he was not given enough tobacco.

Daily News
31 July 1930

216

When it came to half-caste children, Aboriginal mothers were by definition unfit mothers.

217

The decision described in the article following would probably have been different if the thirty-five-year-old 'girl' had been childless, or if she had agreed to surrender her children to the court. The position of the Western Australian Government was clear on this matter: when it came to half-caste children, Aboriginal mothers were by definition unfit mothers. Once remanded to the settlement, Dora Lowe would have been required to relinquish her five children to the care of the white staff.

A GIRL'S OUTBURST.

Dora Lowe (35), an aboriginal woman, charged with drunkenness in the Perth Police Court yesterday, vigorously denounced the Moore River Native Settlement. "I don't want to go back there," she said. "We were starved; all my children were starved. I won't go back."

Mr. A. B. Kidson, Acting P.M., who occupied the Bench, was in a dilemma, since an officer of the Aborigines Department stated that they did not want the woman back at the settlement, and that she was living with a man in a camp at North Perth, and had five children, aged between three and 10 years.

Finally the Magistrate ordered the woman to return to the settlement with her children.

Sergeant Houston prosecuted.

West Australian
26 February 1931

*

The terms of reference for the 1934 Royal Commission were broad: to examine the 'social and economic conditions of aborigines and persons of aboriginal origin' throughout Western Australia. Commissioner H D Moseley tabled the final report of his year-long investigation — all ninety-two typescript pages of it — in early March 1935.

A Police Court Magistrate and former Protector of Aborigines in the north-west, Moseley had begun hearing evidence at Parliament House more than a year earlier, with a *West Australian* correspondent dutifully in attendance. (When Moseley travelled north later that year, he was accompanied by a young journalist named Paul Hasluck, who would later achieve fame as an historian and federal

'We all regard them as human beings. However, humanity is not all on a level plane ...'

politician. Hasluck's powerful dispatches arguably had greater impact on public awareness than the Commission report itself.) Among the first objects of Moseley's scrutiny was the settlement at Moore River — and the press obliged by printing daily highlights from the astonishing testimony of staff, 'half-castes' and concerned members of the public.

The following run of articles from autumn of that year shattered irrevocably the grotesque myth of an Aboriginal 'lotus-land'. This is not to suggest that those giving critical evidence were free of prejudice or misinformation — nor, for that matter, were those who heard the evidence. In the course of these hearings, Moseley himself was reported as commenting, in true Orwellian spirit, 'We all regard them as human beings. However, humanity is not all on a level plane ...' Among the most disturbing comments were those of former state psychologist E T Stoneman, who stated confidently that 'a large proportion' of Aboriginal children were intrinsically 'dull'. Yet even judged against such plainly racist standards, there was no escaping the conclusion that Moore River presented a shockingly 'woeful spectacle'.

Only a month into his inquiry, Moseley tabled an interim report devoted exclusively to Moore River. In a strongly worded plea, he urged the government to attend to conditions there as a matter of urgency. But the report was tabled on the same day as legislation paving the way for Western Australia's proposed divorce from the Commonwealth, and Moseley's warning was lost in the din of secessionist fervour. Not only did Parliament ignore the report, the *West* did too. The next day, it continued its coverage of the hearings by blandly noting that 'a number of coloured people complained about the treatment they had received at Moore River'.

Aboriginal testimony of any kind was rarely reported at length during the hearings, despite the sensational and detailed nature of the allegations made by inmates and former inmates. The few times an Aboriginal person is identified by name in press reports, it is with reference to remarks that were either overtly positive or only mildly critical. In this, the journalistic establishment was taking its cue directly from the government. Neville himself publicly dismissed the testimony of native informants as 'for the most part untrue.'

On the day the final report was released, the more sensationalistic *Daily News* gave the story the full front-page treatment, under the blaring banner headline 'Commissioner Stresses Menace of Half-caste Problem'. Oddly, however, the story omitted all mention of Moore River. The *West Australian* was more sedate but as usual provided much fuller coverage. That the Commissioner bluntly condemned the institution for its 'barbarous treatment' of Aborigines was a watershed. But equally significant was the fact that these charges had been brought fully (if not always entirely fairly) before the general public through the medium of the popular press. The sad irony was that this explosion in public information was never translated into significant action. Like most explosions, it had simply made a terrific noise.

ABORIGINES' WELFARE.
ASPECTS OF THE PROBLEM.
Evidence Before Commissioner.

That the Aborigines Act and regulations have been framed with "criminal carelessness," and in many vital essentials run counter to the spirit and practice of the law of the land, was a view expressed by Mrs. Mary Montgomery Bennett when testifying at Parliament House yesterday before Mr. H. D. Moseley, the Royal Commissioner appointed to investigate the treatment of aborigines in this State.

In reply to a question by the Commissioner, Mrs. Bennett (who commenced her evidence on Monday), said that her knowledge of Australian natives extended from the days of her infancy. She had been brought up on her father's cattle station in Queensland, she said, and her experience of aborigines in this State had been gained by work amongst them at Gnowangerup, Forrest River, Broome and district, and Mt. Margaret, where she lived for two years ...

The Chief Protector of Aborigines (Mr. A. O. Neville): You are something of an idealist. You want to bring about an ideal system all at once? — I want to treat other people like human beings ...

Do you consider it right to marry a half-caste girl to a full-blooded native? That is entirely a matter for the individuals to decide, as it is of such extreme moment to themselves. It is not a matter for anyone else.

You would not regard it from the ethnological point of view at all? — We do not ask the whites to marry ethnologically. Why ask the blacks?

You have referred to half-caste children being taken from their mothers. Do you think it would be better to let them stay in the bush and mate with full-bloods? — That is better than it is for them to commence promiscuous relationship with whites, with the result that they belong to no one and have no family ties. I do not think that there is anything revolting in the marriage of a half-caste girl to a full-blooded aboriginal, if they love one another.

Ill-behaved Natives.

Do these girls never fall when they are living in a mission? — A lot depends on the mission.

Do you know of any who have fallen at a mission? — I do.

Is it not possible that there are some native women whose conduct is so reprehensible that for the sake of the community they must be removed? — I do not know of any.

Is it not possible that there are some native men who are so given drunkenness that a term of seclusion in a settlement is better, as a corrective, than sending them to gaol? — I do not think so.

Have you ever been at the Moore River settlement? — I was there one afternoon.

Your evidence as to that settlement has been supplied entirely by natives? — Yes.

Only a very small proportion of the South-West native population is at the Moore River settlement. The department cannot be smashing many families, can it? — It is terrible to smash one.

Do you know that a large number of South-West natives are unemployable? — I never found that. They have always had the necessary horse-sense to discover that if they give a certain measure they will get a certain quid pro quo.

Do you think that the department is trying to restore the natives' self-respect? — No.

The Commissioner: If natives in a settlement did something wrong, would you pass it over, or merely talk kindly to the offenders, or use some form of correction. What are your ideas on this matter? — When punishing native girls I have found that the most effective way was to withdraw privileges. To remove the privilege of earning was the bitterest punishment they could undergo.

Department's Attitude Criticised.

Mr. Neville: You said that the department was regarded as an oppressor of the natives? — Yes; I do not think there is any sympathy apparent. I do not think that the department's attitude towards the natives is one that will create a sense of confidence.

But that is only your opinion? — Yes.

I am afraid that you have sought for the omissions or misdeeds of the department rather than for its good deeds, have you not? — Good deeds will always speak for themselves ...

The Commissioner: Do you think they will ever be able to mix with whites on equal terms. There are different mental planes among individuals: cannot you imagine different mental planes among races? — I suppose so. Atticus said that Cicero could not get his slaves in Britain because they were all too ugly and stupid.

West Australian
21 March 1934

ABORIGINES COMMISSION.
EDUCATION OF NATIVES.
Views of Psychologist.

Educational aspects of the aborigines question were dealt with by Miss Ethel Turner Stoneman, who occupied the position of State Psychologist from 1926 to 1930, when she gave evidence before the Royal Commissioner (Mr. H. D. Moseley) investigating the condition of West Australian aborigines at Parliament House yesterday. Miss Stoneman also referred to the feeding of aborigines at the Moore River settlement.

Following investigations at the Moore River settlement, Miss Stoneman recommended three separate courses of instruction for black children. The first, she said, should be ordinary school instruction up to the standard four level, and further than that only in exceptional cases. Fully half of the time should be devoted to practical courses in elementary cookery, sanitation, preparation for infant care, sewing, the use of tools, tree planting, and the care of trees, grinding of meal, elementary weaving and net making. These topics were designed for those who would live under native conditions. The second group, those of dull intellect, should have practical courses in personal hygiene, camp order, cookery, spinning, grinding, weaving, the care of animals, and so forth. This was only a suggestive list, Miss Stoneman explained, from which she had cut out reading, writing and arithmetic. These children could also be taught eurythmics and the use of household implements, and be encouraged to engage in the boy scout and girl guide movements where practicable. The idea was that these folk should be able to appreciate and enjoy field interests, and it was of value that they should be trained to do something during their leisure hours. For the poorly endowed, whose maladjustment made it imperative that they be guarded from cruelty, whether wanton or unconscious, instruction should be given in their own dialect where an older aboriginal was able to assist. Early kindergarten occupations, nursery-school training in personal habits, eating, correct posture, and correct breathing should be attended to, and there should be instructional play. Native children were not like white children, who all spoke the same language and came from homes that were similar. In dealing with native children, teachers would have to exercise careful supervision because of the poor physical condition of the black children and because of the fact that a large proportion of them were dull. It was necessary to give them practical instruction. ...

223

The Commissioner: I understand your criticism. You say that the best results are not being obtained from the natives at Moore River?

Witness: That is so. At Moore River I found 97 children allotted to one teacher. The children displayed all degrees of intelligence from average white to imbecility. There were many dialects and the teacher was untrained ... She was working under most disheartening conditions and was jaded and harassed. She was allowed annual leave of only three weeks each year. ...

"You will see," she continued, "why I say that the education attempted at Moore River is inadequate. Those concerned do not know what they are attempting. The work was ill-conceived and it was not possible to obtain the results that could be desired."

The Commissioner. The results were poor compared with what you say might be obtained?

Witness: Yes; the education of the dull group of aboriginal children should be on lines determined by a study of their common interests and achievements. What is required is the teaching of the children to do and make. What the aborigines themselves teach their children to do and make should form the basis on which to build. The aim is to make the attainment of their own goal surer, and to enlarge that goal by adding instruction which would enable the natives to replenish supplies whether of food, water or shade, and to add interest and pleasure to reservation life.

Do you say that there should not be complete segregation or complete miscegenation? — That is so. Some natives are not able to learn what is necessary to keep our laws and to understand our observances. Some of the half-castes prove to be duller than others of full blood.

Question of Food.

The children of Moore River, witness continued, should be given at least a pint of whole milk a day. Palatable home-grown greens and fruit should also be given them each day and they should receive two ounces of boiled sweets each week, not necessarily all at once. The children required more sugar than they were receiving at present. They should be given wholemeal bread, fresh eggs and red meat once daily. Butter or dripping should also be given them and vegetable soup as well. For the adults, fruit and vegetables, eggs and milk should be given in addition to the usual rations. Sweets should be given in lieu of tobacco where preferred. The adults, too, required more sugar than they were receiving.

It should be made difficult, Miss Stoneman went on, for those in the compound to be dirty. Showers should be provided wherever natives were living on the settlement. There should be a daily issue of soap, but the natives not receive a lot of soap at one time because they would merely throw it away and waste it. The natives of the settlement were not provident people. The possibility was that the fact that they were not provident explained their presence at the settlement. They were really the derelicts of the aborigines. ...

West Australian
24 March 1934

THE ABORIGINES.
CRITICISM OF DEPARTMENT.
"Not Protected, but Persecuted."

"The Aborigines Department is controlled by civil servants who are without any practical experience of the aborigines; they really try to protect the natives and I admit that their intentions are good, but sometimes their intentions meet with an unhappy fate." These remarks were made at Parliament House yesterday, before Mr. H. D. Moseley, the Royal Commissioner investigating the treatment of aborigines, by Ernest Charles Mitchell, formerly an inspector of aborigines.

The witness was concluding evidence which he had commenced on the previous day. He emphasised that his criticism of the department did not arise from any personal animus against the Chief Protector of Aborigines (Mr. A. O. Neville). Years ago, he said, he had approached the Chief Protector and stated that reports he had received, as an inspector, from the natives regarding conditions at the Moore River settlement, made it advisable that he (witness) should visit the settlement and inquire into the truth or otherwise of the reports. When Mr. Neville asked why witness wanted to go to Moore River, he replied, "Because the settlement is cracking and will fall down, and you will have to bear the blame." But permission for him to make the visit was refused.

"Not Protected, But Persecuted."

As an instance of what he believed to be the aborigines' attitude towards the departmental administration, witness quoted the case of a native named Peter Jackson, who, with his family, was removed to Moore River, the department stating that it was for their own good. Jackson several times took his children away from the settlement, undeterred by the fact that for these breaches of the Aborigines Act he was sent to gaol at Fremantle. Finally, he had come to witness and said, "Is there not some white law that will protect me from the Chief Protector?" Witness explained to the native that the Chief Protector was acting as his friend, but the man's fixed idea — reflecting the native viewpoint generally — was that he and his people were not being protected, but persecuted. The great difficulty was to provide protection which they could understand as truly being protection ...

A Native Gives Evidence.

A fine upstanding specimen of his race with a laughing eye and a merry smile and speaking excellent English, Wilfred Morrison, a full-blooded aboriginal, was the next witness. He said he had come to give evidence voluntarily, and not acting on anybody else's suggestion: he had come to say that he had "no objection" to the Chief Protector. Witness had always been well treated by the department, he had never been interfered with, and whenever he had sought help he had received it. He considered that his people had no reasonable grounds for complaint about the way the department handled them.

The Commission adjourned sine die. On Monday Mr. Moseley will leave Perth for a short country tour in connexion with the inquiry.

West Australian
7 April 1934

ABORIGINES INQUIRY.
ALLEGED FALSE STATEMENTS.
Protector Replies to Critic.

A reply to evidence given by various witnesses before the Royal Commissioner (Mr. H. D. Moseley, P.M.), who is inquiring into the conditions of aborigines, was made by the Chief Protector of Aborigines (Mr. A. O. Neville) when he gave evidence before the Commission on Thursday. After replying to several criticisms, the Chief Protector suggested that the evidence given by certain aborigines and half-castes was, for the most part, untrue and probably laid them open to a charge of perjury.

The Chief Protector explained the operation of the trust funds, comprising wages of natives, held by him in his official capacity. He said that when the owners of the funds required money, which was generally only when they were on holiday in Perth or out of employment, they applied to his office, obtained a bank slip signed by an authorised officer, presented that to the accountant, and obtained the money, giving a receipt for it. The accountant was the accountant for the whole of the Chief Secretary's

Department in Perth. He, in turn, recouped his cash direct from the bank. It had been suggested that the girls should be given a duplicate of the receipt, but it was found in practice that such documents were not kept. The fact was that the girls were largely improvident, had very little idea of money, and did not carry in their minds any idea of the amounts they had received from time to time. Thesystem in operation ensured that they did have some money to spend when wanted. If the whole of the wages were paid direct to them they would never have any money.

Removals to Moore River.

Much had been said and inferred by the witness, Mrs. Bennett, regarding the so-called "smashing" of families and placing children and others at Moore River, Mr. Neville continued. Since January, 1930, to March 31 last, 1,067 persons were admitted to Moore River and 1,030 departed from the settlement. Included amongst the admissions were 64 unattended or orphan children and, of course, the numbers were augmented somewhat by the transfer of nearly 100 Northam natives. The number of persons removed under warrant in that time was 201. "I say emphatically," he continued, "that there are scores of children in the bush and camps, who should be taken away from whoever is looking after them and placed in a settlement, but on account of lack of accommodation, and lack of means and additional settlements, I am unable to exercise the power which the Act definitely gives me in this respect. If we are going to fit and train such children for the future they cannot be left as they are. Presumably, Mrs. Bennett and others holding her views would wish them to be sent to missions. You, sir, will be able to judge yourself as to whether they will be any better off at a mission than at a Government settlement. In any case, there are enough children and others who should be looked after to fill all the missions and settlements we are likely to have for some time to come."

Little mention, he went on, had been made of those trainees who had left the settlement and were quietly earning their living within the community, and who, if they wished, were free to resume relations with their parents or anyone else from whom they were taken in the first place. Some, in fact, did, though it was best for their own sakes that they should not. Some "went bush" completely, but others maintained their upward course, and did very well ...

Witness continued that Mrs. Bennett had also referred to the matter of incarceration at the Moore River Native Settlement, but he felt sure that she did not appreciate the difficulties. In the first place there were no reformatories for aborigines or half-castes. The material at Moore River was sometimes difficult to handle and correction was necessary. It was no hardship at all to lock up a youngster for a few hours or even a few days in a building which was in the compound with the other buildings, and where the sounds of the settlement could be plainly heard, and where also their food was brought three times a day. Certainly the building was not pretentious, neither was it very suitable, but if it were floored or lined, or built like any ordinary room, some of those placed within it would very soon destroy it internally, at least. The witness could have no idea of the nature of some of the inmates who required to be handled. The superintendent had been asking for a long time for a padded cell, but funds were not available with which to supply it ...

Difficulties in Protector's Path.

The Chief Protector then stated that a number of aboriginal and half-caste witnesses who followed Mrs. Bennett had been induced by her to appear, and that she and certain other persons had gone out of their way to "collect these unfortunate people and bring them before the Commission and prompted them to say what they, the natives, thought she, Mrs. Bennett, would want them to say, and that their evidence was for the most part untrue and probably laid them open to a charge of perjury."

He regretted having to state the facts and thereby hold these unfortunate people up to scorn, but there was nothing else for it.

"I would like to say in conclusion," Mr. Neville continued, "that the path of a man in the position of Chief Protector is beset with difficulties, some of them even occasioned by well-meaning and misguided people who think they understand the natives. The half-caste especially is at all times difficult to handle and it requires years of experience to understand him. He knows no gratitude and the man who may abuse one today will calmly look for favours tomorrow. They are creatures of mood and, as I have said before, must be protected and disciplined to some extent in spite of themselves for their sakes and ours. Most of them can always find a grievance and what better object to aim at than the Chief Protector of Aborigines or his Department? The good we do is hidden and the corrective measures sometimes necessary are made much of and used to flog us when the chance occurs, not only by the natives but by their well-meaning supporters who seldom know the real reasons why things are done. The department should stand in loco parentis to all the coloured people and be their guide and aid until time proves them able to fully take care of themselves."

West Australian
5 May 1934

TREATMENT OF BLACKS.
COMMISSIONER'S REPORT.
TACKLING DISEASE.
NEW PROTECTION SYSTEM.

The report of the Royal Commissioner (Mr. H. D. Moseley), who inquired last year into the treatment of blacks in this State, was made available for the public yesterday.

Problems of disease take a leading place in the report, and among steps recommended are the establishment of a medical clinic at Moola Bulla in the Kimberleys, a complete examination of northern and North-West natives for leprosy and venereal disease, the establishment of a local leprosarium, and the institution of a medical fund for employed blacks.

Recommended changes in the administration of the Aborigines Department include the appointment of full-time divisional protectors in the North and North-West and a reduction in the number of honorary protectors.

Special steps to ensure a better future for half-castes in the Great Southern district are urged ...

NATIVE SETTLEMENTS.
MOORE RIVER CONDEMNED.
Farm Needed for Half-Castes.

Under the heading of "Native Settlements," the report reviews in turn the work being done at the various Government establishments for the care of natives throughout the State.

Particularly strong criticism is made concerning the Moore River settlement. So seriously did the Commissioner regard the position there that on April 19, 1934, in the early stages of his inquiry, he presented an interim report to the Government calling attention to matters which he considered urgent. "Were it not for the very strong feeling I have as to the urgency of these matters, I should be well content to postpone my comments until my report on the whole question is prepared," he wrote. He referred to the settlement as "a woeful spectacle," and added: "My firm impression is that the settlement leaves very much to be desired."

Dilapidated Dormitories.

In the interim report the Commissioner stated that the settlement comprised: — (1) A compound at which were located young people sent there for a variety of causes and children taken from their parents sent to the settlement for education and protection. (2) A camp for indigent natives and their families situated some 300 yards from the compound. The dormitories of the compound presented a dilapidated appearance from the outside. In winter, when the verandahs could not be used, they would be far too crowded. They were vermin ridden to an extent which he suspected made eradication impossible, and the sooner new dormitories were constructed the better. There were no means of keeping the inmates in the dormitories at night. The doors were locked, but lattice walls were easily broken, and many cases were on record of the girls' visiting the camp at night. A strong link meshing should be placed over all openings to the dormitory and the compound should be patrolled at night by a responsible person — not a native policeman.

There was no accommodation for the compound children on rainy days other than the dormitories, the report continued. The head teacher spoke feelingly of her difficulties because of inadequate school accommodation, and the matter required urgent attention. The missionary, who was doing valuable work on the social side, should be provided with a room for her own use. Two more additional wards were necessary at the hospital.

Men and Women in One Ward.

"The nursing sister declares that a labour ward is a necessity," the report continued, "and it certainly seems to me necessary to have an additional ward, as at the present time there is one ward common to men and women. There is no isolation ward and the one bathroom is used as a surgery. The need of an isolation ward was made apparent by the presence of a child suffering from syphilis on the verandah and mixing with other children."

Apart from work in the sewing room and making sand bricks, nothing was being done in the way of vocational training at the settlement, because no equipment was provided. Little could be done in training girls in domestic duties because of lack of equipment. In the dining-room, with few exceptions, the children ate with their fingers as there were no utensils available. There was much room for improvement in the food. Powdered milk was used for the children. No vegetables were grown at the settlement and a totally inadequate supply was imported. There was not enough meat and if fruit and eggs were supplied fewer children would go to the hospital. The view was supported by the doctor and the nursing sister.

"Barbarous Treatment"

Regarding the punishment of inmates by putting them in a small detached room, with a sand floor and little ventilation, for periods as long as 14 days, the report used the phrase "barbarous treatment." If detention were necessary it should be carried out in a more suitable place and the maximum period of

230

14 days prescribed by the regulations should be considerably reduced, the Commissioner said. Records of such punishment should be sent to the Chief Protector.

The camp at the settlement should be removed to another site immediately. Nothing more detrimental to the work of the settlement could be imagined. "The inmates of the compound are admitted for protection and education," the Commissioner continued, "and I found them living within a few hundred yards of a collection of useless loafing natives content to do nothing and always ready to entice the compound girls to the camp."

The interim report admitted the possibility of special difficulties and added: — "I have found it difficult, however, to reconcile an annual expenditure of £5,000 with the present condition of the settlement."

The main report continues that since the closing of the Carrolup settlement in 1922 the Moore River settlement had been the only place in the southern part of the State to which those natives who required care or training could be sent.

The report adds: "Moore River will be of no practical value unless means are found of employing the natives fully. If there is suitable land adjoining the present settlement it should be used. If not, then the location of the settlement should be changed. As it is I can see no hope of success.

West Australian
13 March 1935

*

The Australian Aborigines Amelioration Association, or 'Four A's' was an influential lobby group for Aboriginal interests. Its extensive coverage in the pages of the *West* during the 1930s probably owed much to the influence of respected journalist Muriel Chase, whose personal involvement in Aboriginal welfare was well known. (The practice of identifying journalists with 'by lines' had not yet been adopted by Perth newspapers.) The AAAA, which included former *West Australian* correspondent Paul Hasluck among its membership, published its own journal, *The Ladder*, which a few years later would take a strong stand opposing Neville's 'absorption' policy for 'breeding out the colour' of half-castes. But this publication, like most journals of advocacy, tended to preach to the converted.

Coverage in the *West Australian*, on the other hand, gave groups like the AAAA access to a much more diverse readership, from politicians and policy makers to to the ordinary people who elected and maintained them.

The AAAA report described here, two years after Moseley's visitation, depicts a marginal improvement in compound conditions. The chief complaints, apart from camp conditions and the exploitation of the sewing room girls, relate to dormitory conditions: the lack of linen, beds and supervision. Interestingly, the group's biggest objection was the intermingling between camp and compound — including the fact that some children 'attended school in the daytime' but 'lived and slept with their parents or relatives in the camp'.

As forward-thinking as the Four A's considered themselves (and were considered by others), it is clear that, at this stage, the watchdog shared many of the same basic assumptions as the system it had appointed itself to watch. Among these was the assumption that Aboriginal 'amelioration' depended upon denying children access to their families, their culture and their identity as Aborigines. In one respect, the Four A's took this logic even further. It suggested that the settlement scheme be broadened to provide a permanent — and permanently segregated — environment for half-castes, with appropriate 'womb to tomb' facilities. This was a form of apartheid significantly at odds with Neville's conception of the settlement as a temporary 'clearing house' whose usefulness he hoped would have been outlived in a generation or two.

Aborigines Minister W H Kitson attacked the AAAA report for its 'glaring inaccuracies' but failed to note what they were. He was swiftly called to account for this by a member of the AAAA inspection committee, V H Webster, prompting a much more thorough reply — this time from Neville — a few days later. It turned out that the 'glaring inaccuracies' related to comments about Government expenditures, not in fact to living conditions as described. Other points of contention turn out to be matters of interpretation. The charge that the sewing room girls received no wages is a classic case in point. Whereas the AAAA has interpreted 'wages' as money, Neville considers that wages may consist of unnamed 'concessions' and 'small luxuries.' As we have seen elsewhere, oral evidence suggests that these wages typically translated into a portion of meat in the noonday soup and a handful of chocolates on Saturday.

In other respects, however, Neville's meticulously detailed defence demonstrates a genuine understanding, even an empathy, for his charges at Moore River, defending such 'vices' as sleeping several to a bed and playing two-up for small stakes. He also seizes on the implicitly racist language of the AAAA's description of elderly Aborigines as 'dirty, repulsive old derelicts', in a moving refusal to cast the first stone.

FATE OF HALF-CASTES.
CRITICISM OF MOORE RIVER.
Definite Policy Urged.

The Moore River native settlement formed the subject of a report submitted at the monthly meeting of the Australian Aborigines' Amelioration Association at the Perth Y.M.C.A. on Monday night. The report, which was adopted by the meeting, embodied the impressions of eight representatives of the association who recently visited the institution, the party consisting of Mesdames W. H. Evans and I. A. Greenwood, Miss J. Chinery (minute secretary), Dr. V. H. Webster (who on Monday night was elected a vice-president of the association), the Rev. G. V. Johnson, and Messrs. J. E. Hammond (a State protector of aborigines), P. Hasluck, and W. J. Chinery (honorary secretary).

The institution, explained the report, consisted of two parts; a compound containing all the important buildings, erected on high ground overlooking the Moore River and, a few hundred yards away on lower ground, the native camp. "The compound as we found it," continued the report, "was in a very tidy condition. It seemed reasonably well-equipped with buildings, plant and staff. Members who had previously inspected it noted a marked improvement in this and other respects over the last three years. The Chief Protector of Aborigines (Mr. Neville), who kindly accompanied us on our visit, attributed this solely to increased finance. This came almost entirely from the Lotteries Commission. A creditable and well-equipped hospital block has been built. There are minor deficiencies which may be mentioned; the staff quarters are inadequate and unsuitable and the bakehouse is ridiculously small and must be an inferno in summer. Many of the camp buildings are very bad."

Among the rooms visited was the sewing room. Here were about 20 sewing machines. "We were told," stated the report, "that the older girls, under a white seamstress, turn out some thousands of garments each year, supplying all Government aboriginal institutions and all indigent blacks throughout the State. It is pleasing to see this one attempt to employ the mission inmates in useful work. On the other hand it seems hardly fair that this handful of girls should give such faithful and consistent service and receive no wages.

Dormitory's Disadvantages

"The girls' dormitory is a fairly spacious structure of wood and galvanised iron. It has been found necessary to enclose it with strong wire netting in order to prevent the inmates from getting out during the night for undesirable purposes. The washing facilities were very primitive indeed and thoroughly unsatisfactory. There appeared to be no lockers for the girls to keep their clothes and personal belongings and we learnt with surprise that they were not provided with individual towels. Within the building were a number of beds. Some of these were very decrepit and the mattresses and blankets left much to be desired. The fact that the number of beds in the dormitory did not by any means correspond with the number of girls we had observed in the school led us to make inquiries and we found that the discrepancy was accounted for by two very surprising and disturbing facts. In many instances the children slept more than one in a bed. To those of us who have had to deal with native children, this seemed most undesirable. It was explained that it was not the deliberate policy of the institution but that, owing to lack of supervision, the children had contracted the habit and, owing to the shortage of beds, it was more or less winked at. Secondly, we learnt that quite a number of children, including half-castes of both sexes, slept in the camp.

"To a person who has seen anything of the conditions under which the 'civilised' natives of this State live, the words 'native camp' convey a very definite and not very pleasant picture; a group of unsavoury huts in various stages of disrepair, hordes of huge, wicked-looking dogs; primitive sanitary arrangements, an assortment of inactive natives of all ages, a sprinkling of dirty, repulsive old derelicts of both sexes, and a swarm of half-caste children. To such a person we need only say that the native camp at Moore River is a typical native camp. There seems to be no possible avenue of employment on Moore River for the able-bodied men. As long as they remain on the settle-

234

ment they loaf about the camp. We were told that on most days a two-up game was in progress. We could not help thinking that if this was all the mischief that Satan found for those idle hands to do, his powers are not what they were.

"Dumping Ground for Undesirables."

"The camp is made a dumping ground for undesirable natives from all over the State. The Chief Protector and the superintendent both deplore this, but it is nevertheless a fact. We particularly noticed one strapping half-caste lad who we were told had been committed to the camp by order of a magistrate at Broome in connection with some sexual offence. When we saw in this camp a large number of the children who had previously edified us in the schoolroom, our feelings may be well imagined. To see little quarter-caste girls in such surroundings was a sorry sight indeed. We learnt that some of these had strayed down from the compound, which they habitually did owing to lack of supervision. The superintendent deplored this but admitted that numbers of these children, who attended school in the daytime, lived and slept with their parents or relatives in the camp. The Chief Protector admitted that the practice was most undesirable but said that it could not be stopped at once as it would cause protests both from native sympathisers and from the natives themselves on the ground that it would be cruel to separate children and parents. The superintendent stated that if he had his way he 'would send them up to the compound tomorrow.' It was pointed out by the association's representatives that the same matter had been most strongly brought before the Chief Protector three years ago and that the department had then stated that it was receiving the closest attention.

Permanent Home Required.

"The institution is for practical purposes the Government's contribution to aboriginal welfare outside the Kimberleys and may be regarded as the sum total of the Government's efforts to tackle the half-caste problem. As far as we were able to gather it is the aim of the institution to provide an asylum for children, especially half-caste girls, where their morals may be safeguarded and they may receive the rudiments of education. There is little or no provision for keeping numbers of adult inmates permanently settled on the place. Rather are they encouraged to seek employment in approved outside situations when they are judged to be old and reliable enough. To us, this appeared a futile compromise. We were unable to see that any good purpose was served by gathering these children together, equipping them with the rudiments of religion and education, and sending them out into the world to form an easy prey for undesirable influences. It was admitted that

235

about 20 per cent of the girls who went out into domestic service came back pregnant.

"We are most strongly of the opinion that an institution which occupies such an important place in the national scheme for dealing with these people should be based on the idea of providing a permanent home and permanent occupation for the inmates. There is no real reason why it should not be a model institution, with a well-equipped kindergarten, schools and workshops for training boys as tradesmen and girls in domestic science and with a colony of families engaged in agricultural or other useful occupations. The institution has recently acquired a property some distance away which is said to contain land suitable for cultivation and we were told that it provided employment for a few natives."

Need for More Settlements.

The report referred to the Royal Commissioner's recommendation that the camp should be removed immediately to another site. "This cannot be done until the policy of the Government is widened to include the establishment of further native settlements, one of which would be a place where undesirable natives can be sent without being a menace to the rest of the inmates," the report maintains. "Serious consideration should be given to the question whether it would not be desirable to segregate the children from the influence of adult natives, more or less completely, even from that of their own parents. We are aware that this may be regarded, even by well-wishers, as cruel and heartless, but nevertheless it is done and no one will deny, rightly, to white children every day, by the Child Welfare Department. We are of the opinion that a strong and representative advisory board should be appointed to determine future Government policy on these and other matters relating to aboriginal welfare."

The report will be brought under the notice of the Honorary Minister (Mr. W. H. Kitson).

West Australian
26 June 1936

TREATMENT OF NATIVES.
MOORE RIVER SETTLEMENT.
Detailed Reply to Criticism.

The Chief Protector of Aborigines (Mr. A. O. Neville) has sent to the secretary of the Australian Aborigines' Amelioration Association (Mr. W. J. Chinery) a detailed reply to the report on the Moore River native settlement which was presented by a committee of the association last month. Mr. Neville supported the contention of the Honorary Minister (Mr. W. H. Kitson) that there were glaring inaccuracies in the report.

Mr. Neville said in his reply that the report did not contain the unanimous opinion of those who visited the settlement and did not bear out the numerous expressions of appreciation which fell from the lips of the association members who visited the settlement. He felt sure that if the Royal Commissioner on Aborigines (Mr. H. D. Moseley) visited the settlement now he would be the first to agree that the expression "woeful spectacle" could no longer apply to it, repairs and additions having been made ...

"Reference was made to the fact that the sewing room girls receive no wages. That is only strictly accurate so far as it applies to wages in money. Among the sewing room girls are those who are undergoing disciplinary treatment, who, even if wages were paid, would be unlikely to receive them. Nevertheless, all are provided with special concessions in the way of food, clothing and small luxuries. Here again one detects inconsistency. Would the A.A.A.A. have us refrain from assigning duties to these inmates simply because of our inability to pay them a monetary wage? A little consideration will no doubt convince you that in almost every other similar institution tasks are allotted to the inmates, for which they receive no monetary reward during their training. I think it may be said that the inmates of Moore River in this regard enjoy more freedom and are less subject to stern discipline than is to be found in many other institutions.

Washing Facilities.

"Referring to the dormitories, it is stated that the washing facilities are primitive. If the implication is that hot water, enamel baths and so forth are not provided, then the reproach is just, but nevertheless the facilities provided fulfil the purpose. Water is laid on to a series of wash basins and showers. Most of the floors and basins are of unglazed cement and do not present the nice appearance one would expect to find in one's own home, but that does not render them less useful for the purpose for which they are provided. I do not think any member of the delegation saw the bath-house, where are provided a number of cement baths, with a series of coppers for heating the water adjoining, and where every compound inmate has a hot bath at least once weekly.

"Speaking of the washing facilities, the report expresses surprise that the inmates are not provided with individual towels. That assertion is only partly true. Every adult — that is, the big girls and boys — and every infant in the settlement are provided with a towel. The small girls are provided daily with sufficient towels to meet requirements. The boys are provided with roller towels which are also washed daily. No less than 370 yards of towelling was put into use for this purpose during the past 12 months. In view of the system operating, naturally visitors would not observe the towels in use, since as soon as they are washed they are put away till the next occasion.

"'Within the building were a number of beds. Some of these were very decrepit and the mattresses and blankets left much to be desired.' The superintendent informs me that there is not a broken bed in the dormitories at Moore River, and that the mattresses are clean and also the blankets. The mattresses are renewed with clean straw whenever they go thin, and the blankets are washed whenever necessary. The mattress covers are washed before being refilled. The blankets are manufactured by the Albany Woollen Mills, are of excellent quality, and are large enough where children are concerned for double use.

Two in a Bed.

"Surprise is expressed that children sometimes sleep two in a bed. Is this peculiarity confined to natives? I think not. This is set down to a lack of supervision — an entirely erroneous assumption. Anyone accustomed to the ways of natives must know that whole families sleep together at times, and the children almost invariably do. To eradicate habits of this nature in children taken from the bush is difficult, and one cannot expect members of staff to stay up all night to ensure that the little ones will not creep into each other's beds after being "tucked in for the night" so to speak. It is a fact that in the case of the tiny ones sometimes two sleep in one bed, one at each end. Why should they not? Many of the beds are three-foot beds, and there is ample room for two little children in them. I know perfectly well to what the remarks refer, but this does not apply at Moore River since the older children had a bed each and the little ones are too small to be considered in that connection. I defy anyone, short of staying in the dormitory all night, to prevent small boys from slipping into each other's beds in bush fashion where natives are concerned.

"It does not appear irrelevant to say at this juncture that when I, accompanied by members of your party, entered the girls' dormitory at Moore River during the course of the inspection, certain delegates expressed surprise at finding that the children were even provided with beds and did not sleep on the ground, as it was understood they did at certain other institutions not under the department's direct control.

"Under the heading 'native camp,' reference is made to 'a group of unsavoury huts in various stages of disrepair,' but the existence of a number of camp buildings, clean and ventilated, properly erected by the department, is discreetly ignored. 'An assortment of inactive natives of all ages, a sprinkling of dirty repulsive old derelicts of both sexes, and a swarm of half-caste children' — that is a sorry picture if it were true, but it cannot be said to be so. When the party visited the camps it was a Saturday afternoon. Presumably they expected to find all and sundry at work, but we are more merciful than that. The superintendent assures me, however, that only two adult male natives on the place do no work. One is blind and the other approximately 80 years of age. Every other adult male has his particular job to do whether it is productive or not. The delegation was told, although they did not see it, that as an adjunct to the settlement there is a farm a few miles away where most of the able-bodied males are engaged in farming operations.

"Dirty old Derelicts."

"The reference to the 'dirty repulsive old derelicts of both sexes' is surely to be deplored. Old some of our people are, and indigent, but surely not repulsive or even dirty, at least not more so than might be expected in view of their age and condition. Even among us whites old age is not always associated with ugliness, and we are fortunate if we are in a position which does not necessitate our maintenance at the hands of a beneficent Government, as is unfortunately the case in respect of the old natives referred to.

"There is a reference in this paragraph to the game of two-up. One is well aware that natives are given to gambling, but that is surely not the prerogative of the coloured people. Among the older coloured people it is the exception to find those who can read or write, consequently, they have few interests outside the necessity for procuring their daily bread and one cannot blame them if they indulge in a game of hazard occasionally, though in this regard gambling is officially 'taboo,' even at Moore River.

"To say that Moore River is made the dumping ground for undesirable natives from all over the State is, I maintain, one of the glaring inaccuracies mentioned by the Minister. As the Minister knows, I have repeatedly declined

239

to allow Moore River to be a receiving institution for natives of that character, and have made it quite plain that I consider there should be a special home for these. Apparently your delegates based their assumption upon the presence at Moore River of a half-caste lad from Broome, sent there by the Children's Court in connection with some sexual offence. That is perfectly true. There is such a lad at Moore River, but he is by no means a criminal, or even an undesirable lad. Are there not daily being committed to State institutions such lads, and where else could a half-caste go? This particular boy has led an exemplary life since his arrival at Moore River. He is only a child yet, and will be leaving for Broome again when he attains the age of 16 years.

From Schoolroom to Camp.

"Reference is made to the number of children seen in the schoolroom and subsequently found in the camp. Of course they were. They were interested in the visitors and followed them around out of curiosity, but they did not belong to the camp and certainly would not be allowed to remain there. There are a few children in camp with their parents, but the parents are only at Moore River temporarily, either as visitors the their friends or passing through to other places. It would not be right to separate them from their children for so brief a period, but even so the children go to school and enjoy the usual amenities of the place as do the permanent inmates of the compound.

"It is stated: 'To see little quarter-caste girls in such surroundings was a sorry sight indeed.' There are not quarter-caste children of either sex in the camps, and even in the compound probably not more than one or two. The system is to house such children at the hospital, where they are able to be separately dealt with and receive more intensive care and attention pending the time when they can be removed to some other more appropriate institution.

"The report goes on to refer to the nature of the institution from the point of view of its provision for keeping numbers of adults inmates permanently settled on the place. 'Rather they are encouraged,' it says, 'to seek employment in approved outside situations.' This is characterised as a futile compromise. No good purpose was served, it was stated, by gathering these children together, equipping them with the rudiments of religion and education, and sending them out into the world to form an easy prey to undesirable influences; also that the institution should provide a permanent home and permanent occupation for its inmates. ...

Giving the Children a Chance.

... The policy of the department is not to make the inmates of this settlement permanent prisoners, but to equip them for ordinary citizenship and enable them to earn their living and make good outside. Whatever its defects, whatever its shortcomings, it can be truthfully said that so far as Moore River is concerned the department is attaining this end to an unexpected degree. For a long time past the department has not been able to find sufficient employees to fill the numerous positions offered to it from practically all over the State, stress being laid on the fact that only trained inmates from Moore River were wanted.

What right have we, I ask, to bottle up a large section of the community in a place like this, where they would be principally occupied in propagating their species when work is available for " them in the ordinary walks of life? I repeat here whathave often said before, that I would rather send a youngster out, presuming that such youngster, boy or girl, has had a fair measure of training, even though the result is going to be a failure, than never give them a chance at all. Time enough to make them permanent inmates of the settlement when the failure is evident. Besides, from an economic point of view why should the State be compelled to maintain large numbers of people who in the circumstances could not be self supporting, but who if given the opportunity would be able to maintain themselves?

West Australian
31 July 1936

Curtained windows and brightly coloured clothing: the kindergarten would eventually become only 'a prize exhibit to delude visitors.'

241

Although oral history informant Edie Moore recalls singing 'Rule Britannia' as a schoolgirl at Moore River, this article suggests an even more tangible imperial presence. We know that Neville was grateful, but what the inmates made of this generous donation was never recorded.

MOORE RIVER SETTLEMENT.
Gift of Coronation Photographs.

The Commissioner of Native Affairs (Mr. A. O. Neville) has received from the management of Economic Stores, Ltd., Perth, a collection of 20 enlarged and framed photographs showing Coronation scenes in London for display in one of the State's native institutions.

Expressing appreciation of the gift, Mr. Neville said yesterday that it was the first appreciable donation of its kind that the department had ever received. The pictures formed a magnificent collection. In addition, the Economic Stores had also presented the department with enlarged coloured photographs of the late King George V and Queen Mary. These two photographs would be hung in the school room at the Moore River settlement. The Coronation pictures, dealing with the procession and ceremony at Westminster Abbey, would be placed in the new building for native children which was about to be erected at the settlement.

West Australian
9 July 1937

*

The myth of progressive development — that things were, if not good, then at least getting better — was one of the department's favoured rhetorical strategies for managing criticism about Moore River. This optimism was widely held, and even critical reports of settlement conditions were invariably prefaced with a diplomatic acknowledgment of 'improvements'. This stirring account by an unnamed 'special representative' is no exception.

The position in this report is closely akin to that of the Four A's in its contentious 1936 investigation. Indeed, the 'special representative' may have been AAAA member Paul Hasluck himself — whom Neville had once predicted 'would go a long way'. The settlement kindergarten, which had just officially opened, is lauded as a major victory in the battle to tranform Western Australia's half-caste wards into 'useful units in the community'. As it turned out, the fear that the kindergarten might be used only as 'a prize exhibit to delude visitors' was well founded. Unable to secure the continuing commitment of government resources on the scale suggested here, the department eventually abandoned the dream of giving half-caste children identical bright-red jumpers, enamelled cots and the chance to 'learn white ways' from infancy.

MOORE RIVER NATIVES.
An Improved Settlement.
BIGGER TASKS STILL UNDONE.
(By a Special Representative.)

The Moore River Native Settlement is a much improved place. Several times in the past this settlement on the sandplain west of Mogumber — the chief government institution for aborigines — has been criticised on one ground or another. Some of the general complaints still stand; a number of the particular ones no longer apply.

They were of the kind that a little money could rectify. During the two years to June 30 last the Native Affairs Department spent about £4,837 on new works at the settlement — £3,072 from loan, £507 from revenue and £1,158 from that painless extinguisher of a community's conscience, the Lotteries Commission. Another £100 was a gift from the Youth and Motherhood Appeal Fund.

Two routine jobs done with the money were a new water supply with reticulation among the settlement buildings and an electric light plant serving 150 lamps, including "street" lights.

The first big task was to regenerate the Camp — a section of the settlement where families and other adults live in their individual huts but draw food from the settlement kitchen. This section, which was strongly condemned four years ago by the Moseley Commission both because of its general condition and because of the "contaminating influence" of its "collection of useless, loafing natives" on the Compound (that is the section of the settlement where boys and girls are lodged in dormi-

243

tories), is gradually being altered in its external features and this is probably helping to lessen other evils. The new site is higher up the hill than the old camp and by situation and by the fact that it is now lit at night with outdoor electric lights is more easily subject to surveillance ...

But it is an indication of what may be done rather than a complete vindication. Part of the old "camp" still huddles on the sandhill — rusty iron, torn bags, shabby men, rheumy crones, with a few spindly children down on visits. If money is the cure, the settlement must have more of it to complete the changeover, though one suspects that money will be unable to touch some of the weaknesses in a system that has compelled the department to use Moore River for practically every institutional purpose. To realise the administrative difficulties, imagine one institution attempting to combine the functions of creche, orphanage, relief depot, old men's home, old women's home, home for discharged prisoners, home for expatriated savages, home for unmarried mothers, home for incurables, lost dogs' home and a school for boys and girls. Yet these are the functions which the department is trying to carry out among about 360 people on a couple of sterile sandhills. To improve its old and unsuitable buildings it has received £4,837 and a few odd pence in two years.

The New Kindergarten

The works already detailed, together with minor improvements, have accounted for about £3,000 of that sum. The other big change is the building of a kindergarten on the eastern side of the Compound area. This is now the show place of the settlement; it is the best thing the Native Affairs administration has on view in the southern part of the State ...

The kindergarten building has been in use since the beginning of the year. It houses 30 native children, including a number of fair-coloured ones, between the ages of three and six. It is in the charge of a qualified kindergarten teacher with a good deal of experience of kindergarten work in white schools, assisted by an attendant who has the oversight of the domestic side. Other helpers are two native girls who act as "monitors" in the schoolroom, two to help in the dormitory and two to help in the kitchen, and a native boy as orderly and yardman. These helpers are drawn from other parts of the settlement.

The Children's Welcome.

The visitor goes the rounds. Child faces grin shy welcome to the schoolroom; shrill voices sing it. Little bare feet thump the floor in musical games. Blue-clad, with bright red woollen jumpers, the eager kids make a gay coloured circle as they stand on the floor in readiness for some little make-believe.

But the great event waits while cupboards are opened to show the visitor the wide variety of equipment used, and papers are produced to tell of the daily toothbrush drill, the hygiene parades at 9 a.m., the games, the table work, the recess with biscuits all round, the singing, the housekeeping game and so on through the day until we reach the warm bath at 4 p.m. and tea at a quarter to five.

We came back later for that tea in the kitchen. The thirty little scraps of eagerness were all assembled in the bathroom, freshly polished, noses wiped, hair brushed, bibs tied on, and looking as hungry as puppy dogs. At the order they marched into the kitchen, happily ceremonious, and stood to their places. The perfect decorum of so many children in the sight of food was only equalled by the beatific relish for cornflour and milk and bread and jam once the due formalities had been observed.

Early bed ended the day — thirty white enamelled cots with warm bedding, white sheets and pillowslips and a dusky head on each. The dormitory is clean and airy but snug. The attendant's room overlooks it. The sleeping babies on the white pillows make the most charming picture you can see anywhere in the Native Affairs Department in the State — the sort of picture that would make their women critics gurgle and croon in goo-goo rapture.

But over every cot hangs a shadow and the threat of dark misery; the children lie like victims being prepared in a way to make their slaughter more painful. Under present conditions these children have no proper chance in life after they turn the age of six.

Where the Training Stops.

The children are being taken into the kindergarten, trained in personal hygiene and taught how to behave, and their minds are stimulated and encouraged to unfold. In the few months they have been under such care the way they have developed and the aptitude they have shown encourages hope for their future. But when they turn six, unless something is done and done quickly, they must be turned out and the only place for them to go is either into the dormitories of the Compound, crowded in undesirable conditions with children of a different type, or back to the squalid hutches or bough shelters of native camps. If they go to school it will be to the crowded and unsuitable schoolroom on the settlement where over 100 young tartars carry on a campaign against two greatly-handicapped teachers. Then — (if it may be assured that present conditions are an effect of the present system) — they may go out in their early teens, the boys to become indifferent and discontented farm workers and hangers on, many of the girls to become domestic workers embarrassingly subject to the fate worse than death.

There is little other prospect at present. The kindergarten is an isolated effort. Unless the money spent on it is to be wasted and the present kindness to the children turned into a cruel jest, it is essential that institutions be prepared to receive them when they pass out of the kindergarten and to continue its educative influences. Something along the lines of the cottage homes (so successful at Parkerville, Fairbridge and Sister Kate's homes) seems to be needed. It is needed at once, for already some of the children have turned six but are being kept back because there is nowhere for them to go, while there are hundreds of other candidates for admission who could take their places in the kindergarten.

Needless to say, the department which founded the kindergarten is fully aware of this need. Presumably a Government which did so well in sanctioning the first expenditure will not now abandon the policy of regeneration which it then initiated. It needs something over £1,000 to establish the first cottage home at once to receive children out of the kindergarten and continue the education they received there and this amount (roughly the price of 50 trolley bus route poles or a few days' liberality to coalminers) would surely not be beyond the immediate financial ability of the Treasury.

Several Hundred Others.

But that is not all. A bigger demand lies in the fact that the 30 children now in the Moore River kindergarten are only a handful out of several hundred coloured infants, mostly half-castes, in the southern parts of the State. Most of them now live in rubbish-tip conditions and are being reared in a manner conducive to pauperism and vagabondage and in a way that leaves them quite unfitted to have any sort of satisfactory relation with the white community. Even among the semi-protected children in the Moore River settlement itself there are another 30 children who could also go into a kindergarten if one were available. Even a casual inspection shows that five or six others could be filled at once if established at various centres in the Great Southern district. It would not be hard to find 30 children each in the Quairading, Beverley-Brookton-Pingelly, Narrogin, Williams, Wagin-Katanning, Kojonup and Gnowangerup districts and, apart from the struggling missionary efforts at Quairading and Gnowangerup, at present not a thing is being done for these children — except to issue weekly a shillingsworth of flour and condensed milk in respect of them when their parents happen to be classed as "indigent."

Unless the Moore River kindergarten is going to be a failure or only a prize exhibit to delude visitors, something else must be done. The department has truly realised and everyone associated with the problem agrees that the chief hope of relieving the State of the menacing problem and of doing our human duty by the outcast is to take the children young and bring them up in a way that will establish their self-respect, make them useful units in the community and fit to live in it according to its standards. But taking 30 children out of several hundreds will not do that.

West Australian
3 August 1938

*

There was a long, long gap in reporting on Moore River during the early years of the war. News related to Aboriginal affairs, along with many other domestic worries, seemed to have been quite deliberately censored by newspaper editors zealous to maintain public 'morale'. When Moore River resurfaced in the pages of the *West Australian* in 1943, it was clearer than ever that the idea of attracting thousands of dollars of state funding for kindergartens was a pre-war pipe dream. Now, the situation at Mogumber was flatly described by the new Commissioner as 'desperate'.

An Appeal for Help.

An urgent appeal for help in connection with the Moore River native settlement was made by the Commissioner of Native Affairs (Mr F. I. Bray) during the weekend. Describing the position of the settlement as "desperate", Mr Bray said there were 350 natives, mostly women and children, to care for. At present there were 22 bed patients and 50 outpatients. Immediate help was required to safeguard the health of the natives. A nurse and 4 female attendants were wanted urgently.

West Australian
22 February 1943

*

247

A decade after the Moseley Commission labelled Moore River 'a woeful spectacle', the settlement once again found itself at the centre of a media-driven exposé. This time, the impetus had come not from a Royal Commission's sounding gong but from the small voice of an Anglican deaconess.

Sister Eileen Heath was looking to avert a scandal, not to initiate one. In the three years since the resignations of Neal and Neville, Heath had watched the further deterioration of settlement conditions with increasing despair. Whatever else might be said of them, Neville and Neal were law and order men of the first degree. Under their administration, life at Moore River was harsh but never disorderly or random. The downward slide into institutional chaos which had begun under Superintendent Paget reached its nadir at around this time, under the insolent superintendence of the trigger-happy Mark Knight. As Heath explains:

> I felt terribly frustrated. I just felt that all the work that I had been doing over the years was gradually slipping back and back and back. I thought sooner or later there was going to be a terrible scandal about this place. I thought the scandal would come mainly because of the white people that were there ... I thought, well, sooner or later the church is going to get a terrible name of this. People will say, 'What has the church been doing?'

For Heath, the lack of supervision in the dormitories — especially the habit of some of the older boys of making night-time 'visits' to the girls' dormitory — was emblematic of a deep institutional malaise. She communicated her concerns directly to Commissioner Bray, only to be told that 'inquiries will be made and suitable action will be taken'. That was in June 1943. By spring the following year, nothing had been done. In the meantime, standards of nutrition and hygiene continued on their downward spiral. Schooling had been suspended indefinitely, as the white staff concentrated their efforts on organising 'social evenings' for themselves at the Mogumber Hotel. A sympathetic archdeacon suggested to Heath that she put her concerns formally to the Perth Synod — the

Sister Eileen Heath (left) and former matron Mrs G Campbell, c1939. Five years later, the 'White Angel of Mogumber' became an avenging angel and finally — the pawn in a deal between state and church authorities — a fallen one.

governing body of the Anglican Church in the metropolitan area — 'and that was when I wrote that report, never intending it to splash the headlines'.

Those expectations were realistic, for the secular press of the day reported on the doings of Synod only perfunctorily. That year's meagre Synod coverage did not even mention Aborigines — despite the passage of a motion deploring 'the appalling state of affairs' at Moore River and Carrolup. Sister Eileen's report had formed the basis for that motion, which was moved by Dean R H Moore. There the matter would have rested — as far, at least, as the Perth press were concerned — for Synod motions 'to deplore' have a tendency to gather more dust than momentum. But in this case, the controversy was granted an unusual opportunity for rebirth. Three weeks after the close of Synod, the report which the press had ignored was suddenly 'rediscovered' at a meeting of the Women's Christian Temperance Union (WCTU).

Dean Moore, Heath's mentor and a well-known social justice activist, had been invited to address the WCTU on the subject of Aboriginal welfare on 13 September 1944, the night of the WCTU Annual General Meeting — to which, unbeknownst to Moore, the *Daily News* had dutifully sent a correspondent. By the time Moore finished speaking, that lucky journalist must have known he had hit paydirt. He immediately filed a provocative and rather garbled account, scooping the *West*, whose more restrained version appeared a day late. If Moore himself was surprised — and he was — the 'sister of the Anglican Church', whose identity was a secret to nobody, was shocked.

A flurry of similar reports appeared over the next few weeks, and Bray was kept busy making 'official replies', including the assurance that dripping (the preferred official euphemism for 'fat') was actually a 'wholesome and nourishing' substitute for meat. Public meetings were being called to address the matter, and other women's groups were jumping on the bandwagon. At one such meeting, a participant commented bitterly that the aim of the settlement appeared to be to keep troublesome blacks 'out of sight, out of mind'.

Less than a month after Dean Moore's report to the WCTU, it

His Grace the Archbishop of Perth, Henry Le Fanu (centre). Evidence suggests he bowed to pressure from nervous bureaucrats.

was Heath — the erstwhile 'White Angel of Mogumber', as she had been dubbed by some histrionic sub-editor — who found herself out of sight, out of mind, and out of work. The story of how and why this happened was neither pursued nor presented by the Perth press. In fact, Heath's summary dismissal was the 'story behind the story' of the 1944 scandal — a tale of disturbing complicity between church and state, in which each scrambled to snatch its dirty linen off a suddenly public clothesline.

As the government was well aware, Moore River was not the only Aboriginal institution with skeletons in the closet. The Anglican-run Forrest River Mission had a few of its own — including incidents of alleged sexual misconduct — that had so far been successfully hushed up. If the church refused to reel in Heath and Moore, the Government would no longer participate in this or any other cover-up. All bets would be off. 'Off the record' evidence — including private letters exchanged between Heath, Moore, the

Life at Moore River — once again plunged into the shadows of native affairs administration.

Australian Board of Missions and a number of key figures in the diocesan hierarchy — suggests that Archbishop Henry Le Fanu succumbed to some such not-so-subtle pressure from government sources. It was a classically unholy alliance, a covenant to maintain a mutually protective silence, sealed by the public sacrifice of the 'Angel' herself. The decision was taken behind closed doors, at a meeting in early October between the Minister, Mr Coverley, Commissioner Bray, and the Rev. Leo Parry of the Australian Board of Missions. As Parry explained it to Heath on 4 October, 'Even if the trouble had not arisen ... the Archbishop had already been considering the advisability of changing your work ... it will not be wise for you to think of resuming duties at Moore River'.

By this time, the public controversy had spilled over from the pages of the *West Australian* to the floor of State Parliament. At the same time, its scope expanded beyond Moore River to the settlement system as a whole and to native affairs administration in general. There was claim and counterclaim as ex-staffers told all and current administrators denied all. There was the obligatory call for a Royal Commission. The church blamed the state, the state blamed the church and the Minister blamed the *West Australian*. That 'something was very wrong' was becoming apparent to even the most casual observer, pointed out 'One Who Votes in South Perth'. 'We of the public do want to know just what is to be done', added another exasperated reader. Everyone, it seems, had something to say and said it in print — from housewives and divines to MLAs and editorialists.

Everyone, that is, except Aborigines, whose voices were conspicuously absent from the entire debate. For them, all the sound and fury in the pages of the *West* signified next to nothing. Sister Eileen had been taken away — suddenly and without official explanation. But, although her absence was keenly felt, most people had long since learned to accept the seeming randomness of events shaping their lives. Those who still had youth and vitality enough to protest had no more access to the columns of the metropolitan press than they did to legal counsel or a university education. So they spent their vitality, and their anger, on love affairs and two-up — and doomed escape attempts. Such was the whimper with which the Scandal of '44 ended. The media spotlight had burned itself out, and the settlement was plunged once again into the shadows of native affairs administration. With the possible exception of the *West Australian*'s circulation figures, nothing had changed at all.

Native Treatment "Is A Disgrace"

Appalling conditions under which aborigines were living at the Moore River Settlement would make anyone ashamed he or she was a British subject, said W.C.T.U. President Mrs. M.B. Vallance today.

Conditions in the camp were more like those of a concentration camp, than those which would uplift and help natives, she said

One aboriginal woman who had complained of the treatment given to natives, was moved from Perth to Moore River, isolated from her friends, not allowed to send or receive letters unless they were censored.

All this was done because she showed active interest in the problems of her people, said Mrs Vallance.

Mrs Vallance was speaking after the reading of a report by the W.C.T.U.'s department of the native race at the annual convention.

Report complained that neglect, ill-treatment, repression exist in the State settlements, that workers were not able to help and train the children.

"It was reported by a sister of the Anglican Church that in one dormitory at Moore River where girls of eight to 15 are quartered, there are placed eight working boys," said Mrs Vallance.

"This sister said that Moore River was no better than a day and night brothel.

"The Education Department has not been supporting any aboriginal school for the past 18 months; there is no Government policy for uplifting the natives.

"The pastoralists dictate the policy, thence nothing is done.

"One policeman who has replaced a protector has publicly stated that 'natives should be exterminated.'

"The position is a disgrace to us all."

MR. BRAY REPLIES

Commenting on Mrs Vallance's talk, Commissioner of Native Affairs F. I. Bray said that Mrs Vallance was a well-known critic of the native administration.

Her previous attacks on administration had been found to be unwarranted.

As a moral protection for young native girls, numbers had been shifted from the metropolitan area to Moore River Settlement, said Mr Bray.

Removal was due to their misbehaviour and the adult woman removed was so treated because she refused to camp on the prescribed area.

The alleged statements by the missionary would be investigated, said Mr Bray, but he considered that no credence should be given to Mrs Vallance's outburst.

Daily News
14 September 1944

SEEK 'DECENT TREATMENT' FOR NATIVES

"Living conditions are bad at Moore River Native Settlement. At times families of five or more are compelled to live in one tent."

This statement was made by natives at a recent public meeting on behalf of the natives and substantiated by a former member of the staff, writes "Lorikeet" to the editor of the Daily News.

"The 'good' food alleged by the authorities consisted of: breakfast, bread and dripping; dinner, stew; tea, bread and dripping with an additional treat of jam twice a week," it was stated at the meeting.

"In return for work on the land, on road building, or in the sewing room the natives received the stupendous wage of 8/ to 10/ a month, issued as credit slips to be used in the settlement store."

"On the face of this," writes "Lorikeet," "recent official denial sounds rather hollow. I might add that Mr Bray was invited to but declined to attend the above meeting. Isn't it time we gave the natives a little decent treatment?"

OFFICIAL REPLY

Commissioner for Native Affairs F. I. Bray comments:

"Representatives of the department attended the public meeting referred to. Certain statements were made about the settlement, but they were not substantiated by subsequent inquiries.

"It was also apparent that disgruntled natives were responsible for the allegations, and this, of course, had a bearing on the matter since some of the natives had received disciplinary correction.

"There has been no restriction on foodstuffs at the settlement. Independent observers say that the inmates are reasonably well fed.

"At one time, due to the removal there of a large body of indolent natives from the Guildford district, there was a shortage of accommodation at the settlement, but this shortage was overcome by the provision of tents which were more comfortable than their unsatisfactory camps at Guildford.

"Dripping is on issue at the settlement, but jam, honey and other similar commodities are provided. Quite a number of natives prefer dripping, and we supply it in consequence, and because it is wholesome and nourishing as well, as some white people realise.

"Working natives receive pocket-money allowance. This allowance is not intended as a wage, because we prefer to place natives in outside employment.

"Your correspondent's comments are a re-hash of inaccurate statements made at a Bayswater meeting some months ago, and they refer to conditions which allegedly existed about two years ago."

Daily News
22 September 1944

More Moore River Criticism

Moore River native settlement was likened to a concentration camp by one speaker at a discussion of native affairs administration at the Modern Women's Club yesterday.

The object of such places as Moore River was "out of sight out of mind," said another.

She said that the Department of Native Affairs had the right to send any native to Moore River and, if one of them became troublesome, this was what was done with him or her.

Club president Mrs McEntyre said that it was her opinion that a native woman who had communicated certain information to the Modern Women's Club was sent to Moore River because she did.

It was freely urged that full citizenship be given to natives whether half-caste or full blood and, it was believed, this was one of the aims of the Bill shortly to come before the State Parliament.

Other speakers said that control of native affairs should be the responsibility of the Federal Government and this end should be striven for.

A speaker said that State Administration was tied hand and foot by the small amount of money available but that the department could do better than they were doing.

Another said that after a three hours' visit to the Department of Native Affairs she was convinced that the officers were doing the best they could but that she was "appalled at what we whites were doing to the natives."

"If you read the regulations you will see how natives are deprived of the rights of citizenship in every sense of the word," was another's comment.

Another said that it was the familiar technique of the Natives' Affairs Department [to say] that all natives who gave information were lying.

MISBEHAVED

"The settlement is not a concentration camp," declared Commissioner for Native Affairs F. I. Bray commenting on the statements made at the Modern Women's Club.

"Natives are detained there, of course, by Ministerial warrants, because of delinquency and misbehaviour generally, inclusive of sexual misbehaviour with American negroes, but their cases are reviewed from time to time and mostly the warrants are later relaxed to permit of outside employment. So it is not a question of out of sight out of mind.

"The native woman referred to was not removed because of anything said to members of the club. She was sent away because she defiantly refused to camp at the proper camping place and the health officers objected to her camping place.

"Apart from this she is an unsatisfactory type of woman and has caused endless complaints for many years.

"The Citizenship Bill, I feel, when its provisions are revealed, will be acclaimed as the most forward move in native administration in Australia.

"I think the Commonwealth Government might assist the State in native welfare and have said so in evidence before select committees, putting forward a reasonable financial formula.

"It is not true to say that natives giving information are viewed as liars by the department.

"The majority of natives are good people but we have some very bad types at Moore River at present, due mainly to phases of the war.

"It must be realised, too, that these very phases are causing anxiety with regard to white people as well."

Mr Bray added that an inquiry was made into some previous allegations and the report was now in the hands of the Minister.

He could not disclose details of the report but would say that he was not unhappy about it.

Daily News
23 September 1944

STATE'S NATIVE PROBLEM.
"WILL HAVE TO WAKE UP."
Former Matron's View.

Mrs K. Leeming writes from Brisbane in reply to the criticism of native settlements made recently by Mrs M. B. Vallance at a WCTU conference in Perth:

My husband and I were at one time, Superintendent and Matron respectively, of the Carrolup and Moore River Settlements, and I am desirous of expressing an opinion on this subject.

To begin with I should like all who are interested to take into consideration that natives are essentially without morals, as we understand them, and to think seriously of this fact. The majority of WA "natives" are half-caste, and have their origination in immorality, half white, half black. They have developed through half-caste mating with half-caste, into a "race" of people. (The full blood is almost extinct), and in the south of WA there are possibly 15,000 "castes" who are increasing far more rapidly than are the white population. I know several families (that is the children of one woman) of 16, and 12 or 13 are common.

Take then this race of people, think of their origin, then realise that their native heritage is greater and stronger than their white heritage. Native law, with its cruelties practised for infidelities, etc, do not exist for them. White laws. Well, I ask you is immorality non-existent amongst white people? The strongest urge in a half-caste from the moment he or she has reached early adolescence is "sex."

A Difficult Task.

Now, having contemplated the foregoing facts, try to visualise the task confronting the Super-intendent of a native settlement, endeavouring to introduce and enforce "morality." He probably has under his supervision some 200 of mixed sexes over the age of 12 years. (Yes, they actually reach adolescence at 12). Segregation is neither practical nor possible with the present shortage of funds, and the Anglican Sister, who raised the question, has been resident missionary at Moore River for the past nine years, and devotes her whole time to the teaching of religion in that place, so religion is very evidently not helping greatly ...

My husband and I were forced to encompass in our duties, almost always, what would normally be the work of three or four staff, but the good Sister never, at any time, offered to assist with any work other than that directly connected with the chapel, and I have not heard that she has ever done so.

When I arrived at Moore River scabies was rife amongst the inmates of the dormitories. The department was shocked to hear of this, and readily agreed to the installation of 25 gallon coppers and baths, and nightly baths were instituted, and scrubbing insisted upon, under the direct supervision of the willing horses of the staff. This job alone often took until 9 pm at first, and ultimately ended with the eradication of the scabies. The good Sister of Religion on many occasions came into the dormitories during this scrubbing process, and took out, for religious purposes, possibly 20 unscrubbed inmates, ultimately returning them generally when the unfortunate supervisor was just beginning to imagine her job completed for the night, and that good woman would, of necessity, postpone her retirement, and recommence her scrubbing. Of course, the religious administration was more important, but I never saw one case of scabies cured by it ...

West Australian
14 October 1944

NATIVE AFFAIRS.
MOORE RIVER SETTLEMENT
Superintendent Replies.

To the Editor.

Sir, — May I be permitted to add to the series of letters published recently concerning the ministrations of Deaconess Eileen Heath at the Moore River Native Settlement? I have no quarrel with those who so enthusiastically say that this person has tried to do this, that and the other over a period of nine, ten or eleven years, to make the lot of the native a happier one. I do not for a moment question the sincerity of her purpose over these years but I would like to comment on her sudden outburst of vituperation.

With my wife as matron I have been at this institution since June last. Prior to that we were at Carrolup and in the North-West for a period of eight years caring for and studying the native peoples in sickness and in health. That Deaconess Heath should have found it necessary to call Moore River Settlement a day and night brothel is regrettable. Those words were unkind, unjustified and very rude. Applied to the school kids as they were, they become almost criminal. I would like it to be generally believed that these people are not wicked like that. They are just kids, primitive kids, and their associates are their relatives — their brothers and uncles. And they too are primitive. It requires no Vice Squad to control them. It requires the simplest and yet the hardest of expedients, to wit, a demand that they be clean and decent and fair and an ability to see that these mere fundamentals of ordinary society be carried out. Deaconess Heath could not envisage this. She lacked broadness of mind and a primitive understanding of a primitive people who need guidance so badly and yet resent it so thoroughly ...

MARK KNIGHT,
Superintendent,
Moore River Native Settlement,
Mogumber.

West Australian
28 October 1944

AN INQUIRY NEEDED.

During the past few weeks many serious charges have been levelled against the administration of native affairs in Western Australia, none worse than those quoted by Mr E. H. H. Hall in the Legislative Council on Wednesday. So far the Government has maintained a discreet silence, except to say, on September 21, that the subject matter of some of the earlier charges has been referred to a departmental inquiry and that a statement will be forthcoming sometime. This is deplorable. The institutions that have been attacked are not buried many hundreds of miles away in the Never-Never. Both the Moore River and Carrolup native settlements are relatively close to Perth and are, or ought to be, under the eye of the Government and the Department of Native Affairs. The authorities ought to know the answers to these charges and if they do not know — which would be in itself a grave admission — it ought not to have taken more than a few days to find out. Nor is the result of a departmental inquiry into charges against the department's own administration in the least likely to end the public's disquietude. When a defendant is judge in his own cause a verdict of "Not guilty" — if that should be returned — is hardly calculated to carry much conviction. The public might be pardoned for thinking that when it takes weeks for the judge-defendant to return any sort of verdict at all the case must be pretty bad ...

The Australian public has been shocked time and again by stories of the bestial treatment of European minorities in recent years. Here is a challenge to Parliament to ascertain just how we are treating our own dispossessed, and admittedly difficult minority. Charges have been made. They do not relate to the distant past. They relate to last year. They do not relate to some private or organisational establishment but to a Government settlement run by the department which has power to supervise the work of Christian missionaries. They do not relate to some distant area where Government supervision might be understandably lax, but to areas well within the range of effective Government supervision. The Government, which has admitted the lack of education at these establishments, can surely no longer remain silent. But whatever the Government may do the responsibility devolved upon Parliament to make its own inquiries, by Select Committee or Royal Commission, to ascertain whether this depressed section of the community is receiving tolerably sympathetic and understanding treatment and whether the inmates of these State-run establishments are being trained for citizenship or anything else — except the future visualised nearly ten years ago by the Royal Commissioner (Mr Moseley): "The men useless and vicious and the women a tribe of harlots."

West Australian
3 November 1944

CONTROL OF NATIVES
MINISTER'S ATTACK
Answer to Criticisms

"If an inquiry were held on "The West Australian's knowledge of the native question it might achieve some useful purpose to the public and to the natives as well, but I doubt it, since it is evident to me that an attempt is being made to whip up political criticism in support of the organised attack by certain people on the Department," declared the Minister in charge of Native Affairs (Mr Coverley) yesterday ...

Cells for "Cooling-Off."

"It is nonsensical to say that cells are not required on a large settlement. Natives squabble amongst themselves and the cells are sometimes required as "cooling-off" places. The cells are used simply as temporary places of detention at night-time in the interests of discipline. There is no record of a native being locked up for 14 days. A native deserving of such punishment would be taken before the local justices. The punishment records disclose that natives have been detained in the cells at night time from one night to three nights, but in the day-time the offenders are required to do duties about the settlement.

"It is a pity that the schools had to be closed. The Government has said so, but again astute use is made of the word 'admits.' I do not know what white schools were closed as well in the Southern areas, but the Port Hedland, Broome, Derby and Wyndham schools were closed due to the precariousness of the war situation in these areas. Everyone knows, however, that the Education Department has suffered a grave shortage of teachers, and at least the United Aborigines' Mission School at Gnowangerup was closed for some time, but the Department was able to render some assistance in securing the release of the teacher, and the school is functioning again.

Site Selection Important.

"The selection of a site for a native settlement is an important matter. Many aspects must be considered. If 'The West Australian' does not know of the features to be thought of, then it should see that it is better informed. Its sneering reference to soldier settlement is noted, but there is a big difference between a soldier settlement scheme and a suitable site for a native settlement, and one of the foremost considerations is that the latter should have a copious water supply for at least 250 people, of whom many would be children and need much bathing.

"My previous reply to the criticism mentioned other matters, but apparently 'The West Australian' deems them unworthy of observation...

West Australian
8 November 1944

Suggested Inquiry.

To the Editor.

Sir,- The minister does not deny many of the gross charges brought against the management of the Moore River Native Settlement, but we of the public do want to know just what is to be done about it. It is not profitable for Mr Coverley to adopt the maxim that the best defence is attack, and so attack Mr Hall for daring to bring the matter before Parliament, and attack Sister Eileen in Parliament for daring to report the truth to her official head, and Dean Moore for daring to place the facts before the public, (who surely have a right to know), and also Miss Jones and Mrs Spence for daring to relate what they had seen and done.

The last Royal Commissioner, Mr Moseley, made much the same reports in regard to Government institutions at Moore River, and those of us who have been interested in native affairs have known that things are only going from bad to worse, and cannot be permanently put out of sight, which appears to be Mr Coverley's only "policy." ...

M. E. DEVENISH.

West Australian
8 November 1944

Native Girl Escapee Caught

Seventeen-year-old native girl who escaped from a railway carriage while under escort to Perth on Saturday, was recaptured by the police at Beaconsfield about 9 a.m. today.

On Saturday she attacked two women police escorts, severely lacerating the face of one, who is still off duty and under medical attention.

The native was first taken into custody in Fremantle on Friday night for having absconded from the Moore River Settlement.

Today she was escorted to Perth by Constable Bunce and a woman constable.

Daily News
21 November 1944

*

The facts of this extraordinary case are simple: on Christmas Eve 1945, a teenaged inmate named Ernest Colbung stole some grog from the back of the settlement truck. When confronted, the boy became 'cheeky', whereupon the Assistant Superintendent, William Sutherland, shot him in the leg with a .22 rifle. The case against Sutherland was dismissed. As the Bench put it, 'we consider that it was more or less bad luck that he hit Colbung'.

Both Perth dailies covered the story on the day of the hearing in Moora Police Court — some three weeks after the actual event. From the testimony given, there is no doubt that the shooting was a deliberate — and, as it happened, successful — attempt at crowd control. As we know from other sources, the use of firearms was a matter of open disciplinary policy during Knight's administration. For these reasons, the shooting of Ernest Colbung was not regarded as a particularly extraordinary event, within the settlement or without. As these reports make clear, by the time of the hearing, Colbung himself displayed no outrage and sought no vengeance. Rather, his attitude was contrite, even a little sheepish. Colbung, like the Justices of the Peace at the Moora Police Court, like the reporters who seemed to marvel that the lad could speak 'clear English', like Mark Knight and William Sutherland, would have understood his position clearly. Bullet wound or no bullet wound, he hadn't a leg to stand on.

SHOOTING OF NATIVE ALLEGED

MOORA, Mon — Disturbance during preparations for a Christmas party at the Moore River Settlement led to the appearance of assistant superintendent William Sutherland in Moora Police Court today, charged with having unlawfully wounded 16-year-old half-caste Ernest Colbung.

Shooting is alleged to have been the outcome of an altercation following Colbung's theft of a bottle of wine from a truck which had gone to Mogumber to pick up visitors to take them to the party.

Sutherland denies the charge.

Settlement superintendent Mark Knight told how the truck went in to Mogumber on Christmas Eve to pick up Mrs Cummings, of the Mogumber Hotel, Miss Steiner, who was to entertain the natives, and Mr Ashton, who was to be Father Christmas.

Knight left the truck near the hall in which the party was to be held, later noticed that a parcel left in it had disappeared. He questioned a native boy named Reynold Mogridge about the parcel. Mogridge said that Colbung had been in the truck, had then gone to the river.

Parcel, Knight understood, contained a bottle of wine.

Witness sought out Sutherland, told him of the disappearance of the parcel and asked him to come with him as he thought there might be trouble.

When questioned Colbung and another native admitted having taken the parcel, made a half apology but later hurled abusive language at Knight and the white race generally.

APPEAL FAILS

About 30 or 40 other natives standing and Mr Knight appealed to them to go quietly to their camps.

It was obvious, however, that a disturbance was being created outside and it was found that Colbung and a companion, Ross Oliver, had come up close to the hall. Some of the men were trying to restrain them while others were trying to incite them.

Knight saw that the position was becoming ugly, and he told Sutherland to go and get his gun and that he would get his.

He hoped that by the time they had returned their action would have had a steadying influence.

"Position was still ugly and we decided to arrest Colbung," said Knight. "Colbung threw stones. I dodged the first but the second hit me in the mouth, smashed my plate and cut my gums.

"I grappled with him and threw him to the ground, but in the melee Colbung escaped.

"Later in the evening I head the matron, my wife, say that Mr. Sutherland had telephoned the

Moora police that he had shot a native.

"At the hospital I found Colbung. He was using abusive language, being treated for a wound in the leg, hurled a bottle of carbolic at the door as the matron entered. "Wound could have been a bullet wound. It appeared that the bullet from a 22 rifle had struck the shin and lodged in the fleshy part of the leg below the knee.

SECOND ESCAPE

"Colbung escaped from the hospital after kicking violently at me, just missing my groin. At 9 p.m., about three hours after the trouble started, Colbung sent a message from the camp, said that he wanted to see the matron. Colbung was brought up later and taken to Moora Hospital.

"Sutherland told me that he had gone down to the camp after leaving the hall, thinking I was there. Colbung and other natives were abusive and threw stones.

"Sutherland appealed to them to stop, and decided to run to avoid trouble.

"As he turned, somebody called out, 'Look out.' He turned to see Colbung coming at him.

He fired a shot into the ground to frighten Colbung, who continued to come on but then collapsed. He found that Colbung had been shot in the leg."

To Mr. Seaton, for Sutherland, Knight said that Colbung had become more aggressive as the evening passed, that in his rage he was quite capable of carrying out any threats.

"Colbung threatened to do us all in, to crack our skulls," said Knight. "We do not take much notice of threats unless the natives become violent. Then the position may become dangerous.

"If the first stone had hit me I would not be here now. It would have killed me."

Knight agreed with counsel that Sutherland would have been no match physically for Colbung.

"He is a powerful man and was in a rage," he said.

MEDICAL EVIDENCE

Medical evidence was given by Dr W. S. Myles and an X-ray photo of Colbung's leg submitted.

Bullet had struck at right angles to the limb, and from the front, said the doctor. Taking into consideration the angle at which the gun was held the leg would have been forward when hit.

Small but strongly built 16-year-old half-caste aboriginal Ernest Colbung knew what an oath was when he was sworn.

"It means to tell the truth," he told Prosecuting Sergeant Broun.

In soft, clear English he took the oath and gave his version of what happened on Christmas Eve.

He referred to the removal of the bottle of wine, which he and a companion drank. They also drank three bottles of beer and a bottle of stout, the latter stolen from Mr Ashton's place.

265

"We were getting on," said Colbung.

He admitted that Mr Knight had told him to get off the settlement, that he had become "cheeky" and had rushed to hit Mr Knight.

"I hit him in the mouth with a stone," he said.

Replying to Mr Seaton, Colbung said that there were a number of natives about when Sutherland came along. "I wanted to fight Mr Sutherland. I made some of the other boys wild and they wanted to fight him too," he said.

"I do not know if Mr Sutherland warned me to stop as I was too wild to know what he was talking about.

"I saw Mr Sutherland run away and ran after him to hit him with a stone. There were a lot of stones lying around. When he turned around I heard a shot and fell. I did not feel any pain but my leg started to bleed."

Colbung thought that earlier Sutherland had fired a shot into the air.

(PROCEEDING)

[Before Messrs. E. M. Riley and W. H. Jaques, J.Ps. Sergeant R.N. Brown prosecuted Mr L. D. Seaton appeared for Sutherland.]

Daily News
16 January 1945

*

When Bray retired as Commissioner of Native Affairs in April 1937, the question of who would succeed him was so vexed that Minister R R McDonald fell back on a time-honoured stalling tactic: he ordered an inquiry. Although it lacked the status of a Royal Commission, the Bateman Report — which endorsed an administrative approach combining anthropological insight with public service know-how — cleared the way for an outside appointment. Bateman tabled his report in July 1948 and Stanley Middleton, former Assistant Director of the Papua-New Guinea Department of Native Affairs, was installed the following month.

Read in the context of Moore River's wider history, the Bateman Report induces a distinct feeling of deja vu. Despite a few new recommendations — including the long-mooted issue of 'nominal' and minimum wages for Aboriginal workers — in both form and content, the report was an eerie echo of the previous three decades of official inquiry. As historian Peter Biskup has noted, the Bateman Report merely followed in the 'tradition on such occasions: it was cautious and non-controversial'. In fact, Bateman revealed plenty of controversy — but these 'shocking disclosures' about Aboriginal health, education and welfare were by now so familiar that they had lost their value to shock. Conditions at Moore River were bluntly described as 'hopeless', and its standards of hygiene 'non-existent'.

The new Minister hailed the document as 'an important contribution to the study of native affairs', and alluded to plans for establishing yet more settlements. His predecessor took a less optimistic view. In an oddly self-incriminating outburst, Coverley condemned the report from the backbench as a mere re-hash of familiar departmental data. The irony was not lost on the *West Australian*, which drew the public's attention to the 'distressing similarity' between Bateman's findings and those of the Royal Commission fourteen years earlier.

The headlines came and went — and so, for European Western Australians, did depression, war and recovery. In all of this, the welfare of the state's Aboriginal population seemed somehow frozen in time and space. Moore River was both victim and symbol of a profound public inertia — of a tragedy perpetrated by default, of evil in the passive voice.

Three years after the Bateman Report, the Western Australian Government closed Moore River.

Report Of State Inquiry Into Native Affairs

Payment of a nominal wage to all full-blood natives in the Kimberley district and of a minimum wage to all other native employees throughout the State, with special provision for inefficient workers and domestics and the supply of standard accommodation by employers are recommended by Mr. F. E. A. Bateman, R.M ...

Moore River native settlement also needed reorganisation. Its outlook from an institutional point of view was at present hopeless. Without a change of policy, it was a waste of money and effort.

MOORE RIVER.

Delinquents, indigents and natives suffering from venereal disease mixed quite freely, with the result that many schoolgirls had become pregnant. In view of the ample opportunity for sexual intercourse during daylight hours, it was incongruous to lock girls in dormitories at night. Any good done through schooling was immediately nullified by the children's contact with the undesirable adult population of the institution.

Moore River should be for adult natives only. Its buildings were sadly decayed and neglected. Sanitation and hygiene did not exist. Bedding in the children's dormitories was filthy. Drainage, sanitation and laundry facilities were primitive and, sometimes, disgraceful ...

West Australian
28 July 1948

A NEGLECTED MINORITY

In Western Australia's treatment of her aboriginal and coloured minority since responsible Government was granted there has, we believe, been little deliberate cruelty by individuals and none by Government. But our record towards these people — apart from the praiseworthy efforts of missionaries — has been a compound of ignorance, apathy, parsimony and neglect which has been entirely discreditable to a community professing to be civilised and Christian. Australian natives admittedly are a difficult problem. However we had tried to uplift them we should probably have recorded a fair percentage of failure. Our special disgrace lies in the fact that we cannot honestly claim to have tried.

The recent history of native administration in Western Australia is a story of sincere, conscientious, but not always competent, administrators doing their best in circumstances of extreme difficulty. Inadequate funds, inadequate and often unsuitable staff and disgracefully inadequate, unsuitable and substandard institutions have resulted from lack of any serious governmental drive to improve the lot and raise the status of the coloured population. This applies, broadly, to all State Governments in the past, irrespective of party. They are all more or less culpable.

In many respects there is a distressing similarity between the observations of Mr. H. D. Moseley, who conducted an inquiry in 1934-35, and that of Mr. F. E. A. Bateman who has just completed another investigation. The ground of the two inquiries is far too wide to cover in detail, but a couple of comparisons will illustrate the point ...

In 1934 Mr. Moseley reported of the Moore River Settlement that it formed a "woeful spectacle" of dilapidated, vermin-ridden dormitories and other deficiencies. "I have found it difficult," he said, "to reconcile an annual expenditure of £5,000 with the present condition of the settlement." Mr. Bateman reports that the annual cost has risen to £12,000 and he says that the buildings in general are still dilapidated, many having fallen into a state of disrepair while some are probably beyond renovation. He adds that sanitation and hygiene are words without meaning at the settlement. The bedding in the children's dormitories is "filthy." Fourteen years does not appear to have produced much progress at these institutions or any Government sense of leadership to missions or the community ...

West Australian
29 July 1948

Decision To Transfer Moore River Mission

The State Cabinet yesterday adopted a recommendation by the Minister for Native Affairs (Mr. Doney) that the Moore River native mission be closed as a departmental mission and handed over to the Methodist Overseas Mission on terms to be decided.

Afterwards the Acting Premier (Mr. Watts) said that an agreement to be prepared would contain provision to ensure the best use of the mission station at Moore River in the interests of the native population.

The Methodist Overseas Mission, provided an agreement was reached, would use the station principally as an agricultural school for young natives and as a general school for native children.

In 1949 Mr. F. E. A. Bateman, R.M., as a special commissioner, reported that the outlook on Moore River from an institutional viewpoint was absolutely hopeless.

Mr. Watts said: "During the past two years the Commissioner of Native Affairs (Mr. S. G. Middleton) and all the resources of the department have endeavoured to put the Moore River station on a satisfactory basis but the results have proved that Mr. Bateman's view was the correct one. Costs at Moore River rose from £13,394 in 1947-48 to £23,664 in 1949-50. Inmate costs increased from 18/7 per head per week in 1947-48 to £1/15/ as at August 31, 1950.

"The transfer of the station to the Methodist Overseas Mission has been strongly recommended by Mr. Middleton. Mr. Middleton considers that the institutional accommodation and treatment of natives can be carried out much more efficiently and satisfactorily by missions than by a secular body."

West Australian
9 May 1951

269

Chapter Six

One Half-Caste Girl

ne Half-Caste Girl allows the documentary history of Moore
River to speak in its own voice, in a tale at once unique and
tragically typical. The biography of a single Moore River
childhood, the story is told exclusively through Aborigines
Department documents from the personal file of Gladys Gilligan
Prosser. The chapter begins (as does the file itself) in 1921 as seven-
year-old Gilligan is sent to Moore River from her home at Moola
Bulla, a government-run Aboriginal cattle station in the East
Kimberley; her European father professes to be 'fond' of the girl,
but denies paternity. The chapter ends fourteen years later with a
similar denial — this time concerning the absconding European
father of Gladys' own out-of-wedlock child.

Gladys Gilligan's story contains many of the familiar elements of a
Moore River childhood. She was orphaned at the directive of the
Chief Protector of Aborigines, and became an inmate. She was
clothed, converted and re-named. She received some schooling and
fell pregnant by a white man. She was sent out to work. In all of this,
Gladys' life was archetypal of literally thousands of 'half-caste girls'
of her generation in similar institutional settings throughout Australia.
This is reason enough to tell her story. But at the same time, Gladys
Gilligan emerges from these dusty pages of minutes, memos and
orders as an extraordinary individual. Brilliantly gifted both intellectually and artistically, Gladys was beautiful to look at and, in the words
of her former teacher Eileen Isbister, a 'lovely girl' to know. It is
hardly surprising that this graceful, well-spoken prodigy was displayed with pride to white visitors — a charming advertisement of

what the settlement system was capable of accomplishing.

At the age of seventeen — after years of unpaid service as a pupil teacher at the settlement school — Gladys was given the unprecedented opportunity to prepare for the university Junior examination at a Perth state school. The Department accommodated her at the East Perth Girls' Home (also called Bennett House), an Aboriginal women's hostel, under the watchful eye of former settlement matron G Campbell. According to Neville's plan, Gladys would return this honour by dedicating her life to teaching at native schools. But, like so many other of Neville's ideas, things never quite worked out to plan. Gladys, it soon developed, had an idea or two of her own, and it became alarmingly apparent that beneath her demure facade were depths of passion and pride utterly beyond institutional reach.

Besides Gladys Gilligan, the other main character in the story of 'One Half-Caste Girl' is the Aborigines Department of itself — particularly as personified by its chief, A O Neville. As these documents reveal, Neville exercised his responsibility for directing the lives and fortunes of his 'protectees' with a thoroughness that bordered on obsessive compulsion. It is, of course, well known that the Aborigines Act gave the Chief Protector an astonishing degree of control over the major life decisions of Western Australian Aborigines in everything from employment and accommodation to religion and marriage. What is less well known is the extent to which his dominion extended to even the most trivial concerns — including, as we shall see, decisions regarding the purchase of toothpaste and individual undergarments. Although Gladys Gilligan was in many ways an exceptional case, her file gives unforgettable testament to the extraordinary lengths to which Neville was prepared to go — and the extraordinary effort he was prepared to expend — to 'protect' his charges.

Although she remained the pet of a whole host of European benefactors, no one, not even A O Neville himself, ever succeeded in domesticating Gladys Gilligan. In the unlovely hothouse of the Moore River Native Settlement, she grew to womanhood defiantly, painfully and with dignity. In a final irony, Gladys died at the age of twenty-nine, after a long illness, of a white man's disease which she had inherited.

Gladys Gilligan, 'lovely girl'

Gladys Gilligan. 14 September 1933

Gladys Gilligan, Arthur Prosser with Rev. Sprattling. February 1938.

GOVERNMENT OF WESTERN AUSTRALIA.

DEPARTMENT OF THE NORTH-WEST (ABORIGINES).   493/21.
SUPREME COURT BUILDINGS.

PERTH 1st September,1922.

THE DEPUTY CHIEF PROTECTOR OF ABORIGINES.

      The Wife of the Manager of Moola Bulla Station, who is leaving there in a day or two to spend a holiday in Perth, is bringing with her a little half-caste girl about 7 years of age, and 1 should be very much obliged if you could accommodate this girl at the Moore River Native Settlement.

      The girl's name is Gilligan,and she is a pleasing and well mannered youngster and should well repay any effort on her education and training.

CHIEF PROTECTOR OF ABORIGINES.

Memo

Gilligan arrived by "Bambra" this morning. Pending her transfer to Moore River she has been placed in Salvation Army Home Lincoln St.

12/9/22

DEPARTMENT OF THE NORTH-WEST

ABORIGINES.

No. 493/21

From Manager, Moola Bulla.

MAIN FILE No.

SUBJECT: Recommending removal of half caste girl 7 years of age to a Mission.

"GILLIGAN".

C.P.A

Gilligan left for Moore River on Thursday last 14th inst.

This file might now go to D.C.P.A.

19/9/22

Yes but see me prob
act.
21.7.2

DEPUTY CHIEF PROTECTOR OF ABORIGINES.

I am forwarding herewith the papers relative to the half-caste girl "Gilligan" handed over to the control of your Department.

DEPT. OF N.W.
SEP 25 1922
RECORDS

23rd September, 1922.
L/P.

CHIEF PROTECTOR OF ABORIGINES.

THE SUPERINTENDENT, MOORE RIVER NATIVE SETTLEMENT, MOGUMBER.

With reference to the little half-caste girl Gilligan, recently sent up to your settlement, I forward papers herewith for your information. Kindly return after perusal

4/10/22.
C/J.

DEPUTY CHIEF PROTECTOR OF ABORIGINES.

Recall 25 days

D.C.P.A

Noted

MOORE RIVER NAT.
MOGUM....
6/10/22

495/21.

I have arranged for this little girl to be brought down by Mrs. Woodland when she visits the South about August next. The girl is well featured, and quite worth educating. Mr. Trenouth, late head stockman of Moola Bulla, claims the child as his. He is now doing contract droving for us and others. The mother, an aboriginal named Kitty, wife of Harry, both full bloods, is with Messrs Black and Gliddon at Mount Amherst Station. Mr. Trenouth should be asked to support the child in due course.

21st July, 1922.   C.P.A.
N/S.

Noted 26/6/22

Miss P. Please write up personal card for this child
26/7/24

GOVERNMENT OF WESTERN AUSTRALIA.

DEPARTMENT OF THE NORTH-WEST (ABORIGINES)

Out No. 431/22

MOOLA BULLA ABORIGINES CATTLE STATION.

19 th July 1922   192

CHIEF PROTECTOR OF ABORIGINES

W

PERTH

Sir

I have the honour to advise that I spoke to Mr Trenouth in reference to the Half Cast Child He tells me he does not claim her as his Daughter although he is very fond of her and looked after her while here

Yours Obediently

T Woodland

278

Mr T Woodland   Oct 15" 29
Molla Bulla   Beaudesert St.
Dear Tom
   Just a line as I promised to send
some money to Gilligan
I got a letter from Her last night
and am enclosing a letter containg
cheque for Gilligan as I dont know
her Aders
Will ayou kindly send it along
to her and Oblige
the weather is getting a bit hot of a
day and we have a bit of pluro
in the cattle out here we will
have to enoculate next year if not
sooner
There is no news out this way so
     wi t kind regard to relf an
      Mrs Woodland
       yours faithfully
        G C Trenouth

Mr. G.C. Trenouth,
Beaudesert Station,
HALL'S CREEK.

Dear Sir,

Your letter dated 15th October, addressed to
Mr. Woodland of Moola Bulla Station, has been forwarded to me by
that officer, and the cheque for £10 accompanying your communication has also been received, as well as your letter to Gilligan.

As you appear to take a paternal interest in
this child I think it would be just as well that her position in
this regard should be cleared up. Gilligan's presence at Moola
Bulla was first reported to me in September, 1921, when it was
asked that I should have her removed to some Southern institution.
In July, 1922, therefore, I arranged this, and it was understood
at the time that you claimed to be the father of the child. In
the same month, however, I received a communication from Mr. Woodland, who had spoken to you in the matter, stating that you did
not claim Gilligan as your daughter, although you were very fond
of her. You now write to the child, signing yourself her af-
fectionate father, so I think I am entitled to ask what the
position is, and whether you are really her father or not.

You may not be aware that there is a clause
in the "Aborigines Act" which provides that the fathers of half-
caste children shall be responsible for their maintenance at a
Government institution to the extent of 10/- weekly, and had you
been called upon to pay maintenance for Gilligan the amount payable to date would have been approximately £186 up to the time the
child became fourteen years of age. As this child is now four
teen maintenance is not at present payable, but if you desire
establish your parentage it would be reasonable to suggest th'
you should make a substantial contribution towards the cost c
child's maintenance during the past seven years.

Gilligan, I might say, has turned out very wel
and has even so far advanced in her education as to be able to assist in school in looking after the little ones. She will in due
course be placed out at service, unless any other arrangements
might be arrived at between yourself and the Department. Of
course I am sending Gilligan your letter, and have opened a Trust
Account and placed therein the £10 to her credit. Official receipt for this amount is enclosed.

Awaiting the favour of a reply,

I am,
Yours faithfully,

CHIEF PROTECTOR OF ABORIGINES.

280

X/S

405/29

29th November, 1929.

The Superintendent,
        Moore River Native Settlement,
        M O G U M B E R.

            I enclose herewith a letter which has been
received through the Manager of Moola Bulla Station, which is
addressed to Gilligan by her alleged father. Formerly Trenouth
denied parentage, but at the moment I see no objection to letting
Gilligan have the letter. I think, however, that any letters
which Gilligan writes to Trenouth should be forwarded through me
in the circumstances. Evidently she has written a letter to
this man which has escaped your notice.

                    CHIEF PROTECTOR OF ABORIGINES.

WM/HS
6/12/29

G.P.O.
Perth.

Sir
Yours to hand 3-84" 40/29
Re: Letter addressed to "Gilligan"
The letter stated Mr Frenowith
enclosed $10-. No Money arrived
in the letter. Do you know anything
about it?

It appears- Mrs Rae. addressed, stamped,
+ posted, a letter to Frenouth'
Some time ago - that is how the
letter escaped my notice, the
staff should not seal any letters
from Natives, before they have been
Censored by Myself
yours respectfully

Pendurus St
Hatt[e] creek

Mr A O Nevell

Dear Sir

Your letter Nov 29th to Hand in
Reference to Gillie c.

I would like you to understand
That I do not claim to be the
Father of the child
and State definnetly that I am
not

The child was on mo a Bulla
when I was working there and I did
become fond of her and she allways
looked upon me as her Father
and that accounts for the letter I
wrote to being regard as it was
The ten pounds I Sent her was a
present I never did claim to be her Father

I am

G C Trenoulth

3.1 JAN 1930

C. in C.

        Gilligan is to come down on Monday with Nurse Wilkinson, who is going on leave. Gilligan is to be met at Perth Station by Matron Campbell and taken to the East Perth Home, where she will reside for the future and attend the East Perth School. The arrangement for this has already been made. The girl is to be known as Gladys Gilligan.

        I have told Matron Campbell to see to the girl's clothes, the cost of which will be a charge against her Trust Account. She will have enough Settlement clothes for house use.

                                            CoN.

1st August, 1931.   C.P.A.
  N/S.

Noted.
Mr Campbell advised.

Gladys Gilligan arrived from M.P.H.S. on 3/8/31 & was met by Matron Campbell.

Miss Bishop.
Please card up to date.

Card Brought up to Date
4/8/31

The Manager,
    Moola Bulla Native Station,
       HALL'S CREEK.

        I enclose herewith a letter addressed by Gladys Gilligan to her alleged father, Mr. Trenouth. Possibly you may know the whereabouts of Mr. Trenouth, and be able to hand him the letter in due course.

        In this regard I might say that I do not favour Gladys keeping up a correspondence with Trenouth, who has definitely stated that she is not his child. I can see no ultimate object in her continuing to communicate with him in the circumstances, and I do not think he writes to her.

        It may interest Mr. Trenouth, however, to know that Gladys is now in Perth going to school, and I am trying to educate her sufficiently to enable her to undertake a position of teacher to native children at one or other of our native Settlements. Gladys shows promise, and can do it if she chooses, but she is a little bit harum-scarum at present.

        The money which Trenouth forwarded has been the means of fitting out Gladys with requisite clothing, books, etc., but of course the Department is keeping her as before. She resides with the Matron at the Girls' Home in East Perth, which institution we have recently established.

                           CHIEF PROTECTOR OF ABORIGINES.

Can this be filed ...

C.F.A.

        Mrs. Campbell states that it is necessary for Gladys Gilligan to have a new frock to wear on Sundays during the summer.   Three and a half yards of tobralco, at about 1/11d. a yard, would suffice, and the frock can be made up at the Home.   Do you approve, please?

        Mrs Campbell has given Gladys sufficient summer clothing for school for a time, at least.

        Six yards of elastic are also required, to be used in renovating Gladys' wardrobe.

C.L.

Approved   22/10/31.
C.S.W.
22.10.31   *C.W.*

F/3

2nd December, 1951.

The Matron,
      Native and Half-Caste Girls' Home,
            Bennett Street,
                  EAST PERTH.

Dear Madam,

          In a letter written by Gladys Gilligan to the teacher at Moore River Settlement Gladys says that she hopes to teach in Sunday School every Sunday, and that she is in the choir. May I point out that I have not been consulted in either case.

          Gladys further says that she goes to the G.F.S. every Monday night, with Miss Dee, and choir practice on Friday nights, presumably with the same lady. Will you please let me know whether on these occasions she is always accompanied by Miss Dee or some other lady.

                              Yours faithfully,

                    CHIEF PROTECTOR OF ABORIGINES.

287

Bennett St
E Perth
Nov 5 1931

Chief Prot: Abo
Perth
—Re Gladys Gilligan.—
Dear Sir/
I was quite under the
impression that you knew Gladys
attended Church & all places
in connection with the Church,
& that Mrs Dee, (who is assistant to
Sister Fothers) calles for her & brings
her home. I also understood
it was one of the duties you impressed
on me, to see she attended regularly
to her religious duties, & my
failure to acquaint you with the
fact that she was in the choir, &
hopes to teach in sunday school",
(which is not likely to get past the
hopeing stage for some time), was
that I thought that was inclusive
of religious duties. I quite thought
I was doing the right thing
in allowing Gladys to attend

theses places.
the Dref calls for, - brings Gladys
home on every occasion.
Will you please let me know if
Gladys is to attend theses evenings
in the future.
Yours Obd.
A. Campbell.

10th November, 1931.

The Matron in Charge,
    Native Girls' Home,
        EAST PERTH.

I received your letter of the 5th inst.
re. Gladys Gilligan.

While I have no objection at all to
Gladys attending church it can hardly be said that becoming a
member of a choir and teaching in Sunday School comes within
the category of the permission accorded.

My fear is that Gladys is liable to be
spoilt by these good people and I propose when I get time to
go more closely into the matter. Gladys is susceptible to
influences of various kinds and I do want her to understand
that she is in Perth to work and acquit herself favourably for
the occupation she is to follow in the future. I am afraid if
she takes too much interest in extraneous matters she may forget the main object for which she is here.

CHIEF PROTECTOR OF ABORIGINES.

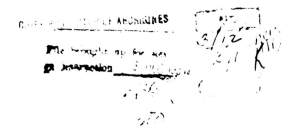

__Report__

Gladys Gilligan

Reading		10
Writing	Ach	5
Spelling		v
Mental Arith.		7½
Arithmetic		(
Composition		(
Grammar		7½

Gladys has improved
greatly during the
three months she has
been in this class,
especially in Arithmetic.
She is now prepared to
continue with Std IV work
in all branches, and
would do so quite well.
She is very ambitious, and
eager to learn, not only
those subjects which give
her pleasure, but

H.T _____ Class Teacher.

I also [...] her more labour.
Arithmetic is the only
subject which is really
laborious to her,
and I think that the
next few months
should do much
to clear her mind
in this subject.
She is very capable.
It is a pleasure
to teach her.

D. Fowler.

R/3

14th January, 1952.

Mrs. E.W. Thompson,
    1 Waylen Street,
        GUILDFORD.

Dear Mrs. Thompson,

             I see no objection whatever to your taking
Gilligan for a walk one day next week.   You may arrange this
with Mrs. Campbell, and also the hours during which Gilligan may
be absent from the Home.

                              Yours faithfully,

                         CHIEF PROTECTOR OF ABORIGINES.

CLERK IN CHARGE.

        Mrs. Campbell brought Gladys Gilligan in to see me as she had not been behaving herself properly. Gladys when questioned informed me that she met a man named Eric Cooper the previous evening. It seems that she met this man once in the Government Gardens when she was in company with Topsy Cross and Linda Nadgi. Cooper sent a message by Kitty Wilson that he wanted to see her and at eleven o'clock the previous evening she had met him in the school grounds, remaining with him for a little while. He told her that he was going away to the Eastern States and she believes that he has gone. *this gel is not known.*

        I have not decided whether Gladys is to go back to the Settlement or not. If she begins this kind of thing all the care and trouble lavished upon Gladys will be useless.

[signature]

CHIEF PROTECTOR OF ABORIGINES.

26th April, 1932.
N/B.

Bennett St
E Perth
May 30 1932

The Chief Prot. Abo.
Perth

Re Gladys Gilligan Clothing.

Dear Sir/
I beg to report that Gladys has grown out of her two winter dresses + overcoat. She also requires shoes (for best) stockings petticoat, pencils, tooth brush, + paste, + her old shoes want mending, + shoe polish. She will require "womens size" in clothing now

Thanking you
I am
Yours Obd.
[illegible]

ABORIGINES DEPT.
30 MAY 1932
PERTH, W.A.

3rd June, 193?.

Mrs. Campbell,
    Native Girls' Home,
    Dermott Street,
    CAN [illegible].

        Before supplying Gladys Gilligan with the
things for which you ask, quite a substantial list, I should like
to have another report as to her conduct and progress.   It is
not worth spending money on this girl unless she is going to
profit by the training she is getting, and if you think that her
progress does not come up to expectations, please do not hesitate
to say so.

        You might also get a report from the school
teacher in this connection.

                    CHIEF PROTECTOR OF ABORIGINES.

295

C.P.A.

        As May Clinch and Gladys Gilligan are now being educated at the Perth Girls' School and East Perth School, respectively, and are receiving hygienic instruction, I think you would like them to have the use of tooth brushes and dental cream at the expense of the Department.

        Personally, I think that it might be advisable to further encourage the girls by a small pocket allowance of, say, 1/-d. a week each. It must not be forgotten that they are now associating with children able to buy little odds and ends of pleasure to children. I feel that it would be very helpful if you could make them some such small allowance.

        At present I understand that Mrs. Campbell is purchasing lots of little incidentals for them and I feel that you would much rather the Department accepted the small cost of their little requirements.

3rd February, 1933.   D.C.P.A.
  B/B.

Also provided /-/

SECTION 12.

Regulation 12A (Form 10).

To.......... **THE COMMISSIONER OF POLICE** .... *and all Police Officers within the State of Western Australia.*

WHEREAS it is deemed expedient by me, the undersigned, the Minister charged with the administration of "The Aborigines Act, 1905," that

GLADYS GILLMAN
....

an Aboriginal, be removed ~~to and kept within the boundaries of the~~

~~.. Reserve (or be removed~~ from the

PERTH
.... ~~Reserve (or~~ District) to

the.......... **MOORE RIVER NATIVE SETTLEMENT** .... Reserve ~~(or District)~~ and

kept therein):

These are therefore to require you forthwith to arrest and apprehend

the said.......... **GLADYS GILLMAN** ....

her
and ~~him~~ to remove from the....... **PERTH** .... ~~Reserve~~

~~(or District)~~, and safely convey within the boundaries of the...................

MOORE RIVER NATIVE SETTLEMENT
....Reserve ~~(or District)~~ and

her
~~him~~ safely to keep within such Reserve ~~(or District)~~ during the Minister's

pleasure.

Dated this........ *Ninth* ....day of.................................193*3*....

.... *Chas. F. Baxter* ....
Chief Secretary.

9th March, 1933.

THE COMMISSIONER OF POLICE.

        Herewith please find warrant covering the arrest
and removal to Moore River Native Settlement of a half-caste deemed
to be an aboriginal named Gladys Gilligan, until last night an inmate of the Native Girls' Home at East Perth.

        I have verbally related to you the circumstances
of this girl's departure from the Home, but enclose a letter which
was recently picked up indicating the christian name of a man concerned in the matter, who is believed to be Frank Craig. There is
another white man known to the girl named Ray Bradshaw, and it is
thought that either one of these men might be responsible for the
present happening.

        I am deeply distressed about this because Gladys
Gilligan was making such excellent progress in her studies, and it
was hoped that before long she would be eligible to become a pupil
teacher in one of our native schools. The girl has a prepossessing
appearance, is well dressed and well spoken.

        Section 44 of the "Aborigines Act" makes it an
offence for any person to entice or persuade an aboriginal or half-
caste to leave any aboriginal institution, etc. etc., while Section
2 defines an aboriginal institution to mean, inter alia, any home
or other institution for the benefit, protection or care of the
aboriginal or half-caste natives of the State. It would appear
that the man concerned has committed a breach of Section 44, and
could be dealt with accordingly. Also, if any such man has taken
the girl to any place of his own, a breach of Section 21 (b) may
likewise have been committed.

                                  CHIEF PROTECTOR OF ABORIGINES.

Merewith St
?? ??
March 1st 1946

The Chief Supt. Police
Qrts

Re Gladys ??

Dear Sir,
        I beg to report that "Gladys
Gilligan" disappeared from the 'Home'
in the early hours of March 1, taking
all her clothes & school books.
I was disturbed by the dog barking,
& three different times during the
night went out to investigate. The
last time about 3.A.M. after that
all was quiet so I think it must
have been about that time Gladys
departed.
It was shortly after 6 A.M. that I
noticed her absence & I at once rang
Police Head Quarters.
Gladys has been particularly quiet for
the past week, she was absent minded

and sulky, & when questioned if anything was the matter, declared there was nothing wrong.

I am
Yours &c
[illegible]

Supported to [illegible] with Olive Harris 11/4/33

Gladys Gilligan arrested at Guildford during night of 21/3/33. & brought to Perth. Interviewed by C.P.A. & returned to M.R.N.S. on (with Mr Neale)

22nd March, 1935.

THE COMMISSIONER OF POLICE.

        I have had a talk with the girl Gladys Gilligan this morning, and while there are one or two people who might be questioned in the matter, I am afraid we have no case against anyone. Mr. Neal, Superintendent of the Moore River Native Settlement, is here today, and will be returning by car tomorrow, and Gladys might accompany him. One of the nurses will also be travelling to the Settlement.

        Gladys says that she left the East Perth Home and went straight to the residence of a man named Cavnova, living at 148 Brown Street. She says that she arranged before leaving that Mrs. Cavnova should take her. Mrs. Cavnova before her marriage was known as Mary Benjamin, a half-caste girl under the charge of this Department. On the contrary Cavnova told Mr. Taylor of this Department that the girl did not immediately go to his place, and must have been elsewhere for a couple of days. It seems that Gladys had arranged with a white man named Frank Morgan to meet him at a wine saloon in Royal Street on the night following the morning on which she decamped, but he did not turn up. She says she has seen Frank Morgan many times, as he made a habit of calling about once a fortnight and speaking to her over the fence, and that he invited her to leave and join him. Apparently we should only have her word against his in this respect. Gladys informs me that there was a photograph of Frank Morgan, who resides at Inglewood, in the "Daily News" last month, when he was described as the inventor of a new burglar alarm. I should think Morgan might be questioned as to his part in the matter.

        So far as the other girl is concerned, Olive Harris, the best thing she can do is to accompany Gladys to Moore River, but I doubt if she will consent to go. Olive evidently induced Gladys to leave Cavnova's home with her, but I doubt whether any charge against her of inducing Gladys to leave the Girls' Home would lie. This girl has no visible means of support, and has not been working for some time. An aunt of hers at South Perth has turned her out. If she could be charged in some way and committed to an institution it might help. Failing that I do not know what I can do, though the Department is anxious to assist her. Evidently Olive prefers not to accept our help, as she knows perfectly well she can apply to us whenever she likes.

        CHIEF PROTECTOR OF ABORIGINES.

301

Moose River
Abanad.
Mozumdea.
6. ?

Dear Sir

Would You please help me in my present situation.?

No doubt You have by now heard that I am in trouble. Really did not realise it. Now that I know I feel I am taking leave of my senses. If you could only help me please Mr Neville. I have confidence in You and feel sure that you will do all you can for me. Although I have been a naughty girl I am sorry for all the trouble I have given and can really and truly say it from my heart. I fully realise now how very ungrateful I have been to You and others who have helped me. I would be very grateful if you could find Frank Morgan's

whereabouts. and let no jet married
please Mr Neville to ask him see him
at it did else small for me but it was
my own foolishness and other that same in
in this present condition

I hope you have forgiven me for what I
have done.

I feel quite ashamed of my self for
not apologising to you.

I trust you will do all you can
for me in this matter.

Yours Respectfully,
Philip Gilligan

GOVERNMENT OF WESTERN AUSTRALIA.

POLICE DEPARTMENT,

COMMISSIONER'S OFFICE,

PERTH, W.A.

2nd August, 1935.

W.A. POLICE No

YOUR No

THE CHIEF PROTECTOR OF ABORIGINES :

        With reference to your memo. of 26th ultimo relative to the whereabouts of Frank Morgan in connection with the girl Gladys Gilligan, I have to advise that his residence is at 49 Third Avenue, Inglewood, and he is a married man with two children.

        He is at present in Sydney endeavouring to place his invention on the market and it is not known when he will return.

W. Douglas

COMMISSIONER OF POLICE.

These papers relate to a girl named Gladys Milligan,
originally from Gula Bella, and one of our most promising and intel-
ligent girls of prepossessing appearance. She had her educational
career at Moore River School and did so well that she became a pupil
teacher. After doing that for a little while I brought her to Perth
with a view to training her as a teacher for native schools, and placed
her at our Home at East Perth, and she did remarkably well at the East
Perth State School. Everything was going on most satisfactorily, and
Gladys was being prepared for the Junior University examination, when
all at once she was missing from the Home. That was in March last.

Gladys was removed back to M.R.S.

When I was last at Moore River Gladys confided in me
and told me that she was in trouble, and that the man responsible was
the same man to meet whom she left the Home in March, but it appears
that misconduct had taken place between the two prior to this. The
man alleged to be responsible for the girl's condition, and her story
is quite consistent, is named Frank Morgan, a married man residing at
49 Third Avenue, Inglewood, and there are two children in the family.
There is no doubt this man waylaid the girl with the full intention of
seducing her. He used to go to the fence of the Home and make over-
tures to the girl and finally took her out walking by some means unknown
to the Matron.

The question is, are we to endeavour to bring such
a man to book by endeavouring to establish that he is the father of the
putative child, which of course presupposes that he will subsequently be
required to pay maintenance. The girl's statement is, of course, not
sufficient to establish the facts, but it is known that the man was hanging round the Home a good deal. This is the type of case which of
course the new Bill is designed to assist. It is heart-breaking to
find that all our endeavours to improve the status and condition of
these girls are destroyed by men of this type.

9th August, 1935.
N/S.

CHIEF PROTECTOR OF ABORIGINES.

C.S.O.

*Certainly. This matter should be followed up
on the return of Morgan to this
place.*

11/8/33.

NOTE :

A man called on me today and said he was the Morgan mentioned by Gladys Gilligan as being responsible for her condition. Morgan said that a Police officer had visited his home and had suggested that he had been dallying with the half-caste girls, which brought him to this office promptly in order that he might deny any charge of this nature. He said he had only spoken to these girls once, and that was when he saw them in the gardens, but as to anything else he was completely innocent. He said that if we proposed taking action in the matter he would immediately consult his lawyer, and further, that he intended to leave again for the Eastern States next Thursday. I asked him whether he would be prepared to confront the girl who had made the statements, and he said he would. I suggested that in the circumstances it might be wise for him to defer his visit to the Eastern States for a week, though he could do as he liked about it.

Meantime I shall see Gladys and have another talk with her in the matter. There is possibly other evidence which we might obtain in the meantime.

Coy.

C.P.A.
6/11/33.

Moore River Native Settlement,
Mogumber.
15th. November 1926.

The Chief Protector of Aborigines,
    P e r t h.

    I have to report the following birth, at 8.40 p.m. on
Saturday last :-

    To Gladys Gilligan, No.469, a son.

The baby's names are "Grady Bevan", and his index number is
1405.

_____ SUPT.

307

C.P.A.
_____

        Gladys Gilligan's baby is now 15 months old. If arrangements can be made for the child to be cared for at the Settlement do you approve of Gladys being sent out to work now?

C.S.

27/2/35.

C. in C.
_____

        Gladys is available to go to work if a suitable place can be found for her. Her boy is at the hospital, and the sister told me that he was better without his mother. He is a very fine specimen.

        Care must be exercised in placing this girl. She should be with people able to adequately care for her, and who would not mind her antecedents which would have to be explained to them. I refer to the association with her mother's husband, who is a leper. She should not be placed where there are young children.

Roll.

C.P.A.
27/3/35.

Noted. 19/1/..

MISS STITFOLD.
_____

        To note.

Roll.

C.P.A.
27/3/35.

308

FORM No. 2.

THE ABORIGINES ACT, 1905.

Application for Permit for Employment on Land.

To the Police Officer in charge of the Police Station at—

Moora 4 May 35

I, *Ch Efremont Orton* of *Petworth Park Moora* hereby apply for a Permit to employ within the *Swan* Magisterial District on land † *Gladys Gilligan* an aboriginal, or a male half-caste under the age of fourteen years, or female half-caste.

Dated the *4th* day of *May* 1935

(Signature) *ChE Orton*

REPORT OF POLICE OFFICER.

To....Chief Protector ....

Protector of Aborigines.

I have to report that I have issued Permit No.6717 to Mr.Charles E.Horton of Puthworth Park Moora.to employ Gladys Gilligan.half-caste girl.Mr.Horton has been the holder of a Permit for some years.

Moora
4/5/35

B McGannan
Const.990
Protector

56 MAY 1935

Orton

Permit No. 6717
Issued ....
.... 7/5/35

13th May, 1935.

Mr. C.L. Orton,
　　"Petworth Park",
　　M O O R A.

Dear Sir,

　　　　　I have to confirm the fact that a half-caste
girl named Gladys Gilligan proceeded from the Moore River Native
Settlement to Moora on the 1st ult. to enter your employ.

　　　　　The wages payable to this girl will be at the
rate of 7/6d. per week, of which please give Gladys 2/6d. per week
as pocket money, obtaining her receipt for each payment. The usual
monthly accounts will be rendered to cover the balance, which must
be remitted to this office to be banked in trust on Gladys' behalf.
In addition, you will be required to provide working clothing for
the girl.

CHIEF PROTECTOR OF ABORIGINES

　　　　　　　　　　　　Yours faithfully,

this brought up for action
or instruction 2 OCT 1935

　　　　　　　　　　DEPUTY CHIEF PROTECTOR OF ABORIGINES.

C/o Mrs. Bitow,
Belmont Park,
Victoria.
June 1935.

Mr. Bray:
Deputy Chief Protector
of Aborigines;
Perth.

Dear Sir

would you kindly
send me as soon as possible. The following
things. 1 overcoat - 2 little shirt one pair
sandals. (Black S.A.)
                    (Women)
Trusting you will do your best
        Yours. respectfully
            Gladys Gilligan

Also previous page

c/o Mr E. Oxon
Network Bank
Moora.
10.9.36.

Mr A. O'Neville,
Chief Protector of Abos,
Perth.

Dear Sir,

Would you kindly permit me to have Frank Morgan's address. It breaks my heart to think he denied being the father of my baby.

So I feel if I could write to him personally and explain things to him, he will understand better. As you having always helped me in other matters. I'm sure you will help me now, please Sir.

Trusting you will do your best for me.
I am
Yours respectfully
Gladys Gilligan

Also previous page

N/B.

405/29.
6th November, 1935.

Miss Gladys Gilligan,
    c/o Mr. C.L.E. Orton,
        Petworth Park,
        M O O R A.

Dear Gladys,

            In reference to your letter of the
10th ult., I have ascertained that Frank Morgan is still
absent from this State and his place of abode is not known.

            However, I do not think I can do anything
more to help you in regard to your claim against this man.
I have seen your child several times and I cannot bring myself to believe that he is the son of a white British subject
born either in England or Australia. It appears to me his
father was either a half-caste or at least a person of colour
or a man of one of the Southern European races. I do not
think you have told me all the truth in respect to this
matter.

                        Yours faithfully,

                    CHIEF PROTECTOR OF ABORIGINES.

C.O.M. c/o Mrs C L Everton
petworthpark
Moora
Nov 7 .35.

Mr A. Oldville,
Chief protector of Abo,
perth.

Dear Sir
I am greatly
troubled by your letter of the 6th ult,,
Not because Frank's present abode is
unknown to you, but chiefly because you
suspect of a half caste being Grady's father.
My baby may be dark skinned, that does
not mean to say he hasnt a white father.
Please Sir I want you to comprehend that
She never associated with a coloured boy
during my stay in perth, not until a
year ago.

But please Sir, just this I know
that many an unconfirmed stories have
been told you concerning me, I do not
want to bore you with my life story

314

I know very well that I rank to in Grady's father and I'll stick to that as I've said before colour doesn't count by any means.

What matters? Why recall the past? It is the future I'm looking forward to. Thanking you for your reply.

Yours respectfully,
Gladys Gilligan

Also page 141

chapter7

The History Lesson

R ead any history of Western Australia and you'll learn the facts about A O Neville. You'll learn that, as Chief Protector of Aborigines from 1915 to 1940, he was a key figure in the establishment of Western Australia's 'settlement scheme'. That he was a British migrant, the son of an Anglican clergyman. That, although he came to the job of Chief Protector with no background whatsoever in Aboriginal affairs, he made it his lifelong business to correct that deficiency, eventually becoming an acknowledged expert in Aboriginal history and culture. That he wrote an ambitious book called *Australia's Coloured Minority* in which he advocated miscegenation as a solution to Australia's 'native problem'. If you read the more recent literature, you'll also learn that, under Mister Neville's exacting administration, Aboriginal people were so well protected they virtually became prisoners in their own land, denied even the most basic rights to control their own lives or those of their children.

The A O Neville of the history books — of the written tradition — is a fascinating construction. But equally compelling, and no less valid, is the A O Neville of oral tradition, the man as he is remembered by the ageing generations of Aboriginal people whose destinies he shaped for a living. Many of these people were still children when Neville retired in 1940. Most of them only saw him a few times in their lives, and spoke to him even less. Yet the reality of his presence in their lives was as bitter as a mug of sugarless tea. In the children — many of whom had been abducted on his authority and in his name — 'Mister Devil' inspired genuine fear. As Chief Protector, he was legal guardian of every last child at the

A O Neville, Chief Protector of Aborigines.

Moore River Native Settlement and indeed of every Aboriginal Western Australian under the age of twenty-one. He held their lives in his hands, and he made sure they knew it.

On the other hand, the children were quick to observe that, in the flesh, Neville was about as menacing as a marshmallow, and they seized on this softness with glee. On the Chief Protector's monthly visits to the compound, they regarded him as just another pompous *wadjala* from the alien world of suits and cities and motor cars, and his smooth, white moon cheeks inspired the nickname 'Mr Cup and Saucer Face'. Had Neville known any of this, he would have been deeply hurt. However misguided, his commitment to bettering the lot of Aboriginal people was genuine. He didn't know many Aborigines well, but those he did — for example, the men and women he employed from time to time on his Darlington property — he liked and treated with kindness and respect.

Neville's writings in the popular press, in academic journals and in his book *Australia's Coloured Minority* mirror these contradictions. They vacillate alarmingly from paeans of praise for a noble culture to viciously racist propaganda. Although in many ways Neville was a man far ahead of his time, in others he was an all-too-accurate reflection of it. Neville considered himself a skilled communicator, and the archival record attests volubly to his elegance of expression. But when it came to communicating with Aboriginal people, Neville failed spectacularly. In fact, although he was charged with their administration and welfare for twenty-five years, he appears never to have addressed himself publicly to any Aboriginal audience. As a functionary of European society, he spoke not only for but almost exclusively to Europeans. In this, as in many other areas of his administration, Neville functioned more as a protector of white interests than of Aboriginal ones.

The notion that government policies should be — or could be — explained to the people in question was quite literally unheard of. Aboriginal children, towards whom so many of those policies were directed, were doubly disadvantaged. Their needs to understand what was happening to them, and why, were overlooked not only on racial grounds but by virtue of their lowly social status as children. Recent histories examining European children's institutions of the period bear this out. The 'lost children of the Empire', for example, interned at places like Fairbridge Farm in Western Australia, understood as little about the forces that had uprooted their lives as the compound kids at Moore River.

When the former children of Moore River were asked in interviews why they thought they had been placed in the settlement, or what purpose they believed the system was designed to serve, the vast majority responded that they had no idea. These were questions they themselves had been pondering all of their lives.

This chapter is an attempt to answer at least some of those questions. Although it is hoped that many other readers will listen in, the real audience for 'The History Lesson' is the children of Moore River themselves. For this reason, they have been allowed to speak for themselves, through the agency of a somewhat unorthodox narrative device that imagines a 'meeting of the minds' between the two protagonists: the children — as they were then — and the man who controlled their fate. The action unfolds in a classroom at Moore River during one of Neville's regular inspection visits. It is shortly before his retirement, and he has been invited to give the children their first (and their last) lesson in Aboriginal history.

Although the scene is an imaginary one, it is not entirely fanciful. It is true that we know of no instance in which Neville actually addressed an Aboriginal audience, let alone a group of half-caste children. On the other hand, Neville took an avid interest in the children's progress, and his regular visits to the settlement schoolroom have been well documented. He was also a veteran public speaker and his illustrated lectures on 'The Native Question' were popular with community and church groups of the day. As a man of conscience, he might well have taken up the challenge of tailoring his standard speech into a 'history lesson' of the kind envisioned here.

The umbrella of poetic licence must also be invoked with regard to the outspokenness of the children, as the scene presents them. Many informants recalled Neville asking their opinions about the settlement, but few were game enough — or silly enough — to answer honestly. As Ned Mippy recalls, 'The kid would say "I like it" whether he did or not. He'd be frightened of him, he'd have to say yes.' The characters in 'The History Lesson' have no such compunction. In this respect they have not been drawn precisely to life, but rather to spirit.

The questions posed by 'Ned', 'Alice', 'Jack', 'Jim', 'Ralph',

'Phyllis', 'Eric', 'Vincent', 'Hazel', 'Doreen', 'Angus', 'Myrtle' and 'Edie' are, by and large, the same ones they themselves asked in interviews. Neville's responses are almost entirely in his own words.

*

Teacher: Good morning, children.

Children: Good morning, Teacher.

Teacher: As you know, children, today we are going to have a very special history lesson, from a very special teacher — Mr A O Neville, the Chief Protector of Aborigines. But before we begin, let's give Mr Neville a nice welcome by singing hymn number 154, 'Do Thou Thy Benediction Give'.

Do thou thy benediction give
On all who teach, on all who learn,
That so Thy Church may holier live,
And every lamp more brightly burn.
Give those who teach, pure hearts and wise
Faith, hope, and love, all warm'd by prayer;
Themselves first training for the skies
They best will raise their people there.
Give those who learn, the willing ear,
The spirit meek, the guileless mind;
Such gifts will make the lowliest here
Far better than a kingdom find.
O bless the shepherd, bless the sheep,
That guide and guided both be one;
One in the faithful watch they keep,
until this hurrying life be done.

Teacher: Thank you, children, that was lovely. Now I want you to listen very carefully to what Mr Neville has to say to you today. It is a great privilege to have a history lesson about the Aboriginal race from an expert like Mr Neville, and I am sure we all look forward to learning many interesting things on this very unusual topic. Mr Neville?

Neville: Thank you Mrs Brenchley and thank you children for that lively rendition of one of my favourite hymns. I am very glad to see that the lamp of learning does 'brightly burn' even here in Mogumber. Ahem. Well, children, let us begin. I have good reason to suspect that you will have some small interest in the topic 'The Australian Native: Past, Present and Future' because each and every one of you has some native blood running through your veins. This is why we refer to you as 'half-castes' — which is a term I much prefer to 'Aboriginal'. Indeed, some years ago, I was successful in seeking to change the name of my office from the 'Aborigines Department' to the 'Department of Native Affairs'. I did this for the reason that 'Aborigine' conjures up an image of inferiority and low status in the minds both of the natives themselves and for the Australian public at large.

Teacher: I'd like you all to remember that, children. 'Aborigine' is not a nice word. It's every bit as bad as 'black'. We are not Aborigines, we are half-castes or natives.

Neville: Quite right, Mrs Brenchley. Thank you for that. Now, getting back for a moment to our definition of a half-caste, sometimes also called a 'coloured person'. According to the Aborigines Act — a very, very important law that was passed way back in 1904 — a half-caste is someone with a native mother and a non-native, usually a white, father. Naturally, a half-caste also results from two half-caste parents. Do you follow me, children?

Angus:	'Scuse me, Mr Neville, but I reckon two half-castes oughta make a whole caste.
Neville:	Well, your arithmetic is correct, young man. Unfortunately, it simply doesn't work that way when it comes to breeding. I shall have to ask you simply to accept my authority on that one. Perhaps it's best if you simply remember that a half-caste is half a white person and half a native person. Not really white, I'm afraid, but fortunately not really black either. Now, some of you may have met children even closer to the white standard — perhaps 'quarter-castes' or 'quadroons', who have only one-quarter native blood. Does anyone here know what an 'octoroon' is?
Jim:	I do! I do, Mr. Neville! I seen a picture once. It's a thing what's got all these arms and lives under the sea. [laughter from children]
Neville:	I think you're a little confused there, son. No, an octoroon is a person with one-eighth native blood running through his veins. You might not even be able to tell that this person wasn't entirely pure white.
Gladys:	Mr Neville, do you got to have eight mums and dads before you can get to be an octoroon?
Neville:	No, indeed, Gladys. Let me explain. You see, several generations back there was one native person who ... Well, the details don't really matter. The main thing to remember is that it is the policy of our department that quadroons not already properly cared for under white conditions must be sent as soon as possible to institutions for white children. They must learn to forget their antecedents, and their parents and coloured relatives should be strictly excluded from any contact whatever with them.

Once upon a time, the native population here in the south-west of Western Australia was mostly full-blood. But today, in 1940, it is overwhelmingly mixed blood. In 1901, for example, the half-caste population of this state was only one thousand. But a mere generation later — thirty years — and it had multiplied four times over. Now, how did all this come about?

Teacher: Mr. Neville, I'm not sure the children are really ready to hear ...

Neville: Nonsense, Mrs Brenchley. As our good Lord once observed, 'The truth shall set you free'. Before the arrival of the Europeans in 1829, the natives of Western Australia ran wild through the land. They were the first possessors of our state, and we must never forget that compared to them, we are all new-comers, dispossessors and despoilers. That is a great sadness, and we must do what we can to make right that wrong. And the best way we can do that is to help the natives to elevate themselves to the white standard. But I am running ahead of my own story here.

Ahem. Yes, the explorers who first discovered our shores, and the first settlers who followed them out, recognised that these natives were a very special people. The settlers were from England — a great Empire with much experience in conquering new lands and civilising native peoples. In Australia, as elsewhere, the British Empire endeavoured to make as pleasant, as profitable and as successful as possible the lives of all indigenous inhabitants.

It has been the privilege of this great Empire to act as the worldwide protector of the native races. Far from decimating these races, colonisation has brought them a thousandfold greater blessings than conquest deprived them of.

I'd like you to think about that for a moment, children, for the point is a very important one. With the coming of European settlement, the native did suffer many losses. We must not underestimate this. The white man destroyed the native's family life, detribalised him, robbed him of his natural rights — even his womenfolk. And by so doing, the European killed the most important things in life for the native race — namely, its customs and its culture. We have ridden roughshod over the native's superstitions, failing to understand the laws which have governed his existence from time immemorial. In our blundering British way we have never learned his language, yet we have expected him to understand ours. And, while professing to look upon the black as useless, many have exploited them. All this has been very sad. But it has also been unavoidable.

Gladys: Why, Mr Neville?

Neville: I beg your pardon, young lady?

Gladys: I said, why? Why was this unavoidable? Why couldn't the white man just have left the native people alone?

Neville: Well, that's a very good question. But I'm afraid the answer is very complicated. It has to do with the fact that the white people had to make their living off the land, by farming and running sheep and cattle. This led to inevitable conflicts with the natives. It needs to be stressed that the white settlers did try to do right, but all of their efforts more or less failed, mainly through ignorance of the people for whose benefit they were designed. They had never known such people before and had no precedents to help them. They tried kindness and conciliation and failed. They defended themselves, their flocks and crops with force, only to make matters 'worse, because to kill meant more killing in return. In desperation they went so far as to extend full British citizenship to those seemingly irresponsible people, only to find their laws utterly disregarded in favour of immutable practices dating from prehistoric times.

Gladys: But you said the land belonged to the natives in the first place — the first possessors of the land, you said.

Neville: Yes, that is correct.

Gladys: So the white people were stealing it. Why didn't they just give it back and go away?

Neville: Dear, dear.

Teacher: Gladys, dear, I think that's enough.

Neville: No, Mrs Brenchley, please let me answer the lass. You see, Gladys, the white man brought civilisation with him. He did not just passively occupy the land — which is what the blacks had done for many thousands of years — he improved it, and developed it. He built great cities with tall buildings, and he introduced delicious crops and livestock for meat, a Christian God and a system of education for the children and nice brick houses to keep people warm and dry. This is what I mean when I say that, although some damage was done, the white man also introduced blessings a thousand times more wonderful than the black man could ever dream of.

Eric: If it's like you say, how come we ain't got them brick houses and that delicious meat and all?

Neville: Well, just look at the very excellent dormitory you now sleep in. It may not be made of brick but it is large and dry and warm, and you are able to sleep on a mattress instead of a pile of old sticks as you would in the bush.

Hazel: My mum makes a break-up in the bush outa branches and we love it a lot better than them mattresses with all the bugs in 'em.

Teacher: Children, children. Order now! I must ask you please to stop these outbursts and to let Mr. Neville get on with his most fascinating discussion. Surely he is the expert these matters, children, not you.

Children: Yes, Teacher.

Neville: Thank you, Mrs Brenchley. It is a bit hot in here with so much 'heated' discussion going on, heh, heh! I don't mean to discourage your questions, children, but you must realise that these are matters that sometimes even grown-ups disagree about. But when they know all the facts, as I do, they always come to understand. I hope that one day you will, too. Now part of the problem of explaining these matters to you is that you are children, and you lack both the maturity and the wisdom that come with years. In that sense, the wild natives that we have been talking about were just like you. They too were like children. The first Premier of our state, John Forrest, understood this. He was opposed to the natives receiving harsh punishments like imprisonment. Instead, he believed it would be 'more efficacious' to 'chastise them ... like one would whip a bad child'.

Even today those natives, whether full-blood or half-caste, who have not had the benefit of a white education are also very much like little children. In fact, it is for this very reason that I have been given the job of Chief Protector. If it is not too immodest, I would like to quote something the *Daily News* said about me not too long ago: 'The Aborigines Department with its Chief Protector' — that is I — 'at its head has become the mother and father to some thousands of full-blooded and half-caste natives'. And I can tell you, having such a big family is quite a responsibility!

So, to summarise what I've been saying, the native race is — by and large — a child race, requiring parental control and protection. That protection will ensure that they do not fall prey to the contaminating influences of civilisation — to drink or to gambling or to loose living — while providing benevolent training and an uplifting environment. And that brings us about up to the present, because that is what your home here, the Moore River Native Settlement, is all about. It has been the proud aim of my department over the past twenty-three years to see to it that every half-caste child is placed at a residential school at a settlement, free from all parental control and oversight. Of course, sometimes that is not strictly possible. But insofar as it can be managed, we like to consider all the children in our settlements to be orphans.

Ned: I ain't no orphan. I got a mum and a dad right here.

Teacher: Ned, that was very, very rude. Please say 'I'm sorry' to Mr Neville.

Ned: I'm sorry, Mr. Neville, but I ain't no orphan.

Eric: I'm an orphan now, I guess, but I had a mum and dad once — till the police come that day and brung me down here. Mr Neville, I want to know why you told them to do that, please?

Neville: First let me say, young man, that however hurt and puzzled you may be right now, one day you will thank me for this.

Ned: [whispering] Watch out! That's what Mr Neal always says before he gives you a hidin'!

Neville: How can I put this in a way that you will understand? Your native parents, children, took no pride in home or care in the upbringing of their families. Here at Moore River, on the other hand, the white staff will teach you the right way to live. Eventually, you'll be able to pass out into the community to enjoy the same conditions as we do ourselves. Well, more or less.

Now I am aware that to some people our policy of taking children away from their parents seems cruel. But the future of the children must be considered first. It is true that in a few instances it might be better to leave half-caste children with their parents, but there are a great many more in which it would be almost criminal to do so. Of course, the half-caste father often objects, vigorously and picturesquely, that he can manage his own family, but seldom can. Neither can mother. As they grow up, the youngsters do just as they like, and if parental coercion is attempted they run away. Father then appeals to Authority to bring back his erring children!

I must speak bluntly. It is a well-documented fact that

native parents routinely leave their children all day and sometimes all night in filthy hovels. The poor children do not dare to move away from the vicinity, and the oldest — perhaps nine or ten years of age — is forced to look after several younger ones while awaiting the return of the absent mother. Such children grow up ill-fed, filthy, unhealthy and untaught.

Edie: I'm starvin' right here, Mr Neville ...

Phyllis: Yeah, and I've had a runny nose and sores ever since I got here. Then I got the chicken pox and then the whooping cough ...

Gladys: I look after twenty little kids every day — only they call it 'domestic science'!

Vincent: I been goin' to school at Moore River for two years now and I can barely spell 'cat' ...

Teacher: Children, that is quite enough. Mr Neville did not come all the way from Perth to hear you complain! On the contrary, it seems to me that what he is telling you should make you very grateful for the good things you have.

Neville: Mrs Brenchley is correct, children. I am aware that the conditions here at the settlement often fall short of perfection, but if any of you had ever had to endure with the horror and degradation of camp life you would know just how lucky you are.

Ralph: But we love goin' campin', Mr Neville. It's our favourite thing to do. See, first we get our kangaroo dogs what we trained ourselves, and then ...

Neville: Excuse me, young man, but I am forced to interrupt
              here and to inform you that you, quite literally, do not
              know what you are talking about. The occasional
              camping expedition is, I agree, extremely refreshing.
              Why, my own children enjoy it from time to time. But
              this is a gravely different matter from living a camp
              life. Under such conditions, children have no 'fun' at
              all. Instead, they grow up to be weedy, undernour-
              ished semi-morons. Is that what you would like to be,
              young man? No, I thought not.

              I was saying that I am aware that conditions here at
              Moore River are not yet all we would like them to be.
              The reason is not a lack of good intentions, but purely
              and simply a lack of funding. Last year, for example,
              our State Government allocated only one pound ten
              shillings to be spent per head of the native population.
              In the other states of our Commonwealth, expenditure
              on native welfare ranges from about three pounds per
              head in Queensland to nine pounds six shillings in
              Victoria. Nevertheless, throughout the Great
              Depression we have just endured, the Moore River
              Native Settlement has managed to do much with the
              very little that it has been allocated. In fact, this settle-
              ment costs the government only half as much per head
              as the Perth Old Men's Home, which is the next
              cheapest State institution.

Teacher: Perhaps that helps to explain my wages, Mr Neville?

Neville: Well, yes, I'm afraid it does. But before we get
              bogged down in a mere accounting exercise, I think it
              is imperative that we keep our goals in mind. I myself
              have been continually frustrated by budgetary con-
              straints over the past twenty-five years. Yet I have
              tried to keep alive my vision of what a settlement
              ought to be — and what it could be — had we only

adequate resources to hand. I have always envisaged, for example, a children's centre wholly separate from the rest of the settlement. The child's whole life from infancy, that is, when its mother hands it over to enter the nursery school, up to eighteen years or there-abouts, would be spent in this centre. These children would sleep in their own exclusive dormitories, have their own classrooms, cooking, dining arrangements and playgrounds.

Edie: That don't sound so hot to me. You mean we couldn't go down the camps to see our rellies?

Neville: Precisely, my girl! You would not be permitted so to do, but more to the point you would have no desire so to do. Indeed, thanks to the excellent training you would have the privilege to receive, the prospect of visiting a filthy, flea-ridden humpy would fill you with disgust. And the mere idea of associating with uncivilised, untutored and uncouth natives ... well, it would no more occur to you to do than it would to me.

Doreen: The kids in the kindergarten, they got their own little centre, like, just what you was sayin'. But we feel sorry for 'em. It's like they're in a cage or somethin'.

Neville: That's a very colourful way to put it, young lady. And yet, cages are sometimes the best places for wild little creatures to be. Even in my own native land of England — and a less wild place is difficult to imagine — we recognise that every child can be improved by attendance at a boarding school. And the wealthiest and most able children there are also taken away at a tender age. It is taken for granted that, thus removed from the softness of parental influence, they will prosper and develop exceedingly.

I need hardly stress how much more necessary is such separation for half-caste children such as yourselves. This is why the Department of Native Affairs, under my personal direction, works tirelessly to save you children from a so-called 'family life' that would fit you for little better than lives of prostitution, ignorance and quasi-slavery. It needs to be understood, of course, that native and half-caste mothers are often mere victims themselves. I am aware that it is white men — usually the owners and managers of stations — who are often the real culprits. They maintain a sort of proprietary interest over their black helpers, and expect implicit obedience from them. These white employers constitute themselves 'lords of life and death' over the natives — and particularly over the native women. And they want the natives kept in ignorance to suit their own purpose.

Alice: My dad runs a station, and he's a white man, and he taught me to read and give me my own horse, too.

Neville: I wonder whether he also contributes to your maintenance at this institution as well, young lady. Indeed, I would stake my life on it that he does not ... As I was saying, these children, left to the devices of the men who fathered them, are going to be no better than those who have produced them and looked after them. In other words, they are going to be white natives.

           I ask you, what kind of a future can such children look forward to? I want to give these children — I mean, you children — a chance. This is why, over the years, we have gathered you up and brought you to places like this settlement. Here you will be taught right from wrong. You will be trained to become decent, self-supporting members of white society.

Vincent: Mr Neville, if we supposed to join the white society
             and learn the ways of the whitefella and that, how
             come you stick us way out here in the bush?

Neville: Ah, yes. That is a potential paradox of which I am
             well aware.

Vincent: Huh?

Neville: There is no doubt, young man, that a permanent isola-
             tion of natives in settlements will not solve the
             problem. In fact, it might even act in quite a contrary
             manner because it will tend to weld all the people into
             an ethnic coloured whole.

Vincent: You mean, we might get to like being black?

Neville: Ah ... well, yes, in a manner of speaking. However,
             the use of settlements as clearing houses and boarding
             schools for the young, preparatory to their transfer to
             the community to live under similar conditions to
             those of whites — well, that is quite another matter,
             and in fact is the object we are aiming at. We could
             not very well place you boys and girls in the public
             schools, now, could we?

Myrtle: Why not?

Teacher: Yes, Mr Neville, if I might be so bold — why are so
             few of the native children permitted to attend the
             public schools? I still remember my history well
             enough to know that the 1871 Elementary Education
             Act made school attendance compulsory for all
             children living within a three-mile radius of a state
             school. So these half-caste boys and girls have the
             legal right to attend public schools, don't they?

Neville: Well, yes, Mrs Brenchley, in the narrow sense, yes they do. According to the letter of the law, if you will. Theoretically native children may attend Government schools, but white folk, mainly through such agencies as Parents' and Citizens' Associations, have seen to it that they shall not. Here in the West the objection of even one white mother to the attendance of a native child is sufficient to debar that child. Often, of course, there are excellent grounds for such objections. There is a natural prejudice against seating white children side by side with native children who ... well, how can I put this? who might be ... unclean or otherwise undesirable. Remember I am speaking here of children unfortunate enough to grow up in a camp or a station setting — not of nice, clean children such as yourselves.

Alice: [under her breath] Yeah, we lucky, we are. We get a bath once a week and at Christmas they give us soap.

Teacher: Hush, over there.

Neville: So for the moment, we have found it necessary to establish separate educational facilities — separate and, unfortunately, unequal. The education our native youngsters are receiving in institutions like this one is (with all due respect, Mrs Brenchley) insufficient to enable them to compete with white youth in after life, and moreover it stops too soon. It would almost seem as though we were willing to accept Herr Hitler's advice in *Mein Kampf* — that it would be an offence against God and man to educate the native for any of the higher places in civilised life. Such an attitude is despicable, and contrary to all we stand for. Indeed, it is my most fervent personal belief that it does not matter what else you do: If you educate, you will solve the problem, but if you fail to do this nothing

335

else can help you. At the present moment, of course, the half-caste child simply cannot be expected to keep pace with white classmates.

But only at the present moment. For it needs always to be remembered that our society is in a state of transition. And this leads me to the main point I'd like to make this morning: that what we are aiming for is complete absorption of the black race into the white. Now the offspring of the present generation — your children, boys and girls — well, they will be acceptable anywhere if the right steps are taken now. So you see, the settlement scheme of which you are all a most important part is only a temporary measure, designed to last only a generation or two.

We white people are trying to make amends for the wrongs we have done in the past. We know that there has been unwarranted destruction of black life for which our race is responsible, but if we work on right lines now it may be contended in days to come that the white man eventually saved the black man from entire extinction.

Angus: 'Scuse me, Mr Neville, what's ''stinction' mean?

Jack: Don't you know nothin'? It's what happens when they put you in the 'lectric chair.

Neville: Well, not exactly, young man. Extinction is what happens to a group of animals when there is a change in their environment to which they are unable to adapt ... uh, to adjust to, if you get my meaning. When that happens, the animals begin to get sick and die, and soon there are none left. Well, the natives are in exactly this danger. Their environment has changed very drastically, thanks to all the wonderful improvements to the land introduced by the white man. If the natives cannot adapt to these changes, they will die out. That would be very sad, and we want to prevent that happening. That's why we have established places like this settlement. Here at Moore River, you will learn how to adapt to the environment of the white man — how to 'fit in' to his society.

Indigenous primitive peoples seem to reach a zero hour from which point they are faced either with extinction or their acceptance of new methods which may save them. Our Aborigines have surely reached that stage, and we must see to it that their acceptance of our way of life raises them to new standards of usefulness, health and happiness and the abandonment of all that is evil in a culture which is outworn and often repugnant.

You see, we dispute the contention that the native is of inferior mentality. Although his mind is in a state of arrested development, he has the natural propensity for evolution. Only recently, for example, I learned of a full-blooded Aborigine, born on a white station, who refused to go through the native ceremonies customary to his age. His evolution — in just a single generation — had already succeeded in turning him against those primitive customs. And he did not even have the benefit of an education such as the one you are receiving here at Moore River. Nor did he have the added advantage of white blood. Thanks to the settlement system for training up you half-caste young people, we believe it will take only a generation or two to achieve our aim: the complete absorption of the black race into the white. So you see it's all really quite simple. Do you understand, son?

Jack: [uncertainly] Yeah, I reckon. It's just that last bit about 'sorption ...

Teacher: Jack, now think back to your vocabulary lessons. You know what 'absorption' means. It's the process by which a substance is fully incorporated into another substance.

Jack: Huh?

Teacher: You know, like when you put a dry sponge in a puddle of water. What happens to the water?

Jack: It all gets sucked up, like?

Teacher: That's right! And the water just disappears.

Neville: If I might offer another example, young man. The position I'm describing is analogous to that of a small stream of dirty water entering a larger, clear stream. Eventually the colour of the smaller is lost.

Jack: So the blacks is like the dirty water, and we gonna disappear into the stream?

Neville: Precisely!

Jack: Then I don't get it.

Neville: On the contrary, you seem to understand perfectly.

Jack: First you say you gonna save us from stink-tion, right? But then you say you gonna make us disappear down some stream somewheres. What kind a savin' do ya call that?

Teacher: I think you're being just a little bit cheeky there, Jack. You know perfectly well that Mr Neville wants only

338

the best for the natives. It's just that his ideas are too complex for you to follow. One day you'll understand.

Jack: [under his breath] Never understand how you gonna save somebody by drownin' them.

Neville: Possibly I can make my meaning clearer by expounding at greater length on some of the problems peculiar to the half-caste. Because it is the half-caste, and not the full-blood native, who is the real problem here. Indeed, I have no case against the full-bloods. They are useful, interesting people whose advancement should run on suitable lines comparable with our own. The half-caste, or mixed blood, or coloured race, on the other hand, has proved itself a people without tradition, lacking culture, spiritual inheritance or guidance of their own. Even their physical vitality has been proved to weaken over a generation or two. The first generation of half-castes were robust, meat-eating people — the women big like the men and as vigorous. They were good, hard workers. It is quite possible, children, that some of your grandparents were among these early hybrids. Unfortunately, however, the offspring were not equal to the parents. They ran to seed through intermarriage and became lazy and lethargic.

Through all the intervening years of wonderful expansion in Australia, these coloured people have gone with fear in their eyes and hearts. Their first fears were of the true Aborigines, who despised them. Next, they feared the white man and his often brutal methods of control. Finally, they feared one another. Often 'knowing fear where no fear was', a sense of inferiority has remained with them all along. Perhaps for this reason, the attitude of the mixed blood is also very selfish. He will not fight for his kind as a whole.

339

He claims his right to freedom, and coercion is repugnant to him, even if it is for his own good.

The character traits we have come to associate with the half-caste — indolence, furtiveness, untruthfulness, instability and moral delinquency — are largely the result of mishandling, and will disappear in proportion to our attention to their needs, both physical and mental. Their half-civilised minds are in dire need of cultural food, and that is precisely what institutions like Moore River have been designed to supply.

Ralph: [under his breath] I knew there was something funny about the food here.

Neville: It is widely believed that I have been personally responsible for devising the ingenious solutions which I have been describing. In all due modesty, however, I must admit that the philosophy behind what has become known as the 'settlement scheme' was established even before my appointment as Chief Protector way back in 1915. Indeed, the very first Chief Protector of Aborigines in Western Australia, Mr Henry Charles Prinsep, was also much concerned about the plight of half-caste children who learned from their parents only laziness and vice, growing up (as he put it) 'not only a disgrace but a menace to our society'. Under Prinsep's administration, the first native settlement was established in 1899. Called the 'Welshpool Reserve', it aimed to establish a self-supporting farming community where native families could live safe and productive lives at a decent remove from white society. The venture failed, however, in no small part because the department then lacked the authority (which it now has) to remove children from their natural parents and compel them to remain on the reserve.

But the settlement scheme as we know it today was actually formulated by Prinsep's successor, and my immediate predecessor, Chief Protector Gale. Like myself, Gale was very critical of the native missions being run by the various church groups. Then, as now, their chief failure was that the young people, once they left the mission, would invariably succumb to the native habit of indolence and become a burden to the state. Nor was the mission-trained native accepted into the white community. On the contrary, he (and particularly she) was being preyed upon by that community. As an alternative to the old-style mission, Gale envisaged a place where half-caste children would be educated and trained in farming and cottage industries, while the adults worked to make the settlement self-supporting. My humble contribution, in association with my Minister, Mr Underwood, was simply to develop the idea a bit further and then to 'sell' it to the Government and the public.

Thus was born the settlement system as we know it today. But the settlement, we must remember, is simply a temporary means to an end. And that end is, I repeat, the absorption of the Aboriginal race by the people of the Commonwealth. To put it bluntly, the only true saviour of the unfortunate half-caste is intermarriage with the white race. For, with the admixture of further white blood, it is known that coloured people can recover some of their original good traits — their robustness and willingness to work hard, for example. But in addition to marked physical improvement, the addition of further white blood also results in distinct moral and intellectual improvement.

Failing this, I am afraid, we may yet witness (if we are not careful) a gradual separation of the coloured people from us in rapidly expanding ethnic groups of a vagrant nature. This has already occurred to a limited extent in certain areas where the coloured people are reverting to the language and customs of their Aboriginal forebears because they find themselves socially unacceptable to the whites, and their growing aspirations denied an outlet. I repeat that the only way to avert such a tragedy is by steadily increasing increments of white blood.

Olive: How you reckon you gonna get that white blood into us, Mr Devil — ahhhhh — I mean Mr Neville?

Neville: Why, by marriage, of course, young lady. You see, while you unfortunately can do nothing to alter the extent of native blood running through your own veins, by making a wise marriage, you can insure that your children will be happier, healthier and more acceptable to the white community. I am sure that you would never consider marrying beneath your caste. If I may speak frankly, it is important that you realise that fate which is in store for a half-caste girl with a black man; he just keeps her as a chattel and leads a life of ease on her hard work. You know it is a fact that she becomes a sort of slave to the blacks and is beaten and ill-treated in a most brutal manner.

Hazel: My sister went and had a baby from a white man, just like you sayin', Mr. Neville, and he was real white and real healthy and all. But they made her give that baby to be raised up at Sister Kate's. She say next time she gonna find herself a black man so's she can keep her child.

Teacher: Hazel, dear, I hardly think this is the proper time and place to be discussing your sister's ... uh, private life.

342

Neville: Thank you, Mrs Brenchley. But simply to put an end
              to the rather sensational turn this discussion has taken,
              may I point out that your sister did not marry the
              white father of her child. Had she done so, and had
              she proved that she was competent to provide a stable
              home life for that child, I can assure you she would in
              all likelihood have been permitted to keep it.

Eric: Mr Neville, there's something bothering me. See, if
              you're hopin' all the half-caste girls is gonna find
              white boys to marry ... well, who's gonna be left for
              all us half-caste boys?

Ralph: That's a dumb question. Didn't you hear Mr Neville
              just say the blacks gotta marry the whites? That
              means we go after the white girls, doesn't it Mr
              Neville?

Neville: NO! I mean, I'm afraid that's not precisely what ...
              Hmmmmm. Uh, well, we haven't exactly ironed out
              all the little wrinkles yet, young man, but you can be
              sure that by the time you're ready to even think about
              getting married, we'll have the answer to that one. I,
              ah, hope so, anyway. For the present, well, I believe,
              Mrs Brenchley, that I have taken up enough of your
              very valuable time. Children, I hope and trust that my
              talk this morning has given you much food for
              thought.

Teacher: Mr Neville, that is an understatement, I am sure.
              Children, would you please take this opportunity to
              thank Mr Neville most heartily for his words of
              wisdom to us this morning?

Children: Thank you Mr Neville.

Teacher: And now, children, I am sure Mr Neville would enjoy hearing another of the songs we've been practising ...

Ned: Yes, talking is good. That's what I say, if we got back,
           back to Mogumber ... we could sit down there and we
           could have our little cry-up, just grab one another over
           the shoulders and cry. People know that you thinkin'
           way back. you cryin' for them old people. Then when
           it comes at night and we're sittin' around the fire we'd
           get a little warning — perhaps a pebble thrown over
           ... we won't panic ... slowly comin' around to see us
           ... they're glad to see us.

Annette: The spirits?

Ned: Yeah, the spirits ...

Index

350